CLOSE-UP ■ 03

THE POLICE SERIES•WEIMAR CINEMA•MEN'S CINEMA

First published in Great Britain in 2009 by
Wallflower Press
6 Market Place, London W1W 8AF
www.wallflowerpress.co.uk

A catalogue record for this book is available from the British Library.

ISBN 978-1-905674-77-0 (pbk)
ISBN 978-1-905674-78-7 (hbk)

Printed in India by Imprint Digital

CLOSE-UP ■ 03

THE POLICE SERIES•WEIMAR CINEMA•MEN'S CINEMA

edited by

JOHN GIBBS & DOUGLAS PYE

WALLFLOWER

LONDON & NEW YORK

CONTENTS

Editors' introduction

The title of this series signals its major intentions: to engage with the detail of films and television programmes and to make analysis of detailed decision-making central to the arguments being advanced in each study. These are modest objectives at one level, since it should be self-evident that any worthwhile study of the arts must engage closely with its objects. But even with the widespread institutionalisation of film and media studies and with a plurality of approaches to the subject being made available through an ever-expanding literature, studies that genuinely focus on the material complexity of films and make this detail fundamental to their enquiries, are rare. The magnetic field of powerful concepts and approaches that dominated film theory from the early 1970s, and which often seemed to discourage engagement with the individual and specific, has weakened but it is still common to find, especially in texts designed for students, films being presented as little more than illustrations of wider concepts or approaches. 'Top down' ways of thinking, in which the general framework takes precedence over the particular text, still pervade the literature and much teaching about film. Yet, if 'top down' approaches can become programmatic, too often finding only examples of their own paradigms, the corrective cannot be to abandon informing frameworks. Theory and concept are required to channel and focus analysis, but investigation of the texture of filmmaking and of the dramatised world, informed by awareness of history and convention, must be able to question and re-shape concept and theory. There is still a huge challenge in understanding what films are and how they work to create meaning and affect. The objective of this series comes to seem less modest when we begin to wrestle with the rich intersection of material elements in any moment of a film or TV drama, attempting to find ways of capturing in language the nuances of action, performance and setting, the degrees of emphasis created by the selection of light, framing and editing, the grading of music, dialogue and other sound. The *Close-Up* series engages with many different areas of cinema and television drama and studies are written from a variety of critical and theoretical positions. What they share is a strong sense of the particular, the choices that make films distinctive and on which arguments for significance and value must rest.

John Gibbs and Douglas Pye
Close-Up Series Editors
January 2009

3.1 THE POLICE SERIES
Jonathan Bignell

ACKNOWLEDGEMENTS

This study is one of the outcomes of the research project, 'British TV Drama and Acquired US Programmes, 1970–2000', funded by the Arts & Humanities Research Council and based in the Centre for Television Drama Studies at the University of Reading. I gratefully acknowledge the support of the AHRC and the helpful comments on drafts of this study made by Elke Weissmann, the researcher working with me on the project. Working alongside my colleagues in the Department of Film, Theatre & Television has invaluably developed my approach to the detailed analysis of visual style in television programmes, and I am grateful in particular to Douglas Pye and John Gibbs for their support and assistance during the writing of this study. The academic staff and postgraduate students who belong to the close analysis discussion group at Reading (known as 'the Sewing Circle') also deserve my thanks for helping to develop the analytical approach I have used here.

Introduction

The focus on close analysis in this study differs from much existing critical writing about television, and within that field it differs also from much of the analysis of the police series. For a long time television criticism on the US police series has been more interested in methodologies of genre grouping (Buxton 1990), institutions and authorship (Thompson 1996) or audiences and ideological representations (D'Acci 1994). The analyses of stylistic choices in selected US police series in this study are not independent of questions of authorship, genre, form, politics and other broad issues, and the chapters briefly address these broader critical contexts in relation to the programme being discussed. But it is a contention of this study that there is a need for detailed analysis to both question and support theoretical ideas about television as a medium, and the police series specifically, that have been developed without much attention to style. The study is structured around a sequence of chapters which closely analyse the style of selected US programmes in the 1980–2003 period. The core content in each chapter consists of detailed analysis of selected sequences from episodes of the featured programme in that chapter. These detailed analyses seek to critically explore the choices made in such aspects of style as camera movement, framing and composition; editing and sequence structure; colour and lighting; performance and characterisation; music, sound and the delivery of dialogue; properties and set decoration; location and the aesthetic significance of urban space. The sequences chosen for analysis aim to be on one hand representative of the predominant visual styles of the series concerned, but also clear and interesting examples that connect to larger critical issues in the study of television dramatic fiction. While the problem of representativeness is a theoretically complex one (see Bignell 2005, 2007a), the motivation for the choice of programmes is to support an overarching argument about television's stylistic restlessness. Aesthetic instability is produced because programme-makers seek to build on perceived successes by alluding to established aesthetic forms, and also seek new audiences and new means of addressing existing audiences by innovating stylistically. Television police series formats are therefore hybrids in which interesting stylistic choices can be tried out.

The close analysis of aesthetic strategies and choices made in the production of television fiction necessarily illuminates critical questions and theoretical approaches to the medium, its genres, its production circumstances and institutions, its notions of audience and its reception. One objective of the work presented here is to assess the critical functions of style in relation to the ideology of police fiction. The structural conventions of the police series include the introduction of an enigma (a crime), its progressing investigation and its resolution. Not only does this support ideologies of law and order by demonstrating the capability of state institutions to deal with social disequilibrium, but also maps this onto the dramatic structure of television storytelling. It facilities the division of the storylines into 'acts', and acts into scenes, where stages in the ongoing narrative are progressively presented and move toward resolution. In the US television context, this suits the division of an hour of television into several (usually four or five) segments separated by commercials. Thus the ideological work of solving crimes is mapped onto a temporal structure characterised by linear progression towards a conclusion, and onto an institutional structure determined by the funding of network programming by spot advertising. Style, especially its rapid definition early in a programme as a marker of the programme's distinctive identity and continuity across commercial breaks, becomes a kind of glue, a differentiating marker, an ideological function and a unifying mechanism for the one-hour episodic form of television police series discussed here. For this reason, chapters pay attention to the opening moments of the selected programmes, and their title sequences, since these establish a stylistic register and dramatic tone with which the main body of the episode will be in dialogue.

Chapters in this study implicitly and explicitly evaluate the effects of stylistic choices in the programmes. Primarily, this evaluation is conducted in terms of the ways in which the style of a shot or sequence contributes to the dynamics of narration and characterisation in the episode chosen. But the significance of style to the episode itself necessarily depends on how it may evoke stylistic registers, narrative forms or specific modes of address that allude to the conventions of the police series genre more broadly, or to other television forms such as the documentary or workplace melodrama, for example. Moreover, the capacities of the police series are shaped by the dominant understandings of what television as a medium can achieve. The critical evaluation of television programmes takes many forms, but it depends on attributing value to a programme either by claiming that the programme makes best use of what the medium is or can do, or because that programme brings into television an aesthetic from outside which redresses an inherent predisposition for the medium to be of low aesthetic quality. The influential US television theorist Horace Newcombe (1974) argued that the primary attributes of broadcast television are intimacy, continuity and immediacy, and his establishment of these criteria led him to claim that the medium is most suited to working on contemporary social anxieties through narrative forms characterised by verisimilitude and involvement with character and story. He associated visual stylishness, on the other hand, with cinema rather than television, and this distinction between media on the basis of their supposed specificities has dogged critical work ever since. Some of the work in this study is directed at showing how visual style has been a crucial component that works together with, and is part of, characterisation and story rather than being secondary or subservient to them.

Modes of performance in television that are suited to the intimate domestic address of the medium and the prominence of character and story are not specific to the television medium. A focus on dialogue and character tends to privilege performance, and in the US context this means the rhythms of psychological revelation through facial expression, gesture and movement that are characteristic of US actor training based on Actors Studio Method. Despite the valuation of screenwriting in discourses about television production, where the visual means of realising programmes' scripts and formats have received less attention, moments of character revelation by bodily means and not verbal ones characterise the series discussed in this study. Indeed in some of the programmes (for example, in *Miami Vice* (1984–89) and *NYPD Blue* (1993–2005)), dialogue is often either spoken too quietly or quickly to hear well, or it is absent from long scenes dominated by music or diegetic sound. The fact that US actors are mainly based in Hollywood and cross between theatre, cinema and television in a typical career both minimises the differences of performance style between these media and also connects television style with film style in terms of performance.

Television scholarship has defined the medium as one in which a distracted domestic viewer glances at relatively simple image compositions with low density of visual information, where images are emphasised and anchored by dialogue, sound and music. These assumptions, made initially in the era of live, studio-based, multi-camera television with monochrome pictures, have militated against detailed work on television's audio-visual aesthetics. However, as technical innovations like colour filming, stereo sound, CGI and post-production effects technology have been routinely introduced into drama production, they have given the police genre new ways of making visually distinctive narratives. The results cannot necessarily be regarded as improvements on a foregoing tradition, since this would imply teleological progress, but new claims for television's aesthetic achievement can be made on the basis of innovations in production and reception technologies. Across the period covered by the programmes discussed here, the difference in these terms between *Hill Street Blues* (1981–87) and *CSI: Crime Scene Investigation* (2000–) is striking. For audiences, the significance of these different production technologies may not be immediately noticeable while viewing, but they do contribute to the audience appeal of programmes when they are launched, and to the appeal of 'landmark' programmes when they are seen again years later. Images of busy urban settings, investigative technologies, as well as punctual narrative moments which foreground spectacular physical action, are aesthetic components that address and retain viewers through distinctive forms.

The institutional context of competition between networks in US television has led to the use of 'must-see' programmes such as these police series to create programme 'brands' and network identities. As filmed series made with extensive use of location settings, a matching colour palette and lighting style in exteriors and also studio-shot interiors, place is an aspect of a branding effort to produce distinctive programmes in a competitive institutional environment. Thus mise-en-scène is highly significant in its literal meaning of where and how the drama is staged. New York, Miami, Las Vegas or Baltimore locations (and, interestingly, the unspecified location of Hill Street) are discussed in this study as key contributors to the meanings of the programmes. Places are distinctive parts of their identity and act as means to make distinctions from other programmes broadcast in the same period and programmes made in the past. Institutionally, however, television executives, producers of programmes, as well as actors, politicians or journalists, make distinctions that are not primarily dependent on the programme text itself, but in terms of popularity, value for money or the 'quality' status of programmes' majority audience. Building fan audiences and developing a 'cult' aesthetic in niche programmes were not very significant in Britain's 'era of scarcity' (Ellis 2000: 39–60) or in the USA's period of network dominance, when three UK channels and three US networks provided a restricted diet aimed at satisfying mass audiences. After this period of what NBC executive Paul Klein (1975) called 'least objectionable programming', both British and US network television underwent considerable change during the 1980s and 1990s, and this led to a reconfiguration of the aesthetic criteria through which television quality was understood. The emergence of a culture of 'cult' programmes, repeated viewing, programme-related merchandise and exploitation of franchised formats was significantly dependent on the visual and aural aesthetic developed in the specifically televisual form of the episodic serial and the long-running action series. Each of the series discussed in this study was made after 1980, and belongs to that specific epoch in television history when visual style gained increased importance.

Series were designed to reward sustained viewing and involvement, through the creation of distinctive visual styles, serial character and storyline development, and generic hybridity such as blending the comic or the fantastic with the hermeneutic puzzles of detection in the crime series (see Curtin 2003). This questions the continued purchase of the concepts of the glance and flow for describing television viewership, because these are programmes that demand and reward attentive and repeated viewing. These police series also emphasise visual brands or signature styles in combination with, for example, a continued emphasis on the star performers who characterised earlier phases of production and marketing of television police and detective drama. As Simon Frith (2000) and Jane Feuer (2003) have shown, discussing UK and US television respectively, the quality of contemporary television is simultaneously defined in relation to its aesthetics, mode of production and audiences. The confusing term 'quality', which has gained increasing prominence in academic work about television, has different meanings in these different contexts. Quality television drama means an aesthetically ambitious programme by comparison with what are seen as generic, normative television productions. In this study, each police series discussed has been thought to stand out distinctively from among other programmes in the genre. Such a programme's creative imagination, authenticity or relevance might even suggest links with cinema, visual art or theatre and thus quality comes to mean 'not-like-television'. As a mode of production, it is where writing and mise-en-scène are prioritised, and the names of key creative figures responsible for these things, like Steven Bochco or Barry Levinson, become widely known. Quality television is also valuable television in that it is what valuable viewers (relatively wealthy and educated ABC1 social groups) enjoy and what they will pay for through a licence fee in the UK, but more significantly, through subscription to paid channels in both the USA and UK. Each of the programmes discussed in this study was imported and shown in Britain on one of the five terrestrial channels, and each had claims to be among the best of acquired US series. This study is one of the results of a larger programme of research about relationships between US and UK programmes, in which analysis of style is just one of a range of methodological approaches. Work on the style of the US police series is part of that project to document and evaluate the similarities and differences between US and UK television towards the end of the twentieth century. Attention to how television style operates, and the evaluation of its significance, provide specific evidence that can add another dimension to arguments about what quality in television means.

Evaluating the significance of style in the meanings of programmes implicitly suggests that choices about mise-en-scène could have been made differently, with different effects, and thus it is sometimes relevant to consider who made these choices and why. Although this study does not document the institutional structures of production teams or the story of how programmes were made in any detail, it does contextualise the analyses of programmes with brief explanation of some of these points. The production processes of US television in the 1980–2003 period have given greater creative control over programmes to creator/producer/writers rather than episode directors or screenwriters. US writer/producers and series creators have been the devisers of programmes' formats, setting up the 'look' of programmes along with their main characters, settings, generic components and other continuing aspects of their identity. Adopting a series format means that a robust production system can be established in which numerous freelance writers and directors may contribute to a stable format overseen by this creator and manager. While not exclusively the product of decisions made by this figure, since many collaborators such as episode directors and cinematographers make important contributions, visual style in the programmes discussed here is contextualised briefly in relation to the key personnel who devised and realised it, and the production processes and technologies they used.

Each of the series discussed in this study was shot on film, as part of a long history of series production for television based in Hollywood. Production uses the resources of studios and personnel originally established for cinema and its institutional mode of production. While made for television, the emphasis on mise-en-scène associated with the greater depth of colour, contrastive lighting and more elaborate camera movement of production on film is responsible for much of the stylistic interest attributed to these programmes. This contrasts with other television forms, such as the sitcom or soap opera, which are shot with multi-camera setups and less investment in the look of the finished programme. By shooting using single cameras, with film stock used for both interior and exterior sequences, planned and consistent visual signatures are made possible for these police series, and thus programme 'brands' are set in place partly by visual style. This distinctiveness works together with other factors such as the planning of narrative arcs across episodes in a series, and the continuities of settings and character that are determined by the series 'bible' that specifies the ingredients of programme format. Because of the production system using single cameras, each shot can be individually lit and its camera positions planned to exploit point of view as much as possible. Post-production can harmonise aesthetic patterns of colour and contrast through grading processes, producing further opportunities for creative intervention after the period of shooting itself. All of these aesthetic effects are tried out in the pilot episodes for series, which are one-off television films designed to interest network executives and audiences in the possibility of a long-running series. The analyses of *Hill Street Blues*, *NYPD Blue* and *Homicide: Life on the Street* (1993–99) here are each of pilots or first episodes because of their importance in setting up the parameters of a series' style. But the work on *Miami Vice* and *CSI: Crime Scene Investigation* discusses episodes further into a series run, in order to avoid over-emphasis on episodes with the specific initiatory functions of introducing settings, characters and style.

Having introduced some of the theoretical, historical and methodological issues that have prompted this study, the following five chapters each focus on a single police series, and within it on one selected episode. The analyses of *Hill Street Blues*, *Miami Vice*, *Homicide: Life on the Street*, *NYPD Blue* and *CSI: Crime Scene Investigation* are intended to function as free-standing discussions, but there are continuing strands of argument that connect them. One is the simple argument that visual style is significant to the meanings of these programmes, and is not a factor that can be separated from their generic narrative components, character dynamics or ideological stance, for example. Following from this, visual style is argued to be the crucial means that determines the nature and degree of the viewer's access to a programme's fictional world. By offering and also denying knowledge to the viewer, visual style shapes how that world can be known and what the parameters of access to it may be. This epistemological dimension can be expressed as a relative proximity or distance between the characters and the viewer, where the viewer may know more or less than the characters at each moment in the drama. To introduce a difference of knowledge between the viewer and a character impacts on the effects of suspense, comedy or pathos, for example, that the narrative may generate. But it also forms the basis for the viewer's evaluation of the fictional world as one where knowability itself can be put into question. The conventions of the police series suggest that the ordering of narration and the ordering of the world parallel each other, with the expectation that narrative patterning mirrors the possibility of understanding people, action and society. While this is one of the forces evident in the programmes discussed here, this study argues that the police series as a television form is equally concerned with what can be only incompletely seen, known and resolved (Bignell 2007b). Visual style, since it is concerned with how seeing and knowing works for its characters, how this is presented to the viewer and how the viewer is able to see and know in similar and different ways to them, is bound inextricably into the problems that the police series works on.

1. *Hill Street Blues*

This precinct drama follows an ensemble of uniformed police and detectives. It was scheduled as a one-hour late-evening series introduced in the US as a January mid-season replacement for a cancelled series, and ran from 1981–87 on the NBC network. It was created and executive produced by Steven Bochco and Michael Kozoll for the MTM company, and was the first in the long run of successes that established Bochco's reputation as a television 'auteur'. The pair had been contributing writers to long-running series and had co-written the short-lived police drama *Delvecchio* in 1976–77, while Bochco himself had written for the detective dramas *Ironside* (1967–75) and *McMillan and Wife* (1971–76) for example, and was story editor and chief writer for *Columbo* in 1971. So *Hill Street Blues* was created by a team that had long experience of the genre conventions of police and detective drama, and the ensemble of actors in the programme overwhelmingly consisted of performers who had already worked either in Bochco's previous pilots and series, with the MTM company in other workplace series, or in the *Police Story* anthology series of 1973–77 (see Kerr 1984: 150). *Hill Street Blues'* complex serial and series storylines were woven around about a dozen recurring characters (see Stempel 1996: 227–36), in a highly-wrought structure that claimed a level of 'realism' that was ground-breaking at the time. It depended significantly on stylistic cues drawn from US direct cinema documentary, especially *The Police Tapes* (1977), made on portable video cameras for PBS in 1976. Reviews of *Hill Street Blues* on its US debut in January 1981 and its British premiere in early 1982 focused on its realism (see Jenkins 1984: 184–6) and its cultivation of authenticity. The US television critic Todd Gitlin (1983: 274) opened his chapter on the series with the bold statement that '*Hill Street Blues'* achievement was first of all a matter of style', by which he meant its blending of dramatic and documentary forms. The series' focus on character and comedy have been eclipsed by discussion of this documentary-like realism, which is in fact a relatively minor aspect of its style.

Around the beginning of the 1980s it became increasingly common for prime-time fiction television to combine the single setting and episodic storylines which are components of the series form with the serial form's ongoing development of characters and storylines across episodes. Alongside this structural pattern, television drama adopted a style involving rapid cuts within and between storylines, using temporal ellipsis to omit establishing detail and get straight to moments of action or psychological revelation. The historical and institutional background to this development was the attempt by US television networks in the 1980s to wrest audiences in high-income and well-educated demographic groups from the emergent cable networks, and *Hill Street Blues'* fate was determined by the change in perceptions of the audience occurring at the time. Initially the series was not a ratings success and finished its first season as the 87th most popular programme that year (see Feuer 1984: 25–8). However, *Hill Street Blues* was renewed by NBC because it gained significant numbers of affluent urban viewers in the

18–49 age group for whom advertisers would pay premium rates. The series was also critically praised and eventually won the Emmy award for Outstanding Drama Series five times.

The chosen director for the pilot and the first four episodes, Robert Butler, had a long career in television drama going back to the live studio psychological realism of *Playhouse 90* (1956–61) and including Bochco's time on *Columbo* (see Gitlin 1983: 290). Making the episodes subsequent to the pilot in blocks of four enabled Butler (and later directors) to save time and money by shooting locations for more than one episode at the same time, thus providing opportunities for more elaborate lighting and rehearsal than was common. The overall effect of casting decisions, choice of director and production schedule was to prioritise the visual look of the series, and to allow for the interaction of the performers with each other to develop an ensemble style. This focus on performance as well as visual look made it possible to develop a hybrid of comedy and realism that depended on choreographing multi-character scenes in a crowded studio set, with relatively few exterior scenes. Nevertheless, the large cast and complex filming process that derived in large part from the series' stylistic innovations made production very expensive, and Bochco was asked to leave MTM (and thus *Hill Street Blues*) in 1985 as a result (see Marc & Thompson 1995: 225).

Although *Hill Street Blues* might be seen as an exceptional or even unique programme, it is in fact a hybrid of many different generic components. Its workplace ensemble drama was inherited from successful sitcoms of the 1970s, including *M*A*S*H* (1972–83) where a similar ensemble was transposed to the Korean War (paralleling the Vietnam War of the time), and *Hill Street Blues'* verité style portrays the city as a 'war zone' while infusing it with comedy in a similar way. According to Paul Kerr (1984: 148–9), NBC network head Fred Silverman prompted the creation of the series by asking for a hybrid of *M*A*S*H*, the police precinct sitcom *Barney Miller* (1975–82), the film *Fort Apache, The Bronx* (1981) and the anthology drama series *Police Story*. The particular form of this hybrid product, from its colour palette, sound montages and apparent 'wildtrack' background sound textures, to its camera style and modes of performance, are certainly unique in combination, however, and have been rightly understood as marking a step-change in episodic US network drama. Camera movement and unstable framing and composition signal to the audience that knowledge of the fictional world is partial and provisional, as discussion of specific sequences will illustrate later in this chapter. Indeed, this chapter's focus on the dynamics of how the giving and withholding of knowledge works stylistically in *Hill Street Blues* will establish this issue as a key theme of this study as a whole. These stylistic choices are matched at a structural level by the decision to use parallel montage to shift back and forth between storylines, and often to arrive at a complex and only partial closure at the ends of episodes.

Unstable viewpoint is introduced as a signature aspect of the series in the opening minutes of the pilot episode, in the ways that its music, title sequence, shooting style and editing are presented and integrated. Because the television image is small, and television competes with other activities for the viewer's attention, sound is conventionally used to call the viewer to look at the screen (see Kozloff 1992: 79). Music and other sound in television programmes signify the emotional significance of images, and have a vital role in directing the viewer how to respond to action and characters. So *Hill Street Blues'* eschewal of music except in the credit sequence and scene openings after commercial breaks is a crucial signifier that operates through absence rather than presence, withholding the guiding tonal register that music would more normally provide. The pilot's and subsequent episodes' opening theme music is organised around a three-note piano cadence echoing the syllables of the title, in a minor key. Over this relaxed, even mournful tune by a small ensemble, a montage sequence shows the first of a series of white patrol cars leaving the underground car park of Hill Street Station to drive in a loose column along the rainy streets of the inner city in the grey early morning, interspersed with static shots of each main character and a caption showing that actor's name. This choice is significant in itself, for it blends a grey urban environment with conventional head and shoulders stills of actors in character. A claim for gritty contemporaneity is mixed with the privileging of performers in role, thus opening up a question for the viewer about the dramatic emphases of the series.

Each episode is structured by a day in the life of the police station, beginning before the credit sequence with a caption announcing 'Roll Call' and a dimly-lit scene in the basement of the station in which the duty sergeant Phil Esterhaus (Michael Conrad) updates the day shift officers about ongoing investigations and assigns patrol tasks, ending with the refrain 'Let's be careful out there'. This scene enabled some of the storylines to be introduced as duty assignments were given to the continuing characters, and those characters could also be briefly established through their reactions to the assignments and each other. The roll-call sequences were shot with two cameras rolling simultaneously, on tracks positioned at ninety degrees to each other (Gitlin 1983: 293). In the pilot (Fig. 1.1), the camera shoots the sergeant in long shots, mid-shots and close-ups alternating with pans and brief tracking shots in which the camera searches

Fig. 1.1

around the busy room showing individual officers and partner teams. This observational style, as if following action not planned in advance, continues when the camera moves further into the space to witness officers removing unauthorised personal weapons including flick-knives, coshes and concealed pistols and shotguns. They load these onto the tables as instructed, only to pick them up and keep the weapons when the sergeant ends the meeting. A barrage of talk in the scene makes it difficult to locate either storyline points or character cues that may become important later, however, and this busyness and sense of lack of dramatic structure is supported by the supposedly unplanned documentary filming style. The rather shocking revelation in the pilot that the officers are fully loaded with both legally held and also illegal firearms and other weapons is reminiscent of an investigative documentary. But that tonal flavour is accompanied by the pronounced comic effect of the officers' legerdemain in hiding the weapons in and under their clothes, the excessive accumulation of weapons that results when they are revealed, and the casual re-equipping of themselves as they leave the room. The opening scene establishes not only generic and storyline premises, for example that effective policing might involve bending or breaking the law and internal police regulations, but also a hybrid dramatic tone that runs throughout the series and is crucial to its instability of viewpoint.

The series draws on conventional documentary shooting techniques, in which shots may be unsteady because of the use of hand-held camera, composition is not always harmonious and the observed action may be captured in movement, or partially obscured by objects or people in the frame. These characteristics connoting the observation of actuality are combined with editing techniques associated with drama. The line producer on *Hill Street Blues* (responsible for day-to-day shooting control) was Greg Hoblit, a graduate of the Film Programme at the University of California, Los Angeles (UCLA), who said, referring to Sidney Lumet's 1973 film about an undercover New York cop : 'I read the [pilot] script and immediately a whole visual scene came to me about what it ought to be. Hand-held camera. Let's get the film as dirty as we can. What I said is, "Let's go for the *Serpico* look"' (in Gitlin 1983: 290). Butler and the producers considered using hand-held camera for the whole pilot, and also considered using 16mm black and white film to get the look of observational documentary. But the Los Angeles processing labs were unable to produce finished film in 16mm with the required speed and regularity for a long-running series so instead the pilot and subsequent episodes were shot on 35mm colour film. The hand-held technique was also too difficult to control so it was used only rarely (see Gitlin 1983: 293) and was often simulated by camera movement in shots produced by dolly-mounted cameras as in the pilot's roll-call sequence.

Nevertheless, Butler and his successor directors aimed for the aesthetic of observational documentary. For example, he encouraged supporting actors to walk through shots, sometimes obscuring principal actors, and requested that the processing labs did not optically clean or enhance colour or definition in the daily rushes that were sent to them. Wardrobe and lighting were dull in colour and designed not to look polished or over-designed. An improvisational acting ensemble, Off The Wall, were hired by Hoblit to create ambient soundtracks including scarcely-heard conversation, radio chatter and crowd noise to be laid over the final cuts of the episodes in post-production (see Gitlin 1983: 294). Scenes outside the police station were structured around following the police characters, rather than establishing a scene before their arrival, thus setting in place the expectation that the fictional world will be realised through the experience of the police officers. The consequent withholding and gradual revelation of information places *Hill Street Blues* in contrast to investigation programmes (like *Columbo*) that give the viewer privileged access to the fictional world in advance of the main character's encounter with and comprehension of it, and the variant ways that police series make use of these possibilities will be considered in later chapters of this study.

The opening roll-call sequence in each episode and the patrol sequences shot on location (but not most of the scenes in the precinct interior) eschewed the shot/reverse-shot convention familiar from cinema, in which scenes are performed several times with the camera positioned differently each time in order to capture the reactions of one character to another and to provide a coherent sense of fictional space. By contrast, *Hill Street Blues* aimed to give the impression of unrehearsed action occurring in real time. This references the conventions of documentary, where a single camera operator tries to catch the action as it occurs, and is often forced to pan quickly between speakers, and to carry the camera physically as action moves across a space. This form requires the audience to observe the police and interpret their actions without the camera providing the dramatic contrasts and movements from wider shots to close-ups which usually offer an interpretive point of view on the action. The visual style was paralleled by a style of writing dialogue that allowed for incomplete sentences and the interruption of one speaker by another. *Hill Street Blues* demanded a more active and interpretive viewer than is usual in television drama, with the camera technique implying observation and investigation as much as identification with the characters. Its structural and stylistic qualities work together to signal genre conventions but also to blur them.

Hill Street Blues borrows, via their inclusion in the repertoire of television documentary, from the French tradition of *cinema verité* and the American direct cinema documentary. *Cinema verité* openly admitted the role of the filmmakers in constructing the film and shaping the behaviour of its subjects. The ordinary people who they filmed were seen interacting with the filmmakers, being asked questions or interrupted as they spoke, and sometimes filmed as they looked at the rough cuts that had been produced. Direct cinema largely did away with analysis and argument, aiming instead to reveal individual and social truths through the camera's apparently objective witnessing of a situation. Having been given apparently unmediated evidence, the audience is invited to draw its own conclusions. Since they are necessarily unscripted, direct cinema films use the juxtaposition of editing to energise a sequence of shots into a revelatory and dramatic structure, producing narrative and involvement with their subjects by shaping the films to provide pace, a narrative arc and a sense of development (see Winston 1995: 149–69). Conversely, French *verité* filmmakers saw themselves as participant observers, like anthropologists, taking part in the situation and putting pressure on it and its participants in order to reveal what they saw as a deeper truth. The spontaneity of these American and French documentary traditions can present police procedure effectively in drama, since police work can be shown as a succession of minor incidents that have been captured by an observing camera as they slowly unfold. The experience of duration can then contrast with the camera's efforts to capture unexpected and surprising moments as the police go about their business.

These two related but very different traditions of factual filmmaking exemplify two important components of *Hill Street Blues* as a series/serial hybrid. The first concerns the characters, who are largely police patrolmen and women, and are witnessed as if the camera makes no intervention into their situation (as in American direct cinema). Yet secondly, the scripts put them into situations that pressurise, manipulate or invite them to reveal character (as in the French *verité* tradition) that will gradually become more complex across the series arc, and episodes of *Hill Street Blues* were usually written in blocks of four, to allow for about four continuing storylines (see Gitlin 1983: 274). Noting the use of apparently disordered *verité* style in the roll-call sequences, Jenkins accurately points out that 'it is used to mask, or render less obvious, the specific ways in which our attention is being directed and fixed, the ways in which the upcoming contents of episodes are being laid out. There is very little in the roll-call sequences which is not later developed; they are tight rather than, as they are made to appear, loose' (1984: 194).

Fig. 1.2

In the pilot's pre-credit sequence, the roll call segues into early scenes in the precinct house which are choreographed to connect the main characters as members of a collective and temporally unified fictional world. For example, as one brief interaction between Bobby Hill (Michael Warren) and Andy Renko (Charles Haid) ceases, itself partially obscured by extras walking across the frame, Mick Belker (Bruce Weitz) and a suspect walk into the shot and begin a new brief scene (Fig. 1.2). The shift of interest onto a new pair of characters takes place within the same shot, rather than cutting to a new shot, suggesting that the camera is able to access the space of the action coherently and fluidly, despite the occasional obstruction of its visual field by activity in the station. This shot then continues as a tracking shot that follows Belker's direction of movement along the booking desk, admitting the camera into the inner space of the station and again suggesting its capacity to follow action and select dramatic incidents at will. Spatial and temporal continuity are produced by choices of camera position in relation to the set and performers, and these choices of camera position privilege brief dialogue exchanges that reveal character rather than story. At the same time, this emphasis on character is embedded in choices of shot which have sufficient depth and mobility to include the documentary-like capture of action occurring in motion and in which the presence of both foreground and background action makes the viewer's focus on the main characters' interactions more difficult to sustain.

Hill Street Blues' narrative world is character-centred, and the initially documentary-like roll-call scene gives way to a gradual settling-down of camera style into relatively conventional two- and three-character sequences using establishing shots, two-shots and close-ups in shot/reverse-shot patterns, most evident in the pilot's many scenes in Captain Frank Furillo's (Daniel J. Travanti) office. The style in the main body of each episode is motivated by character revelation and storyline progression, and the more conventional visual style has the effect of privileging dialogue and centring attention on the performers, in contrast to the busyness of the precinct setting in the roll-call scene. The series established regular characters with extended back-stories that were gradually unravelled. Some of these back-stories were revealed early on, such as Furillo's moral authority and efficiency being undercut by his status as a recovering alcoholic, his difficult relationship with his ex-wife Fay (Barbara Bosson) or his 'secret' affair with the public defender Joyce Davenport (Veronica Hamel). This affair produced a character pairing where their antagonism at work (Furillo's quest for convictions versus Davenport's high legal standards) contrasted with their romantic scenes in the bedroom or in their bath in the final sequence of many episodes when they discussed the day's events. Further character pairings, usually motivated by the practice of sending police on patrol in buddy teams, included the conservative and prejudiced SWAT team leader Howard Hunter (James B. Sikking) with pacifist Jewish hostage negotiator Henry Goldblume (Joe Spano), the sexually rapacious white John LaRue (Kiel Martin) with black former drug addict Neal Washington (Taurean Blacque), black civil rights supporter Hill and Southern redneck Renko, and the macho Joe Coffey (Ed Marinaro) with the anxiously unfeminine Lucy Bates (Betty Thomas). Within individual characters, similar conflicting binaries were established such as plain-clothes detective Belker's propensity to exaggerate violence and threats to suspects versus his inability to escape his stifling mother's constant phone calls. These pairings and internal conflicts permitted comedy and irony, for example when the practical joker LaRue loaded blanks into the militaristic Hunter's gun, so that when the depressive Hunter tried to shoot himself he was fortuitously saved. When Furillo told LaRue to deal with his alcoholism or be fired, LaRue happened to attend an AA meeting at which Furillo was present, thus revealing Furillo's 'secret'.

In the pilot episode, the introduction of these characters is carried out by pacing the lengthy first sequence in the precinct house to include dialogue exchanges between pairs and small groups of characters where shot/reverse-shot and reaction shots are motivated less by storyline information than characterisation. The initial exchange between Hill and Renko in the pre-credit sequence revolves around the vain Renko's flashy new boots, while the animalistic Belker is shown growling at and threatening a pimp who he has just arrested. The camera dwells on the tall and elegant Davenport as she walks through the station, to be offered a coffee by the squad's lothario LaRue in a conversation filled with comic double entendres. Davenport's arrival is witnessed by Bates who looks disapprovingly and enviously at her while framed by a group of ogling male officers (Fig. 1.3). The composition of the shot offers the possibility of comparing her expression to the mens'. Since sharp focus and more light are given to her than her colleagues, the shot emphasises her and makes a point about her frustration with being undervalued by the men, and compared unfavourably by them with the alluring Davenport. The well-meaning Goldblume is shot in a head-on mid-shot when the episode moves to an exterior scene beginning the first major storyline about a liquor store hold-up (Fig. 1.4). However, the lengthy forty-second shot of Goldblume is

Fig. 1.3

Fig. 1.4

motivated not by the plot significance of the scene but by the visual information it offers about his juggling of police procedures, his concern for the perpetrators of the hold-up who are teenage Hispanic boys, and his determination to forestall the violent resolution of the crisis by Hunter's SWAT team. This juggling is represented visually by Goldblume's management of a telephone, a notebook, a baby's dummy from his pocket, his spectacles and a page torn from the phone book all at the same time.

So what *Hill Street Blues* achieves, by means of a blend of documentary with drama and comedy conventions, is a form dominated by the investigation of character. The visual style of the series serves characterisation by highlighting the contrasts and parallels between characters, made possible by numerous pairings of officers with each other, romantic couples (especially Furillo and Davenport), encounters in the populous space of the squad room and the sporadic or one-off interactions between suspects, perpetrators and witnesses encountered in the multiple storylines. This largely psychological emphasis is embedded amongst the signifiers of realism present in the adoption of documentary conventions, overlapping scene construction and the aesthetic choices of dull colour palette and costume, unobtrusive lighting and busy, mobile shot composition.

The compromises between the character familiarity necessary to *Hill Street Blues'* serial components, the documentary realism of some of its visual style and its selfconscious aestheticisation as 'quality' television can be seen in the final sequences of the pilot. The original pilot's long sequence at the end is an exception to the visual style of the rest of the episode, and features an unsteady camera which selects details of Hill's and Renko's shooting by a drug addict and offers static shots of the abandoned building in which they are left for dead. The scene is considerably shortened on the Channel 4 DVD version of the series presumably because of the DVD's 12 certification, and the original will therefore be described in some detail. The scene was preceded by a series of scenes of characteristically mixed tone in which Hill and Renko respond to a call where they find a couple arguing as their daughter tries to hide from her sexually rapacious stepfather. Hill and Renko emerge from the building to find that their patrol car has been stolen. Looking around the area, they walk into an apparently abandoned building that is being used by drug addicts. A point-of-view shot picks out the group of young men as they react to the policemen's entrance, then a close-up of the floor beneath their feet shows a spoon, plastic bag of heroin and a syringe falling to the ground. The camera returns to a mid-shot of the addicts and a reverse shot of Hill and Renko reaching for their pistols, then a close-up of Hill's hand drawing his gun. The camera reverses again to show one of the addicts approximately from Renko's point of view as he aims a gun at the policemen and fires. At this point the images slow down to about half normal speed, and the sound texture changes to remove all noise except the gunshots so that their aural impact is emphasised. Reversing to show Renko in medium close-up, the camera sees him cry out and fall backwards (Fig. 1.5), with a cut back to the addict's gun in shallow depth of field that favours the gun barrel and its bright blast-flash obscuring the front of his blurred body. A cut back to Renko sees him falling towards and to the side of the camera. A second mid-shot of the gunman shows him fire again, with a cut to Hill who falls backwards. The camera position moves to floor level to show Renko's shiny new cowboy boots slipping as his body begins to twist and fall. A

Fig. 1.5

mid-shot shows Hill falling too, tilting down to see that he collapses into Renko's arms. On this shot all diegetic sound disappears, and is replaced with the simple piano phrase that begins each episode's opening credit sequence. The camera returns to the close-up of the floor where drug paraphernalia lies on the ground, and this is followed by a floor-level shot using a distorting lens that takes in the policemen's legs, the floor and stairs of the building, framed by a partial iris border at the edges of the screen. Another shot picks out a detail of the stairway before cutting to a slightly elevated wide shot looking back towards the building's doorway, in front of which Hill's and Renko's bodies lie still. The previous two shots are repeated with the camera pulled back to show more of the background of the hallway in the first shot and the policemen's bodies in the second, with the piano theme music still playing in a slowed-down tempo, then the episode fades to black for the final commercial break as the piano phrase resolves to its final chord.

The sequence enforces a focus on Hill and Renko as key characters in the episode and among the ensemble of their colleagues, since no other characters are favoured with the foregrounded stylisation of action that occurs in this scene. However, on the other hand, it seems that they are both dead and this surprising turning-point both raises the stakes of the audience's involvement with them and displaces the comic tone of much of the foregoing drama in exchange for a tragic one. It was Bochco and David Milch's intention that at least one of the pair would be killed, but test screenings of the pilot showed that audiences particularly liked the two characters and it was decided that they would both survive and become fixtures for the whole series. At the end of the episode Furillo learns that Hill's and Renko's condition is critical but that they are alive. The aesthetic and emotional impact of the long sequence remains in the screened version of the pilot, but is framed by material that remodulates it as a hook to entice continued viewing rather than as a bleak downbeat conclusion.

Throughout the next and final segment of the episode there is a sense of gathering pathos achieved by introducing cross-cutting that contrasts the epistemic position of spectator and characters. After the commercial break the narrative leaves Hill and Renko entirely, and cuts to the resolution of the liquor store hold-up where Furillo protects the Hispanic teenagers from the shooting of a SWAT team who had misheard a falling champagne bottle as a gunshot endangering the hostages. In a moment of comic physical business, Hunter accidentally breaks the shop's windows and walks away before anyone can notice. Back in the precinct house, Davenport pours coffee over LaRue's crotch, saying 'No hard feelings', resolving the comic sequence of double entendres that began their relationship and reversing its dynamics of gender power with a joke about LaRue's potency. A scene in which Furillo and Davenport kiss in bed, revealing for the first time that they are a romantic couple as well as rivals in their professional roles, is intercut with the discovery of Hill and Renko's bodies. None of the characters the audience sees completing storylines and reinforcing character profiles know about Hill's and Renko's fate until near the end. While the comic business and verbal wit of the closing scenes matches the tone of the preceding drama, these scenes are interestingly counterpointed by the hovering significance of the patrolmen's shooting, whose impact is assured by the length of that sequence, its different and self-conscious visual style and its positioning just before the commercial break that precedes the last part of the episode.

The style of *Hill Street Blues* is a more complex and less unified entity than has often been supposed. The style is a hybrid assemblage that draws on cinematic and televisual antecedents, belonging to the different dramatic modes of heightened naturalism and comedy, and the rhetoric of documentary forms of both European and US origin. The connective tissue that holds this series together stylistically and dramatically is the central significance of character. This became increasingly pronounced as the series continued, as the potentially confusing parallel montage and partial resolution of storylines reduced because NBC demanded more conventional storylines with a single resolved plotline in each episode (see Gitlin 1983: 305). There was progressively less radical stylisation in the episodes' visual form yet greater stylisation in the performances of the lead actors. Despite the acclaim of *Hill Street Blues* for being (in loose terms) realistic, which derives from its evident but actually sporadic and fragmentary adoption of documentary conventions, it is much more like *M*A*S*H* than *The Police Tapes* because of the greater emphasis on performance and characterisation. The visual style gives the viewer access to a confusing and down-at-heel precinct environment, alluding to observational documentary but picking out aspects of the visual field that will be taken up as significant to character development or storyline progression. The use of more stable and harmoniously-framed shots of characters, matching the conventions of drama that privilege tensions between them, especially in terms of character pairings set up by the narrative, again demonstrate the camera's ability to know them. Even the extended sequence of Hill's and Renko's shooting, despite its unconventional visual form, works to foreground the dramatic stakes of their apparent death in counterpoint with the immediately following scenes where their fate remains unknown. The hybridity of *Hill Street Blues'* style is thus far from incoherent or deconstructive, though it does draw attention to its innovative status in the police series genre.

2. Miami Vice

Miami Vice, which ran from 1984–89 on the NBC network in one-hour slots on Friday evening prime-time, is widely regarded by academic critics and television aficionados as one of the most innovative television series of its time. It centred on vice-squad detectives Sonny Crockett (Don Johnson) and Ricardo Tubbs (Philip Michael Thomas) from the Miami Metro-Dade police department and their undercover investigations of drug, prostitution and firearms crime, but paid much more attention to design and production values than earlier cop series. Contemporary (men's) fashion was selected to match a consistent colour palette for sets, architectural backgrounds and props, and pop music was laid under a greater proportion of action sequences than was usual in filmed US police drama. *Miami Vice* was one of the first series to be broadcast (in the USA) with stereo sound, and significantly increased the market for stereo television sets (see Marc and Thompson 1995: 232). Episodes featured pop stars and celebrities including Phil Collins, Frank Zappa and Ted Nugent as guest stars in non-recurring roles. Moreover, contemporary chart pop was laid not only under car chases but also dialogue scenes, so that these celebrity voices functioned as aural 'guests'. These uses of music had already been tried when *Miami Vice*'s creators, Michael Mann and Antony Yerkovich, had worked on the pilot for the series titled *Gold Coast* (1984), and in a famous anecdote it is claimed that the series was created when an NBC executive sent Yerkovich a memo that read simply 'MTV cops', and that Yerkovich and Mann created *Miami Vice* to fit this brief.

Before *Miami Vice*, Mann had made commercials and documentary shorts, and written episodes for genre series such as *Starsky and Hutch* (1975–77) and *Police Story* as a way of getting into the cinema business (see Hillier 1993: 107). He made television films and directed the theatrically-released *Thief* (1981, also known as *Violent Streets*) which combined the rain-washed streets and underworld settings of neo-noir cinema with a stylised soundtrack featuring avant-garde electronic pop music by the group Tangerine Dream. His subsequent feature *The Keep* (1983), a gothic horror mystery, was unpopular with both audiences and critics. Making *Miami Vice* for television rescued Mann's reputation at a low point in his career, and offered the chance for the aspirant film director to create a television form in which visual style and uses of music enriched a relatively conventional generic police drama format. Partly because of its relationship with the burgeoning pop music culture of 1980s television (especially the MTV channel), there has been some significant critical writing about *Miami Vice* which uses the series as evidence of postmodern style in popular television and as an example of how postmodern themes are expressed in popular culture (see Ross 1986; Schwichtenberg 1986; Rutsky 1988; Wang 1988; King 1990). This chapter looks much more specifically at the aesthetic of *Miami Vice* and how it is constituted by mise-en-scène and by the manipulation of conventions of genre and format.

Stylistic distinctiveness was established by Mann in the series pilot and the first 1984–85 season (see Hillier 1993: 113), which introduced a number of key elements.

Miami is presented as an environment of consumption, pleasure and wealth; the terrain of the commodity. For example, the connotations of the main title sequence relate pleasure to wealth, leisure to style, bound together in a sequence invoking visual excitement in a similar sense to the mobility and fast cutting of some television commercials and MTV videos of the period. The title sequence consists of a rapidly-edited montage in which many shots involve camera movement, and includes palm trees, flamingos, a sailboarder, a pelota game, horseracing and dog racing, a line of parked Rolls Royces, a parrot, bikini-clad young women and helicopter shots of Miami's seafront hotels. These shots alternate with a shot of the sea from a low-flying helicopter, flying rapidly towards the city's beachfront, and over this the title is superimposed in peppermint green and pink (the colours alluding to the strip worn by the Miami Dolphins football team), and lettered in an Art Deco graphic style. The sequence is accompanied by a pulsing musical theme to which the particular episode's generally driving and repetitive rock-based musical components are related. The music was composed by Jan Hammer, whose title theme and the oft-repeated 'Crockett's Theme' were chart hits when an album of the series music was released in 1985. The title sequence remained almost unchanged across its several series, and establishes Miami as a setting rather than introducing the main characters. Clearly, the meanings of place and the tone and mood of the city are to be understood as the key signifiers of the series' identity. Indeed *Miami Vice* is preoccupied with the tone or atmosphere of the city and its moral problems, and the music of its title sequence and in the episodes themselves can be seen as a way for the series to 'speak' about this through using music as a metaphor. What the music has to say is not information but tone, sometimes working as a commentary but mostly as a discourse about the world of feeling that the fictional world generates for its characters and the audience.

The stylistic components of camera movement, exaggerated colour, asymmetric framing and elaborately styled sets in the series as a whole have led some commentators such as David Buxton to complain that they 'display an overt formal force that seems extravagant in comparison to the traditional television series' (1990: 140). This attack on the series' style is driven by both a materialist political position which critiques its fictional world as cynical and shallow, and also a desire for adherence to the conventions of the police genre. Buxton continues: 'In an attempt to maintain constant visual and sound excitement, the series uses aesthetic devices from the clip (aggressive camera movements, "unnatural" colour schemes and mood music) to fill out the story rather than resorting to "irrelevant" complications of plot and dialogue' (1990: 145). Music video sequences (what he calls 'clips') are, according to Buxton, 'simple time-wasting devices from a narrative point of view' (ibid.) because although the series often deals with the problems of rampant capitalism and the failures of liberal social policies to match up to the success of capitalism and associated criminality, it is unable to resolve these contradictions and so ends up in fatalism, world-weariness and a posturing with signs that lack an organising narrative. In contrast to this view, the analysis of the 'Buddies' episode in this chapter pays special attention to the relationship between storyline construction and visual and musical style, and will argue that style is not a supplement to or diversion from narration and characterisation but a key means of foregrounding the motifs that organise them.

The relationship between the attenuated narrative conventions of the police series and the foregrounding of style in *Miami Vice* can be seen in the frequent displacement of the structural convention of introducing a mystery that the narrative will solve. In *Miami Vice* what is introduced is more often a problem of deceptive appearance that the narrative may not find the right means to 'read'. Episode narratives are explicitly concerned with applying the law and dispensing justice, which is articulated as a problem of correctly recognising the good guys and the bad guys. The narrative of the pilot episode, for example, is not a completed or closed presentation of an achieved order, and it is commonplace across the series that Crockett and Tubbs arrest the wrong people, ineptly allow criminals to escape or their quarries are shot before they can be captured. These problems of moral action are linked to problems of maintaining a fragile sense of self, expressed in both visual and aural choices. For example, one distinctive feature of the pilot was its music, most notably in a long night-time sequence in which Crockett and Tubbs pursue a suspect across the city in a Ferrari sports car accompanied by the non-diegetic pop song 'In the Air Tonight' by Phil Collins. Thomas Carter was responsible for the sequence, and explained: 'What I wanted to do was not to use the music as just background, but as psychological subtext' (in Friedman 1985: 9). The song signifies Crockett's emotional status, where at this point he has just broken up with his wife, as Collins had done when the song was written, and Crockett has just discovered that a fellow officer is leaking information to the episode's antagonists. The music is an expressive device to register Crockett's feelings of disconnectedness and failure, and the car chase is thus not simply a digression from the storyline. Its rapid cutting between shots from camera positions on the car and at road level as it speeds past, for example, convey urgency and forward progression alongside the music's expression of being mired in despair and disappointment. While this can be interpreted, as Buxton does, as evidence of 'fatalism' in the mood of the series as a whole, the sequence has specific significance in the pilot as a realisation of character and as an expression of the counterpoint between Crockett's failures in his personal life and the vigour of his working role as a detective. Failure and powerlessness are consistent themes, and in *Miami Vice* generic narratives of investigation are problematised by the limitations of its undercover vice cops, and visual style is a key component in expressing the lack of knowledge that they have of themselves and the city's moral ambiguities.

The episode 'Buddies' (1985) has a broadly generic plot in which Crockett and Tubbs investigate a murder, but the detectives' ability to read the fictional world correctly and thus both identify right and wrong and also resolve the crime story are disturbed by confusions around the significance of family and masculine identity. There are three families in the episode: Crockett's friend Robert Cann (James Remar) celebrates the arrival of a son; Dorothy Bain (Eszter Balint), sometime cocktail waitress and battered wife, tries to protect her young baby and kills a nightclub performer; and 'The Family', a crime syndicate organised on patriarchal and hierarchical lines. Cann's family is especially ambivalent, for he not only comes to terms with being a father to his son, but is also a member of The Family, son of its 'godfather' Johnny Cannata (Tom Signorelli). The tensions between these family obligations are brought to the surface when the innocent Dorothy becomes a fugitive from The Family and Cann is asked to kill her for them. These non-recurring characters and the theme of family relationships are connected with Crockett in the 'Buddies' storyline because of his relationship with Cann's family. But the series format deals with familial relations on a larger scale, since Crockett and Tubbs are the most prominent members of a 'work family' that also includes their boss Lieutenant Castillo (Edward James Olmos), and buddy teams of two female and two male detectives. In the series pilot, Crockett broke up with his wife, leaving his son in her custody, because of his devotion to his job and his 'family' of colleagues. Tubbs arrived in Miami to pursue the killer of his brother, motivating his initial role in the series as a quest to avenge a family member.

Problems of knowledge are raised in the episode's opening pre-credit sequence, where the audience is introduced to Cann in one of Miami's glossy bars before Crockett arrives to meet him. Cann enters the bar, and wide shots establish it as visually disorienting because of its mix of relatively low-lit and undefined spaces versus a bright open area lit by a large circling overhead lighting fixture that casts multi-coloured hues over its occupants. This is a minor example of the influence of film noir (see Butler 1985) that has been discerned in the series' canted camera shots, high-contrast lighting and use of strong shadow, and deep focus to generate dynamic shot compositions stressing spatial depth and interconnecting spaces within settings. Loud diegetic rock music reinforces the visual connotations of confusion in the opening scene and makes the dialogue difficult to follow. An exchange between Cann and the barman shows that Cann is drinking too much because he is celebrating his son's birth. Crockett arrives and proposes a toast, 'Here's to the family', initiating the narrative question of what 'family' may mean. Cann draws a photograph out of his jacket, asking Crockett 'You know who's in that picture?' This moment is privileged by a close-up, to show that the photograph is of Cann and Crockett arm-in-arm as soldiers in Vietnam. Crockett identifies them as 'you and me', to which Cann replies 'No – that's me, and the godfather of my son'. The scene therefore offers two identities to Crockett, one of which is based on his complementarity with Cann and derives from their shared experiences in war. Second, Crockett is being invited into a family, with the quasi-paternal role of godfather. The close-up on the photograph, showing Crockett and Cann in a very different time and space from the narrative present, emphasises how different they may now be from each other and from who they were in the past. Cann is now a well-to-do husband and father, and Crockett a police officer, and the ways in which their identities are now different is expressed by the action that follows. The drunken Cann begins to dance on a pool table, provoking one of the players to pull a gun. Crockett, from trying to soothe with friendly words, has to draw his gun, announce himself as a police officer and save the situation. The camera takes a position from where Crockett, dressed in white, can be seen dominating the open space of the bar in a standing position, wielding his gun then manhandling the humiliated Cann out of the bar like a police suspect. Crockett is forced to invoke his authority as a policeman to control Cann's disordered behaviour and control the space of the action. But while the audience was privileged to see Cann's lack of self-control before Crockett's arrival, Crockett's changed understanding of and response to his old friend happens in the moment. This pattern of giving the audience more knowledge than the protagonists continues in the episode and consistently undercuts the detectives' mastery over the fictional world and its characters, because they act on incomplete or incorrect knowledge or fail to act effectively on the basis of what they know.

Miami Vice is reflexive in its foregrounding of genre convention, but by quite different means from *Hill Street Blues'* allusions to hand-held style and a large number of characters in unconnected storylines. Policing in *Miami Vice* is all about surface appearance. Crockett and Tubbs mark the difference between good and evil, just and unjust, by being and looking as ambivalent as their quarries and with a contingent relationship to Miami that changes as they adopt undercover identities. In a subsequent sequence of episodes including the aptly titled 'Mirror Image' (1988), for example, Crockett is afflicted by amnesia and lives for some time as a gangster, confusing his undercover and 'real' police identities. 'Buddies', like the series as a whole, explores Crockett's separateness from Miami's fascinating but duplicitous appearances. In the Miami of *Miami Vice*, the vice cop has the same style and status as Cann the nightclub owner, for example, and to conserve a principle of differentiation and social responsibility which underwrites this world of appearance becomes a difficult enterprise. Commodities like clothes, cars and stylish homes or nightclubs are signs of wealth and the possibility of pleasure, and might be gained by the sanctioned American ideology of upward mobility and gaining wealth, but they may also be the masks and dubious rewards of crime. Crockett and Tubbs take on these signs as a disguise, but in doing so they become fetishised objects of fascination for the camera's look and for the looks of other characters, for the narrative is frequently displaced by attention to the visual appearances of the two cops, as well as the sumptuousness of the locations. Fetishisation is the elision or concealment of lack and difference, and the emphasis on how things and people outwardly appear poses a problem for the police genre's processes of separating good from bad, and moving from the unknown to the known.

In 'Buddies', Morty Price (Nathan Lane), inept comedian and partner in crime with Cannata and Doss (Frankie Valli), The Family godfathers, is knifed to death by the innocent Dorothy Bain after an attempted rape. The visual style of the scene begins with stable and conventional shot/reverse-shots, when Price welcomes Dorothy into his hotel room and offers to use his influence to get her job back. This stylistic pattern changes, however, when Price tries to initiate sex with Dorothy in exchange for his help. The camera circles them at a distance, suggesting a shift from an innocent social encounter to a more threatening one and Dorothy's confusion about what is happening. In another shift in camera style, Price's attempt to rape her is shown in slow motion produced by step-printing parts of the scene's footage (Fig. 2.1), with slowed-down sound, producing a dreamlike sequence of sexual violence where the camera is close to Dorothy's

Fig. 2.1

face. Positioning the camera close to her point of view and using slow motion reinforces the viewer's alignment with Dorothy's shock and confusion, both emphasising the assault by lengthening its duration but also distancing it to some extent by rendering it in a different style from the established means of conveying time and space in the episode. The two forms of shooting share techniques and possible connotations, since both the circling and the subjective slow-motion camera movement register threat, but the slow motion accentuates horror and disturbance so that the violence itself is more evidently out of place and excessive. It is rare for *Miami Vice* to show hand-to-hand or bodily violence, and violence onscreen is elided in favour of an insistent and underlying threat of violence, conveyed by the almost omnipresent music and the restless movement of the camera.

Following a lead that Dorothy was seen with Price, Crockett and Tubbs locate her as gunmen are trying to find the betting records that she used to wrap her baby in when she left Price's room. Typically, Crockett and Tubbs fail to catch the gunmen or Dorothy following an exchange of fire. The members of the vice squad meet to discuss Morty Price's murder, which they suspect has something to do with Cannata and Doss, and Lieutenant Castillo instructs the detectives to locate Dorothy Bain. At this point her name is an empty signifier for the police. As the cops discuss the mystery, the camera circles twice around the table at their head-height, paralleling the circling around Dorothy in Price's room and with a similar effect of impending threat but lack of plot movement. Circling seems to signify indirection and confusion, and the movement of the camera is not arrested until the naming of Dorothy Bain. The narrative's concern with the difficulty of interpreting the evidence is concretised by camera movement and unanchored point of view. This uncertainty about where to look is then taken further by the narrative, as Castillo orders the video surveillance of Cannata and Doss in the hope of finding clues to Dorothy's whereabouts and her link with the crime syndicate.

One name which appears from the surveillance is Cann, Crockett's buddy, who features in a scene where he pays a tithe of his club's weekly income to Cannata and Doss while attempting to remain separate from their illegal activities. Again, the audience is shown the evidence of Cann's involvement in The Family's vice before Crockett is aware of it, and thus the challenge it represents to Crockett's separation from vice and also his ability to discriminate good from bad in the narrative world. Crockett and Tubbs visit Cann's club, which is glittering and stylish, where Cann denies involvement in The Family's pursuit of Dorothy. But Crockett's relationship with Cann makes Tubbs suspicious and threatens the relationship between the detectives. As the two sit outside the club in Crockett's Ferrari, Tubbs accuses Crockett: 'You're not facing reality, man', to which Crockett replies 'And you're not hearing me. He's my friend', while angrily stepping on the car's accelerator to rev the engine as the pounding chords of Jan Hammer's synthesised electric guitar rise in the sound mix to match it. 'Reality' is represented as a matter of reading people correctly, and the audience already knows that Crockett has misread Cann while Tubbs has accurately seen beneath Cann's outward appearance of respectability. Again, the detectives' lack of knowledge is clear to the viewer, and the implications of this threaten the detectives' relationship with each other. Sound and music are used to underscore this, in an otherwise conventional shot/reverse-shot exchange between them in the car.

Fig. 2.2

Cann's godson's christening features Crockett in a white suit matching the priest's white surplice (Fig. 2.2), and a gradually intensifying musical accompaniment by Hammer's driving synthesised guitar. Visually paralleling Crockett with the priest in this sequence establishes Crockett as a moral authority, welcoming Cann and his son into the community as the ceremony confirms their names. The next shot is of Crockett splashing water on his face at police headquarters, explicitly linking this scene with the christening because of the use of holy water to anoint the child's head. Crockett looks in the mirror above the sink as Tubbs enters and announces that Cann's real name is Cannata: he is Cannata's son. Not only is Crockett party to the inclusion in the community of the changeling child (Cann/Cannata), but Cann himself as a father, businessman and friend is revealed as masked, undermining his buddy relationship with Crockett. Crockett and the camera look into the mirror at Tubbs, the other buddy, whose mirror image visually complements that of Crockett's in the frame (Fig. 2.3). Looking in the mirror, or at a character who functions as a complementary mirror image, become visual means of representing the truth or duplicity of identity. After she had killed Price in self-defence, Dorothy noticed her reflection in a huge mirror in his room (Fig. 2.4), in another instance of the audience being given more information than the characters. She stopped for a moment, but had no difficulty in looking at her image 'because' she was innocent. Right and wrong, truth and duplicity, are expressed visually as a matter of correct seeing. Identities are tested by mirrors, and looking in the mirror is a way of trying to see oneself and other people correctly. This motif is available both to the characters, since Dorothy

Fig. 2.3

Fig. 2.4

and Crockett (and later Cann) reflect on their situation by looking at themselves in mirrors, and also to the camera since camera positions are chosen to permit the seeing of a character and his or her reflection. What works on one level as an expressive device of the narration is also present at another level as part of the fictional world. Thus the camera's interest in mirroring appears in the episode not as an added layer of commentary by stylistic means, but as an appropriate complement to the ways the characters think about themselves.

After the mirror sequence in which Cann's true identity is revealed, the gap between the detectives' knowledge and the audience's knowledge progressively narrows. Crockett confronts his buddy, and Cann confesses that his repudiation of the name Cannata and the identity of his father is because: 'It's like a scar Sonny, being related to these people. It's like having a cancer growing out of you – I mean, do you show that to somebody?' Metaphorically, Cann's patrimony has excised some organ or caused some part to grow out of control. These references to mutilation and disfigurement not only reflect back on the buddy relationship but also on the representation of the social body as the human body. The social body is expected to be a regulated set of relationships whose central metaphor is the human body's harmonious articulation of parts, so that the propriety of the physical and social bodies are mirror images for each other. Cann's dissimulation threatens the propriety of this ordered relationship between healthy body and properly functioning society, but Crockett as the representative of its order is delegated to heal the wound and thereby to repair Cann's 'cancerous' body and the fractured social body that it represents. Cann has to sacrifice his father to the law to retain his identity as a proper father himself, and this is done by his recognition and affirmation of his own true name (Cannata). For the mixing of these issues of family and patronymy reveals that the patriarchal order of The Family of crime is a distorted mirror image of conventional family relations and also the distorted mirror image of the capitalist economy. As a buddy, Crockett asks that Cann accept his 'real name' as Cannata and thereby purge his lack and social disease by speaking it to 'Sonny' Crockett. Crockett is then the godfather to whom confession is given in exchange for absolution, presiding over inclusion and exclusion from the social body as he did for Cann's child. Crockett is empowered to recognise right and wrong amid Miami's appearances, but a complete (masculine) identity which the 'scarred' Cann lacks is not coherent in itself and needs to be supplemented and complemented for Crockett by Tubbs and for Cann by Crockett. In other words, there are lacks everywhere that need to keep being filled up, or wounds that keep needing to be healed, in order to maintain the fragile law, bodies and identities in *Miami Vice*'s fictional world.

Again, this problem of restoring both moral and social order is addressed in terms of visual style through the repeated motif of the mirror. Crockett insists to Cann: 'The only obligation you've got is to yourself. If you can get up in the morning, look in the mirror, and be proud of what you see, then you fulfil that obligation.' The obligation is for Cann to recognise his own image in the terms of an already-present capacity to conform to the law and to social-moral norms. Crockett's remark is visually instantiated as Cann catches sight of, and turns away from, a mirror (Fig. 2.5). The imperative is then to take on this literal image, specifically to be able to see his family of wife and baby son and not feel guilty about connections with The Family. But as well as the set's mirror which expresses this issue visually, Crockett himself is a 'mirror' for his buddy, a moral guide. In the shot, Crockett is positioned so that he can be seen in the mirror alongside the reflection of Cann, suggesting the possibility of their complementarity. In the frame of the mirror's glass the two men share

Fig. 2.5

visual space and are complementary to each other, as Crockett and Tubbs were (in Fig. 2.3). One buddy relationship is compared and contrasted to the other by means of the same visual technique.

The narrative and style of '*Buddies*' work together to express persistent questions as to who the characters are and how their environment should be interpreted. This is a problem for discourses of law and justice in police drama, which are premised on the possibility that the moral status of the characters and the fictional world can be decided upon. Although Crockett and Tubbs are agents of narrative movement and embodiments of the law's identifying look, this does not fully account for the complex audio-visual construction which puts their ability to do their jobs and to know themselves in doubt. They have to be immersed in the confusing world of Miami's vice when they are undercover and it is only their efficiency and moral legitimacy which enforce ideological closure. However, the motifs such as mirroring, doubling or washing tend to problematise and confuse their identities as much as their antagonists'.

Neither the kinds of family introduced in 'Buddies' nor the certainty of the police's ability to master Miami's criminality are stable or reliable, and this is expressed in a characteristic use of music and visual style when the song 'No Guarantees' by The Nobodys is played over a car chase at the climax of the episode (Fig. 2.6) when Crockett and Tubbs race to rescue Dorothy from Cann (characteristically,

Fig. 2.6

Cann escapes from Crockett at Cann's nightclub). The song's refrain is 'No guarantees in the Western world' and, like the car chase in the pilot, fast cutting, unusual camera positions conveying the speed of the chase and close-ups on the policemen's worried faces express both generic action and the risk of failure. An overhead shot shows the car skidding out of control and, typically, Crockett and Tubbs arrive late as The Family's hit-men have already started shooting at Dorothy.

A momentary closure takes place in the final scene of 'Buddies', after Cann goes to save Dorothy from Cannata and Doss's gunmen. The camera position shifts repeatedly to show the hitmen's eruption into Dorothy's room in medium shot, then Crockett and Tubbs bursting into it and the ensuing gun battle between them. The sequence is edited together as a series of rapid cuts, matching the staccato sounds of gunfire and fast-paced rock music on the soundtrack. The scene is a generic action sequence that functions as the climax of the episode. It would conventionally be followed by a slowing down in the pace of editing where a scene, perhaps in the detectives' squad room, would parallel the imposition of order by the police with an exchange of friendly banter between Crockett and Tubbs, returning the narrative world to a sense of normality. However, the episode ends at the close of the action sequence. Cann rescues Dorothy Bain and her baby and is injured by a flesh-wound in the shoulder from a henchman's bullet. The alternation of brief shots separated by cuts in the action sequence is completed with a mid-shot of Cann lying on the floor, cradled in Crockett's arms. He receives Crockett's benediction, 'Yeah man, you did the right thing', and the frame freezes as credits appear over it. Tubbs is not present in the shot, and there is no return to another space unmarked by the disorder of furniture and gunshot damage that the camera witnessed in the room. Visually, then, there is little sense that the fictional world has been restored to normality and the episode ending seems abrupt and curtailed. Nominally the problems of identity and justice are resolved, and the end-titles reprise the opening title sequence, re-establishing the visual paradigms of the series. But the representation of social order and its legitimacy have been threatened by the ambivalence of appearances throughout, and the ending itself only appears to restabilise the fictional world by virtue of the fact that it is the last shot.

Stylistically, *Miami Vice* seems to acknowledge the provisional and deceptive nature of what and who its characters see, by expressing their own uncertainty through the visual motifs that the camera adopts. Structurally, the screen time given to passages of psychological and emotional confusion, car chases and failures of the protagonists to achieve their goals undermines the expected conventions of the genre. The impact of these decisions is to challenge a coherent vision of society at both the literal and ideological levels. Mann and the other creative authorities in the production seem to have regarded visual style as both a vehicle for storyline and characterisation and also as a relatively autonomous feature that produced *Miami Vice*'s audience appeal and distinctiveness as a 'brand'. The example of 'Buddies' shows that storyline and characterisation on one hand, and the cultivation of distinctive visual and aural style on the other, are certainly aspects of the programme which can yoke together uneasily. But attempts to link them through motifs such as mirroring or circling camera movements produce effects that comment in interesting ways on the moral dilemmas of the detectives in the specific fictional world of Miami, and the problems of knowledge and action with which that world presents them.

3. Homicide: Life on the Street

Homicide: Life on the Street was screened on the NBC network from 1993–99 in one-hour evening slots, was syndicated on the Lifetime cable network and has been sold abroad including screening on Channel 4 in Britain. This chapter returns to the development of a dramatic form adopting the aesthetic of hand-held filming that was used in *Hill Street Blues*, but also some of the self-conscious dramatic stylisation discussed in the chapter on *Miami Vice*. *Homicide: Life on the Street* was based on the book *Homicide: A Year on the Killing Streets* by the *Baltimore Sun* reporter David Simon, who spent a year with Baltimore police's homicide unit, and the series' producer Barry Levinson initially considered the book as the source property for a cinema film (see Troy 1997). Levinson is a native of Baltimore, and wrote and directed the Baltimore-based films *Diner* (1982), *Tin Men* (1987) and *Avalon* (1990), having begun his career in television as a writer for various series including the comedy *The Carol Burnett Show* (1967–78) in the 1970s. Comments by cast and production team (see Fretts 1993) reveal that Levinson was not only attracted by the dramatic potential of Simon's book but also by the idea of setting the series in an American city with a distinct sense of place. Positioned between New York and Washington DC, Baltimore lacks the cosmopolitan glamour of the former and the political profile of the latter, and its economic health as a centre of heavy industry was severely affected by the recessions of the 1980s. Furthermore, Baltimore as it appears in the series has been shot to distinguish it from the more usual locations for prime-time drama of Los Angeles, New York or Chicago. So not only does Levinson's conception of the series emphasise the particularity of its locations, but also the difference of those locations from urban environments associated with the police procedural genre. To further this particularity of place in the scripting of episodes, Levinson required that *Homicide*'s writers worked on the series on-site (see Troy 1997), to accustom themselves to the milieu and its characteristic regional accents and idioms.

A further advantage for the production team was that the NBC executives overseeing the process were located in the main production centre of Los Angeles. This meant that their visits to the shooting locations were rare and Levinson could work with considerable freedom on the style and structure of the early episodes that established the form of the programme. For this reason, the close analysis in this chapter deals with the opening episode 'Gone for Goode', which was directed by Levinson and set the visual parameters of the series. NBC's strategy for *Homicide* was to advertise it both by emphasising its generic characteristics as a police drama with gritty storylines and strong characters, and also to appeal to a sophisticated audience familiar with the discourses of auteurism, 'adult themes' and high production values associated with the emergent cable channels and cinema. By promoting Levinson through his films *Diner, Good Morning, Vietnam* (1987) and *Rain Man* (1988), the audience was being offered the attractions of visual style and creative distinctiveness. The first episode was shown directly after the Super Bowl to bring the series to the attention of the largest audience of the entire year.

The first episode begins with two characters walking slowly at night towards the camera, which is hand-held and unstable, and moves quickly to focus down onto their feet. They are holding a conversation about a book one of them has read that says life is a mystery. As the camera reverses to share the direction of their movement, it is apparent that they are police detectives in a rainy street arriving at a murder scene. The opening moments of the programme raise questions for the audience about who the characters are and what kind of programme this is, though some of this mystery will already have been dispelled by the series' widely-seen trailer in the Super Bowl television coverage. The camera remains hand-held throughout the first sequence where the

police walk into the centre of the crime scene and talk to uniformed policemen. Throughout, lighting is relatively low in the exterior setting and the illumination provided by the policemen's torches and the flashes of camera bulbs at the crime scene is prominent. Colour is muted, emphasising the grey suits, white shirts and black ties of the detectives and the black night sky (Fig. 3.1). This produces allusions to documentary and news footage, where low levels of available light in night-time shooting are likely to give rise to the same lack of colour definition and

Fig. 3.1

loss of visual detail, and strongly distances the programme from the highly coloured and brightly-lit conventions of shows in the preceding decade such as *Miami Vice*. The use of hand-held Super-16mm cameras (rather than 35mm) lent greater possibilities for camera movements to be tried out in the different takes of the same scene, responding to the performers. In the episode's first sequence, the camera moves around and up close to the detectives in the crime scene, as if following action that has not been planned-out for its convenience.

A very short interior close-up shot follows, of a hand writing with a red marker pen on a whiteboard, where the number of this crime is recorded together with the name of its victim, a Mr Becker. Punctuating the episode as a repeated motif, close-ups of the board mark the arrival of new cases into the detectives' purview, and the confirmation of their solution when victims' names in red are erased and the names are re-written in black (Fig. 3.2). Across this episode, night scenes shot with little supplementary lighting and reduced colour density repeat

Fig. 3.2

the aesthetic of the first scene, and the episode ends with another arrival at a crime scene by the new detective Tim Bayliss (Kyle Secor), shot in a similar style. Amidst heavy rain a pale body is laid out on the ground in a park, covered by a white sheet soaked in red blood, shot from above and contrasting with the black earth. The last shot of the episode is when a uniformed officer's flashlight, white against the black night-time trees and pallid moonlight, illuminates Bayliss's torso and hand but not his face as he pulls his reflective silver badge from his coat and says 'Homicide'.

The opening credit sequence follows the almost monochrome first scene, and comprises over a minute of rapid montage. The title sequence was shot on an 8mm camera, thus producing grainy images further processed in post-production to blur definition and increase contrast. It begins with a canted camera shooting through a car window as it drives along the empty street of a city, with colour bleached out from the buildings. This is followed by rapid camera movements panning very quickly across an indeterminate urban background, then the camera follows a car turning into a street, partially obscured by an object in the foreground. Colour remains almost entirely bleached out. Further very rapid alternations of shots show a city monument, another street seen from a car, a close-up on an office wall clock, a cobbled street with tram tracks, then a close-up of an eye and further fragments of street scenes. Next a tracking shot, again from a car window, shoots through a chain-link fence behind which a large dog barks and follows the movement of the car. The music throughout the sequence is relatively rapid but lacks strong melody and is based on an extended development of percussion and simple keyboard phrases, with intrusions of fragmented police radio communication. The sequence continues with further alternations of fragments of street scenes, men's faces and an extreme close-up of longer duration in which the camera pans slowly across the top of a police badge, revealing the word 'police' embossed on it. There are more shots of city centre monuments, which for some viewers will lead to the realisation that all of the exterior shots so far have been of the city of Baltimore. Interior shots follow, including a baseball sitting in a cup on a desk, extreme close-ups of parts of the face of a black man, and an occasional flash of red colour, which thus stands out against the black and white of the rest of the sequence. Among more brief close-ups of men's faces, the sequence returns to the police badge and pans slowly over its lower edge where the word 'Baltimore' can be seen. Following this are shots of the keypad of a telephone, more men's faces, more fragments of both the city streets and an office. The sequence draws to a close with the series title against a very strongly red-tinted photograph, in which the steps and railings at the front of a building can be made out. Only at the end of the sequence does a series of captions list the actors in the series, separately from their visual appearance, against a black background across which streaks of white light move quickly. Finally, a bleached, mainly white shot shows the reverse side of the glass door to the precinct office, on which the word 'Homicide' and the room number 203 are written.

Overall, the title sequence identifies the place in which the series is set, by fragmenting the city of Baltimore into relatively anonymous domestic buildings along with public parks and statues. Interior office settings are prominent, signified by such metonymic objects as the wall clock and telephone. The sequence identifies the faces of the lead actors (these are the men who are briefly featured) but without giving their names or providing clear visual introductions to them. The police badge, of course, identifies the series generically and geographically, and together with other elements it suggests the sub-genre of the police squad procedural. Most significantly, the title sequence establishes the fragmented, barely-coloured and self-conscious visual aesthetic of the programme which is analysed in greater detail below. But the sequence is distinguished stylistically from the main body of the episode in which fragmentation takes the form of cuts between different takes of the same shot, rather than a montage of different shots. The title sequence's speed and complexity are also different from the use of long takes and lengthy dialogue exchanges in the episode's narrative. But what links these styles is their shared evocation of place and procedural office-based policing.

The complexity of the opening episode's storylines requires a brief summary here in order to avoid unnecessary explanation later in this chapter. The opening teaser introduced the first storyline, in which Becker's murder is investigated by Detectives Meldrick Lewis (Clark Johnson) and Steve Croseti (Jon Polito) who visit a hospital to interview a suspect and Dollie Withers (Oni Faida Lampley), the woman accompanying Becker when he was shot, who is recovering from a head wound. It becomes clear that the attack was part of a conspiracy by Dollie's aunt to kill her for her life insurance, a crime the aunt already committed against five dead husbands, one of whom the detectives exhume from a cemetery. A new detective, Tim Bayliss, arrives to join the team and is shown around the squad room by its commander Lieutenant Al Giardello (Yaphet Kotto). John Munch (Richard Belzer) and Stanley Bolander (Ned Beatty), interview a suspect in a double stabbing. Kay Howard (Melissa Leo) and Beauregard Felton (Daniel Baldwin) are called to a scene where the decaying body of Henry Biddle has been found in a basement and they interview a suspect, Jerry Jempson (Jim Grollman). Over a group lunch, Giardello decides that Bayliss will partner Frank Pembleton (Andre Braugher). Munch and Bolander investigate the death of a young woman, Jenny Goode, a case they have previously failed to close, visiting her parents and then finding a suspect with long hair and a black sports car. They interview him on his porch, where he admits to running her down with his car. Pembleton and Felton investigate a death at a motel, taking Bayliss with them, then they interrogate a young man seen with the victim who turns out to be his killer. At the end of the episode, Bayliss takes his first phone report of a murder and goes to the scene, on a dark rainy night. These storylines begin at intervals through the episode and are intercut as they develop, thus emphasising the process of detection rather than the witnessing of crimes themselves. Point of view is thus focalised through the detectives, and the viewer's access to the fictional world is restricted to what they know. Storylines are initiated by the detectives answering telephone calls that send them to a crime scene from their squad room, and the arrival at the scene of a crime is usually the opening moment of each narrative strand.

The episode's unconventional style is evident in the scene from the first episode when Munch is interviewing a suspect in a hospital room. Throughout, the scene is segmented by a large number of cuts where the camera position changes but continuity of dialogue and action are maintained. There is no master shot from where the camera offers a whole view of the space and to which it could return to confirm the parameters of this space. The camera repeatedly 'crosses the line', breaking the 180-degree rule which conventionally requires that camera positions are always on one side of an invisible line connecting two speakers filmed in shot/reverse-shot. The camera usually favours the person speaking, but set-ups shift without any obvious reason so that by the end of the scene we have viewed the action from various points around a roughly circular perimeter surrounding the performers. This draws attention to the visual style of the sequence, but not to serve a marked interpretive narrative system (as the motifs of *Miami Vice* did). Instead it references the attempts of a documentary filmmaker to find the best place to witness an interaction that he or she does not control, without subservience to the spatial conventions of drama. The flow of dialogue is unbroken, and since *Homicide* was shot with a single camera the different takes of the scene would require the performers to perform the same dialogue many times so that the camera could be moved to a new position for another view of the interaction. This scene might then resemble documentary inasmuch as the camera seeks out an appropriate position rather than seeming to know where the performers are going to be, but the continuity of dialogue shows that this is scripted, rehearsed and precisely performed fiction. *Homicide*'s visual style often draws on two contrasting conventions. Camera position and camera moves suggest the observation of action that was not staged for its benefit, while continuity of action across cuts and different camera positions makes clear that this is drama. There is an assertive quality to this repeated adoption of both unconventional camera positioning and editing, which draws attention to the series' style as a deliberate differentiating strategy within the police series genre.

The first season of *Homicide* predominantly comprised episodes with three and often four separate storylines, though this number reduced in later episodes. Narrative pace within scenes is created by the placement and movement of the camera rather than physical action itself, and created also by the varying rhythms of cutting between parallel storylines as opposed to following complete scenes in sequential order. Storyline segmentation and cross-cutting take the place of action scenes. One effect of this is that the conventional structure of four acts is much less evident in episodes of *Homicide* than in the writing of previous series. The action consists not of generic car chases, shootings or pursuit through the streets, but of how the camera establishes a relationship with the mood and pace of dialogue and physical performance. This can be seen in the very unusual practice of jump-cutting between noticeably different takes of the same scene in this episode and more generally in the series. The sequences omit a passage of performance time without changing the camera position, resuming shooting the performance with no significant change of composition or focus. This practice is anathema to the conventions of dramatic television (and cinema) and also rare in factual programmes since, conventionally, cutaway shots to another view are used to cover up the join between the parts of the performance, so that the slight jarring or 'jump' in the image caused by cutting the two together is unnoticed. However, 'Gone for Goode' uses numerous joins between takes of the same shot, some more noticeable than others, and it quickly becomes clear that this is a consistent strategy.

One example is when Howard is interviewing Jerry Jempson about what he knows

Fig. 3.3

regarding the murder of Biddle. A short preceding sequence has introduced the character by showing his arrival in the squad room and his entry into 'the box', an interrogation room with two-way glass in which many scenes are set. Quickly there is a cut to a mid-shot of Jempson sitting still at the table, facing the camera but with sunglasses obscuring his face so that relatively little information is offered by his physical performance. A lengthy sequence, in which there are three obvious cuts without cutaways, stays focused on his face (Fig. 3.3). Although he is still, small movements of his head and shoulders make these cuts clear to see, and they have three predominant effects. The first is to render the man's rambling discourse comic, since at first he vaguely suggests he knew the victim, and a cut resumes this denial with further extraneous digression, then another cut resumes the denial again, until finally he claims he knows nothing at all. In this case the style portrays Jempson comically, and in the episode as a whole its function is to offer evaluative comment on character. Howard's questions can be heard though she cannot be seen, but a tedious process of Jempson's distraction, time-wasting and defensiveness is being abbreviated, ending up by showing that he is both guilty and ridiculous. The second effect is therefore to privilege speech rather than physical action and to allow characters to speak at length and reveal themselves through tone, turns of phrase and minimal gesture. Thirdly, the long sequence with noticeable edits between takes foregrounds the visual style of the sequence by refusing expected conventions of continuity. Taken together, these effects show that *Homicide* is interested in people, rather than forensic investigation, physical pursuit or the detail of police procedure. The audience's knowledge of the fictional world is primarily available from what characters say and how they react to each other, and interrogation scenes like that of Jempson are important ways of staging this across the series.

A stylistic device with parallel effects to jump-cutting is evident when Munch investigates the death of Jenny Goode. Early in the sequence Munch is at his desk, looking through photographs of men to find one matching the description of the man with long blond hair whose car was seen when she was run over. Brief jump-cuts omit parts of his repeated movement of putting one photograph to the back of the pile to reveal the next. Thus the sequence, shot over Munch's shoulder in medium close-up, seems to be looping the same shot over and over again, though in fact the photographs in his hand change at each repetition. While notably stylised, this is less marked as a technique than what follows, when Munch and his partner drive to a suspect's house and interview him on his porch. Here, different takes of the man's performance shot from different camera positions are cut together. The changes of camera position make the cuts very noticeable, since the man repeats the same line of dialogue, 'I don't know, I was drinking' over and over again as he is being questioned, with the camera shooting in close-up on his face but from suddenly different angles. Here the effect is also to make the man seem helpless to protect himself from the truth, finally evident in the change of the victim's name on the precinct's whiteboard from red to black, confirming that he was the killer. So, rather than marking an abbreviation of time, as if to cut out unnecessary detail, jump-cuts and the editing together of different takes of the same shot actually introduce far more detail into these scenes, though it is always detail of performance. Facial expression, the relationship of the performers to the background behind them, minimal gesture or movement and details of costume and appearance become intensified because they are extended in time or repeated.

The final aspect of camera style to be discussed in this chapter is the use of long takes, both where the camera is still and where it is moving. These, like hand-held camera operation and jump-cutting, are persistent features of *Homicide*'s style, and occur across all of the series. Long takes produce the impression of temporal continuity, and allow the camera to follow characters in a space that they interact with to reveal themselves and the relationships between character and environment. The extended look at the character places pressure on him or her, by enforcing the viewer's concentration on the detail of how the character acts and reacts across a sustained passage of action. In 'Gone for Goode' some long takes are static dialogue scenes comprising two-shots where both speakers are fully visible to the camera in mid-shot or long shot. An early example in this episode is when Lewis and Croseti are waiting in a hospital room for the shooting victim Dollie Withers to wake up from her operation. They decide they can afford the time, and stand leaning against the window frame talking. They are not discussing the case, or giving any of the expository information that might be expected in the opening episode of a television series. Instead, Croseti talks about his ongoing studies of the murder of Abraham Lincoln, about which he has been reading for some time and which is something of an obsession for him. A large part of the scene consists of a static two-shot of this conversation, whose main purpose is to reveal character by privileging performance both by the speaking Croseti and the mainly listening Lewis. As part of this, it suggests the long familiarity that the men have with each other, and also the tenacity and attention to detail that are the hallmarks of a homicide detective. This sequence does not contribute to their detective work and is a digression from the storyline, so it suspends the conventions of detective fiction. Furthermore, such an exchange would usually be edited as a sequence of shot/reverse-shot angles, so the duration of the static two-shot draws attention to it and its style. The character structure of the series is based around the partnerships of Baltimore police detectives, where each detective has extensive interaction with his or her colleagues and long-standing relationships and rivalries between them are explored. At the same time, this occurs together with evident self-consciousness of style in how these interactions are presented.

Later in the episode, Pembleton and Bayliss are standing in the dark room next to 'the box' in which the young suspect in the motel murder is sitting alone. The camera is positioned some metres behind them, and the dark room contrasts strongly with the bright lights inside 'the box'. The difference in light levels makes it difficult for the cam-

Fig. 3.4

era to pick out any detail in the detectives' bodies, and their faces are almost wholly turned away from the camera. An internal frame produced by the edges of the two-way mirror in front of them further emphasises their static positioning in the shot, and their lack of engagement with the seated suspect (Fig. 3.4). Pembleton tells Bayliss in a long speech that he is like a salesman, whose job is to sell a prison sentence to a perpetrator who is assuredly not desirous of one. The unchanging lighting and composition forces attention onto Pembleton's delivery of this key speech. It reveals him to be extremely insightful and thoughtful about his profession, and presents his sense of himself as both akin to a rather seedy salesman peddling something to a consumer who does not want it, but also as a highly skilled interrogator who very often succeeds in securing a confession. Once again, the long take privileges a verbal performance and sets up a difference between the characters. Bayliss finds Pembleton ruthless and cruel because his technique aims single-mindedly for results, even though Pembleton's expertise in securing confessions is a kind of efficiency and thus valuable to the squad. A moral issue about whether the detectives are pursuing truth, their own ambition or a better clear-up rate is expressed by character interaction. Pressure on the characters from their jobs and from each other is expressed by adopting the visual style of static camera in a long take whose visual field is constrained by darkness and an internal frame.

There are three scenes which make use of long takes with moving camera in 'Gone for Goode', two of which combine exposition with character development and one which is largely centred on the relationship between Pembleton and Felton, and thus offers characterisation more than any contribution to storyline progression. When Lewis and Croseti are working on the investigation of Dollie Withers' aunt and her dead husbands, they visit a cemetery to witness the exhumation of one of the husbands. Long hand-held tracking shots follow the detectives as they converse with the graveyard attendant (Leonard Jackson) while walking towards the grave. The camera position is alongside the line of men walking three abreast, occasionally moving ahead of them to see their faces more clearly and at times finding only two performers in the frame as their speed of movement slightly changes or the camera closes in a little on one or two of them. The camera tends to favour whoever is speaking, giving equal attention to the non-recurring character of the attendant and the two detectives. As in other sequences discussed here, this prioritises dialogue at the expense of forward movement of the storyline. Although some of the dialogue is blackly comic, concerning the process of decay of bodies in the cemetery, and is supported by the changing background of white gravestones behind the men, it also serves to inform the detectives about what they might be able to discover from the exhumed body and thus the evidence they might gain. Later in the episode, another similar visit to the cemetery is shot in the same way.

In another example, Lewis and Croseti visit the city morgue to speak to the pathologist about the exhumed body from the cemetery. In this very long, mobile and stable take, the camera is always ahead of the detectives as they move towards it, thus keeping their faces and bodies in shot throughout. It begins as the officers walk down a long corridor. When moving around a corner, talking as they go, they stand back to make way for a stretcher carrying a body which is wheeled in front of them. Resuming their original direction of movement along the corridor towards the camera, they stop and stand in the doorway of the morgue, and finally the pathologist (Ralph Tabakin) approaches to speak to them. This shot contains little storyline information, and is instead centred on the reaction of the detectives to the environment in which they find themselves. While Lewis is relatively unconcerned, the scene's long take and wide angle permits the

Fig. 3.5

viewer to see at length and in detail the reaction of Croseti to the space. Throughout the scene, he is sweating heavily and repeatedly mops his face with a handkerchief (Fig. 3.5). The reading of his bodily movement is thus much more significant than his words, and establishes his uneasiness with the morgue, its smell and its enclosed interior space. It is also significant in relation to this dramatic function of the scene that it cuts to another long take sequence where Croseti and Lewis return to the cemetery (because the wrong body was exhumed), thus drawing further attention to the motif of encountering dead bodies in different locations and circumstances and also to the visual means by which this is represented.

Continuing the development of Pembleton's character which was discussed above in relation to the static long take outside 'the box', a short scene between Giardello and Pembleton leads to his departure with Felton from the squad room. In two long takes, with hand-held camera, they move through the precinct building and down into the police garage where long lines of white police cars are parked. Pembleton has a car key, and while the dialogue continues he tries one after another of the 100 or more identical cars to find the one which his

Fig. 3.6

key will fit (Fig. 3.6). This scene is comic, in that it is based on physical business where Pembleton repeatedly approaches a car, talking with Felton all the time, and tries a key, only to find that it is the wrong one and he moves on. When asked why he does not give up and go upstairs for another key, Pembleton replies that the next car he tries might be the right one, so going upstairs would only risk wasting more time. Of course this demonstrates Pembleton's tenacity and thoroughness, but here in a context that also suggests that his very strengths as a detective in these respects might also be a character weakness that amounts to obsession. The dialogue between the detectives is based on Pembleton's view that Felton does not like him because he is black, and reflects on racial tension that runs through many of the scenes in this episode. By shooting the scene in long takes, the episode counterposes dialogue with physical activity that has nothing to do with it, setting up the distance from, on one hand, Pembleton's preoccupations and on the other Felton's and the audience's reading of them, leaving space for both humorous and serious reactions to the performance.

This analysis has shown that *Homicide* favours characterisation and complex dialogue interaction over the conventional generic components in police series of action sequences and narrative momentum. Across the seasons of this series, character profiles were developed that emphasised the problems for the individual detectives, whether within their jobs or in their domestic lives. For example, Munch has been married three times, Bayliss is a survivor of childhood sexual abuse by his uncle, Lewis carries the supposed bad luck of having a series of partners killed and Pembleton is a control freak who had a debilitating stroke after which his wife left him along with their daughter. By paralleling working relationships with the detectives' lives outside their work, notably their interactions about and within the bar which they decide to buy together later in the series, *Homicide* as a whole addresses the challenges to individual masculine identity that being a detective poses, and the boundaries between public and private identities. The co-executive producer Tom Fontana commented that 'Homicide detectives are the elite – the best of the best – but the procedure they do is fairly dull. What attracted Barry and me to the material is that these are thinking cops ... they can be articulate. They can be a way with language that the audience will enjoy watching as these guys verbally joust with each other' (in Troy 1997). As this chapter has discussed, visual style prioritises characters speaking at length, and the viewer's access to the fictional world is through their interaction with it and each other, primarily in dialogue. The use of long takes with still and moving camera to extend the viewer's experience of time, and repetition of moments of the action, permit the evaluation of the characters. Shifts between comedy and drama were understood as representations of the real behaviour of police detectives, masking both masculine aggression and a compassion that might signify weakness by defusing them with off-hand humour. This mixed tone is most evident in the complex writing of the episodes, with the effect of realising character and the narrative world with greater depth. But by denying the viewer any knowledge of the narrative world except what the detectives have themselves, the conventional mastery of that world achieved by the detectives' solving of crimes is rendered insecure. Instead, what the viewer is given by means of visual style and narrative structure is the detail of inter-personal interaction, and it is the detectives themselves to whom the camera and the viewer have privileged access.

4. NYPD Blue

NYPD Blue is another of Steven Bochco's productions, co-created with David Milch, beginning on ABC in 1993 in a late-evening Tuesday slot and running until 2006. The precinct-based drama maintains some of the stylistic texture of *Hill Street Blues*, including the extensive use of mobile camera, but unlike the earlier series it uses prominent music to underscore emotional tone. This matches *NYPD Blue*'s emphasis on performance by the lead actors, characterised by richly detailed facial expressiveness and physical gesture to convey moral and emotional turmoil, especially by Dennis Franz as Lieutenant Andy Sipowicz. Franz is one of a loose ensemble of actors who have appeared in other Bochco productions (*Hill Street Blues*, *Bay City Blues* (1983) and Milch's *Hill Street* spin-off *Beverly Hills Buntz* (1987–88), for example). *NYPD Blue*'s commitment to the development of its lead performances, and to what US commentators and some US audiences have regarded as challengingly 'adult' sexuality, earned the series numerous Emmy award nominations, of which Franz won four. This chapter will give most attention to the opening episode from September 1993 in which the 'signature' stylistic elements were first aired and were at their most prominent. These include moving camera and fluid shot composition, a percussive and pervasive music track and a marked use of slow motion and shots with different depths of field. The decision to apparently fatally wound the leading character Andy Sipowicz in the opening episode, and to include a lengthy sex scene, make clear the programme's ambition to innovate in the police series genre while also connecting it to the heritage of 'quality' work associated particularly with Bochco.

The first and second episodes of *NYPD Blue* were written by David Milch, and shot in a single twenty-day period on sets built in Los Angeles at 20th Century Fox and on location in New York's Lower East Side (see Milch and Clark 1996: 27). Paul Eads was the production designer for the series, aiming for a down-at-heel urban setting for interiors and exteriors. New York location sequences were planned to include recognisable signifiers of place such as parks, the city's skyline or subway stations, where as many as possible of the regular characters would be featured. Having created establishing sequences in this way, a second unit in New York without the presence of performers provided a selection of further establishing shots that could be integrated in post-production. The series' cinematography aimed to recreate the light and colour palette signifying New York in both interior and backlot exteriors in Los Angeles, using backlighting and areas of natural light to signify the strong shadowing created by New York's tall buildings and the leakage of fluorescent or neon lights into both interior and exterior spaces (see Fisher 1996). Light bounced from steel mirrors onto scenes shot on the shadowed side of Los Angeles backlot streets produces the effect of sunlight reflected from unseen buildings, and shooting on Eastman film stock gave stronger contrast. In interiors, performance areas were lit through the motivated apertures in the set (like windows and doors) and choices of lens aimed to compress the space to make it appear smaller, urban and claustrophobic. By painting the walls of the sets with gloss paint, light in interiors could be bounced off the walls and floor to simulate indirect natural light, and overall the decisions on lighting and setting were made to prioritise verisimilitude of location and a sense of spatial confinement that would match the characters' embattled relationships with their jobs and each other.

These settings establish a sense of place for the series and offer the viewer a consistent understanding of the fictional world as a busy, grimy and morally confusing environment, where the routine processes of police investigation make sense of its complexity only barely, temporarily and at considerable cost to the detectives themselves. The opening of the first episode announces this strongly by combining mobile camera shots in a rapid montage of exteriors and interiors, within which the lead characters are first seen, shot with a consistently muted brown and blue colour palette. Each episode of *NYPD Blue* begins with an opening 'teaser' unique to it, and is then followed by a title sequence common to all the episodes in the series. In the first episode, this teaser is a rapid montage of moving shots that denotes relatively anonymous parts of Manhattan and street scenes with numerous cars and passers-by. Over this sequence, a rhythmic percussion soundtrack is played, and as the sequence concludes there is a series of moving camera shots showing fragments of the exterior of the Criminal Courts Building. It would be conventional in television series episodes for the opening to comprise one or more stable wide shots that denote the location of the subsequent action, often panning along a street then moving in close-up to a specific doorway or window, followed by a cut that implies the narrative's entry into that building for an interior scene. The opening of *NYPD Blue*'s first episode abbreviates and fragments this conventional establishing sequence, but does not abandon its role in establishing place. The stylistic choices of moving camera where the subject of the shot is not clearly identifiable, shooting parts rather than the whole of buildings, bridges and streetscapes, and cuts within the montage that are so frequent as to confuse the movement from the generality of the city to the Courts building specifically, are in dialogue with convention but destabilise the viewer's sense of knowing this fictional world with any security.

The first scene presents a courtroom in which Sipowicz is giving evidence against local crime boss Alfonse Giardella (Robert Costanzo). The camera moves restlessly, following the exchange between the Assistant District Attorney Sylvia Costas (Sharon Lawrence) and Sipowicz on the witness stand, and repeatedly breaking the 180-degree rule to shoot from the back, front and each side of the space. Changes of camera position suggest that the camera 'knows' what the characters will do and say next, so that it can be in an appropriate place to show the audience what they say and do from a frontal position. But on the other hand, the camera pans unsteadily as if attempting to place each speaker in a central position within the frame, reframing during the shots and often arriving 'too late' to privilege a speaker at the centre of the frame at the moment they begin to speak. Overall, the camera appears to offer privileged access to the fictional world by being in the right place at the right time. But it lacks sufficient insight into the motivations, intentions and emotions of the characters to anticipate specific moments in the drama and present them with the assurance that stable camera and harmonious framing would conventionally achieve.

Sipowicz delivers his testimony as if it were thoroughly rehearsed, in a rapid and inexpressive official discourse, but this moves to vehement self-justification as it becomes clear that he illegally searched the boot of Giardella's car by puncturing his tyre with nails to provide an excuse for stopping him. The camera's emphasis is on distinctions of bodily movement as well as the dialogue, representing a contest for authority between the Assistant DA, Giardella's lawyer, James Sinclair (Daniel Benzali) and Sipowicz. Sipowicz is relatively still, even lumpish, on the witness stand, while Costas and Giardella's attorney control the space by moving around in the open floor in front of the judge's bench. A brief long shot introduces John Kelly (David Caruso) who is yet to be identified as Sipowicz's partner, sitting at the back of the court and smiling grimly as the deception is revealed. The climax of the sequence plays out outside the courtroom when Sipowicz asks Costas whether she is accusing him of lying in court, to which she replies with learned authority that she would say 'Res ipsa loquitor' (the matter speaks for itself) if Sipowicz could understand it. Franz's performance physicalises Sipowicz's rejoinder 'Ipsa this, you pissy little bitch' in a quite shocking way by

Fig. 4.1

speaking the line as he stands erect and thrusts out his crotch towards her with his hand (Fig. 4.1). This demonstrates his determination to regain his masculine ascendancy over her, and the choice to shoot this moment with both characters facing the camera, with Kelly as a judging onlooker, provides for comparison and evaluation of their expressions and postures. Costas' weary endurance of Sipowicz's sexism and his own desperate need to assert himself are economically communicated by the composition of the shot.

By means of this first scene, the ongoing vendetta of Sipowicz against Giardella is established; Sipowicz's misguided, prejudiced and high-handed personality is introduced; and performance styles conveying varying levels of physical control and sublimated violence set up these issues as the primary undercurrents of the narrative world. The visual style of wandering and restless camera follows character interaction and discursive contests of authority. The editing style counterpoints these mobile close shots with wider shots that permit observation of physical movement, gesture and character interaction. But in both close and more distant shots, off-centre composition and constant reframing, with the apparent uncertainty about the centre of action that this implies, parallel the moral and emotional ambivalence of the fictional world with a corresponding uncertainty of focus embedded in the style.

The main credit sequence, following the episode-specific opening teaser discussed above, remained the same across the first season and signalled the series' interest in New York as a confusing, racially diverse environment that has been associated with violent crime. Representations signifying New York much more clearly than the shots of the city described in the teaser were combined with still shots of the main characters, each captioned with the actor's name. The prominence of the actors in the credit sequence draws attention to the significance of performers in a way that the credit sequence of *Miami Vice*, for example, did not. The sequence opens with a shot of the 'El' elevated railway at night as a train thunders past, followed by shots that include the demolition of an apartment block and the busy entrance of a subway station. These are interspersed with shots of the detective team and other main characters such as Kelly's estranged wife, Laura (Sherry Stringfield), and fragments representing police work such as a crime scene attended by uniformed officers and a police patrol car. The sequence closes with the white and red lights of distant cars on a freeway at night, the fireworks, traditional drumming and dragon costumes of a Chinatown festival and finally the dark tunnel of a subway seen from a train driver's cab. The music for the sequence comprises the percussion rhythm identified in the opening establishing teaser, together with an overlaid woodwind motif in a minor key with occasional intrusions of found sounds including police sirens. The sense of New York as a multi-ethnic, noisy and messy environment is connoted by these fragments of busy streetscapes, forms of transportation and crowds of people, and the percussion itself is to some extent motivated by its components (train sounds, drums, fireworks). The slow woodwind melody suggests an ageing urban fabric (as opposed to the choice of a synthesiser or electric guitar, for example) and a weary, dispirited mood that matches the grim expressions of the main characters in the sequence's stills and their placement in the untidy and dully-coloured settings of the squad room.

Greg Hoblit was the producer for the whole of the first season and also directed some of the episodes, ensuring continuity in the style of the series. In later seasons, the introduction of newer producers and multiple directors gave greater creative autonomy to the cinematographers responsible for the continuities in the distinctive visual look of the series. The cinematographer working on the series from the eighth episode onwards was Bob Reynolds, who described in an interview (in Fisher 1996) how by the time of his involvement a style of camerawork had been embedded into the aesthetic template of the programme. In his view, the style of filming used throughout the first season derives from imagining the camera to be a participant character in the scenes, present as an unacknowledged onlooker. However, as we have seen in the discussion of the courtroom scene, the camera is positioned not as if it were the ocular point of view of a character familiar with the people and places that it witnesses. Instead, the camera is able to anticipate passages of action but without the precision of framing and composition that would enable it to have mastery over the fictional world and deliver knowledge of that world confidently to the audience. In this respect, the camera's role is parallel to that of the detectives, who are competent and effective but also unable to master their environment and their own emotional and moral problems.

The effect of the directorial style of the series on establishing shots and the beginnings of scenes is often to diminish the emphasis in the shot composition on what or who will become the centre of the dramatic action. In Fig. 4.2, for example, in which Kelly arrives at the precinct house, the camera is shooting through the chain-link fence of a small public playground across the street, and Kelly is obscured not only by this but also the parked police vehicles and then some of the officers standing outside the building. In scenes with several performers, like this one, the effect is to greatly diminish the conventional television prac-

Fig. 4.2

tice of offering a master shot of the action in a scene supplemented by singles, two-shots and close-ups. In the brief sequence showing Kelly's arrival, the camera tracks his movement as if it were the subjective point of view of someone behind the fence, trying to pick Kelly out from among the vehicles and police officers. This locates Kelly at the station-house in preparation for the subsequent dialogue scene, thus operating as an establishing shot, but the decision to place the camera behind the fence rather than in front of it, leaving the wire mesh in shot, works together with camera movement and reframing to introduce a sense of difficulty and uncertainty in the camera's and the viewer's access to space and significance. The series producer Greg Hoblit labelled this the 'flicking eye' technique or 'dektoring' (after the prominent US director of television commercials Leslie Dektor; see Fisher 1996), and in the early seasons this shooting style was NYPD Blue's distinctive trademark. The fluid camera style is hardly ever hand-held though it might appear so, and was created by using a wheeled dolly and a Sachtler camera mounting which has settings that variably resist jerky camera movement, allowing levels of panning or tilting speed and smoothness to be adjusted either for stability or a deliberate approximation of hand-held camera wobble. As versions of this style began to be adopted by other network series, the impact of the style became less significant and by the later 1990s Reynolds diminished its vigour while still aiming for an aggressive prominence of camera movement. In contrast to Homicide: Life on the Street, aesthetic stylisation throughout the series was orientated around the moving camera's attempts to locate the centre of action in space (by means of what Reynolds (in Fisher 1996) called a 'fishing pass'), or following character dynamics in a dialogue scene where whip-pans, focus pulls and reframing match the byplay of interaction or suggest the shifts in power evident in a confrontation between characters.

The visual style of NYPD Blue raises again the epistemological issues discussed in earlier chapters of this study, which have explored the ways in which the police genre's focus on the acquisition of knowledge and processes of moral evaluation are connected with style and narration. NYPD Blue has partial knowledge of its fictional world and its characters, rather than total access to them. The ways the camera is used to demonstrate this are sometimes described by suggesting that the camera represents a character, because this suggests the embedding of the camera within the fiction but also the camera's limited mastery over the drama's progress. In an example given by Reynolds (in Fisher 1996) referring to his work with the later pairing of Franz with Jimmy Smits (playing Bobby Simone) as the series' protagonists, the camera might show that Sipowicz is looking for a newspaper by tilting down from a mid-shot of him, following the direction of his glance, to see one on a desk. Tilting up to see Sipowicz point to Smits in a wordless request for the newspaper, pans back and forth between them are shot wide enough to show Smits pick up the newspaper and hand it to Sipowicz as he walks past, all in a single shot. In this wordless exchange, the relationships between the two policemen are communicated by their interaction in a shared space and a shared shot, without cuts back and forth between each of them or to the newspaper. While the camera cannot anticipate or fully know their thoughts, its movement between them and around the space is motivated by a sense that observing such simple details brings the camera and the viewer both physically and emotionally close to them in the context of a seamless passage of time and action.

Studio sets for the series were made to provide the actors with relatively realistic spaces in which to perform, where rooms were constructed with ceilings, and scenes were played beginning to end several times, shot from different camera positions, in order to allow continuity of performance for the actors. Cutting between these different set-ups, together with the tendency to keep the camera moving as it reframes the actors and follows their movement, produces the overall effect of bringing the viewer close-up with the actors' performances, but also of troubling the viewer's access to the drama. The detectives are themselves not wholly in control of their relationships with each other, or their professional and personal lives, thus aligning their rather precarious knowledge of themselves and their world with the viewer's restricted access to them. The extent to which Sipowicz is unable to control himself or his surroundings is shown by the events leading up to his shooting, and the shooting itself, towards the end of the episode. These scenes are filmed in different ways, and continue the pattern of giving and withholding knowledge. Narratively, it is shockingly unconventional for a main character such as Sipowicz to be apparently fatally wounded in the first episode of a new police series. Some of this surprise is also communicated at the level of style by the intensification of privileged access and also the denial of access that have been discussed so far.

The narrative progression towards Sipowicz's shooting begins when he retreats to Patrick's Bar to drink a long series of whiskies after the opening courtroom scene. He is confronted by Kelly about his drinking and Kelly refuses to keep covering for his partner's inadequacies. Kelly visits his estranged wife, where a sub-plot involving robberies in her apartment building is introduced. Sipowicz confronts Giardella in a restaurant, goads him about his toupee and forces him at gunpoint into the street where they tussle, interrupted by Kelly who rescues Sipowicz from further trouble. Next day, Kelly meets Detective

Janice Licalsi (Amy Brenneman) to arrange surveillance of his wife's apartment block. Sipowicz admits his failings, is interviewed by Internal Affairs and is suspended from duty. The depressed and defiant Sipowicz reacts by going with Lois (Shannon Cochran), a prostitute he knows and meets on another visit to Patrick's Bar, to her apartment where Giardella shoots him several times in the back and legs in a pre-arranged assassination attempt.

In this scene, Franz's performance emphasises Sipowicz's physical decay and grotesqueness, drunk, chain-smoking, overweight and balding, approaching physical and psychological collapse in a parallel and opposite movement to the similarly overweight, balding and crude Giardella's triumph over him. Sipowicz is on the bed with Lois in his inelegant singlet, shirt and boxer shorts, as Lois comforts him and initiates sex. Remaining close to Sipowicz's pallid and sweating body as he descends

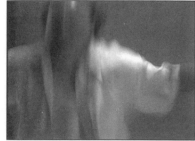

Fig. 4.3

further into degradation by exploiting Lois seems at first to amplify the withdrawal of the audience's sympathy for him, initiated by his lying on the courtroom witness stand and then his evident alcoholism and dependency on Kelly covering-up for him. The camera roams over their bodies in mid-shot, tilting slightly upward to notice Giardella's arrival in the room. After an exchange of insults, the sequence moves into step-printed slow motion as the camera witnesses Giardella's gunshots from a position close to Sipowicz's optical point of view, reversing to show Sipowicz catapulted back into the wall (Fig. 4.3), then falling onto the bed as further shots hit his back and buttocks. Slow synthesised chords in a descending phrase accompany the sequence as Sipowicz lies face-down on the bed, barely moving. The impact depends on the sudden abandonment of the episode's rapid speed of information delivery and rapid pace of cutting and camera movement. Focusing on Sipowicz's body almost exclusively, the sequence leaves little room for doubt that he has been killed.

This remarkable narrative turning-point is emphasised by the adoption of a different visual style from what has preceded it, and is very reminiscent in both visual style and narrative impact of the slowed-down shooting of Hill and Renko in the pilot episode of *Hill Street Blues* (see chapter one). But showing Sipowicz as a victim, lying lumpishly on the bed in his underwear with bloody wounds in his back and buttocks, modifies the feeling of revulsion for his physical and moral decay. Instead he becomes much more sympathetic, since Giardella's actions are excessively violent, and Sipowicz has been deliberately lured into vulnerability by Lois who is revealed to have been complicit with Giardella in setting him up. The emotional tone shifts from revulsion for Sipowicz to revulsion for the fictional world in which he could suffer such self-disgust, moral degradation and violent retribution. The slowing-down of the sequence at its end, finishing with

Fig. 4.4

the still mid-shot of Sipowicz on the bed, allows a space for contemplation and reflection, and seems to indicate the end of the episode.

The shooting is not the end of the episode, however, and the following scene centres on Kelly's arrival as Sipowicz's body, covered by a sheet, is brought from the doorway to a waiting ambulance, accompanied by the same slow music as the shooting scene and completely without dialogue. The camera is positioned in the street, some metres from the action, and a series of pans and cuts locate Kelly as he arrives and follows his movement towards Sipowicz's body. However, the action is partially and sometimes fully obscured by a large number of obstacles in the frame, which include police vehicles parked across the street, barriers protecting the crime scene, uniformed officers, bystanders and detectives who stand there uselessly and look around in distress (Fig. 4.4). Moreover the camera's panning movements and occasional shifts in focus convey its lack of privileged access to the action, as if it occupies the point of view of a member of the public being held back from the crime scene. This develops the series' characteristic use of the camera as an observer, but at the same time the camera's attempts to identify and isolate Kelly as he moves towards the body demonstrate that the camera is aware of his significance as Sipowicz's partner and friend. Placing the camera amid the clutter of the street scene situates the drama firmly within the spatial context of New York and the confusing street-level activity that can be seen at its most dense from the waist-level position and with the deep focus lenses used here. Overlapping planes of people and objects seen against a busy and detailed background thematise the problems of making sense of this milieu and of the excessive violence that erupts from the vendetta between Sipowicz and Giardella. The problems of seeing through these layers of foreground and background action, like the camera's attempts to centre subjects in the frame, dramatise epistemological issues stylistically.

The lighting system adopted in the series as a whole makes some of the problems of identifying the significant visual elements within a shot less difficult for the viewer. Its effect is to exaggerate contrasts of light and dark, 'hot' and 'cool' colour temperatures, and to produce the series' dominant colour signatures of blue, brown and green. By developing a relatively dull colour palette, bright colour achieves greater significance. So the red sweater of Donna Abandando (Gail O'Grady), the glamorous precinct secretary, marks her out from her surroundings, for example, and in exteriors yellow police crime-scene tape or red blood appear more emphatic. Reynolds reported (in Fisher 1996) that the final arbiter of visual style was Bochco himself, who supported experimentation with low light or long lenses, for example, as long as they matched his aesthetic vision for the series. An example of this kind of experimentation occurs after Kelly has confronted

Giardella's mafia boss Angelo Merino (Joe Santos), and news arrives that Sipowicz is alive. Kelly and Licalsi go back to Kelly's apartment and have sex, only to be interrupted by a visit from Kelly's wife wishing to sympathise over Sipowicz's shooting.

Fig. 4.5

A series of dissolves, in contrast to the cuts used in all other scenes of the episode, abbreviates Kelly's and Licalsi's arrival and initial kissing in his apartment, before they undress and begin to make love accompanied by a non-diegetic pop song. The scene is shot in very low light, with motivated high-lights from an open window picking out the curves of their naked bodies in a series of mid-shots and close-ups. The highly aestheticised sequence uses the same colour palette as the majority of scenes in the episode, emphasising blue in the room's curtains which are lit as if by a neon sign outside it, and brown in the skin tones of the actors' smooth naked bodies (Fig. 4.5). But here the tone of the sequence is completely differ-ent from either the urban drama of policing, or the otherwise closely related sex scene involving Sipowicz and Lois. The dramatic function of the scene is to represent Kelly's desire for release from the day's traumatic events, and Licalsi's attraction to Kelly who she perceives as a role-model (though it will later be revealed that she is in the pay of Giardella's boss, Merino). Its visual style contrasts with the grittiness of the preceding scenes and corresponds to aestheticised portrayals of the body in other media such as magazine photography and advertising.

The way that the style of the scene positions the audience is interesting because the scene's relative length, its use of dissolves and its unusually smooth camera move-ments contrast with the rest of the episode. Although the lighting system is similar, the love song laid over the scene is quite different in mood from the percussive sound used elsewhere and suggests both romance and the narrative's willingness to endorse the relationship between Kelly and Licalsi. The first part of the scene seems calculated to lull the audience into an acceptance of the narrative's shift to Kelly rather than Sipowicz, and encourage an eroticised mode of engagement with the action. But while the couple are in bed Kelly's wife arrives at his door, and the music and visual style change to a relatively conventional shot/reverse-shot exchange between her (clad in dark-coloured outdoor clothing) and Kelly whose nakedness is partially covered by a white sheet. She has come to sympathise with Kelly, having heard that Sipowicz has been shot, but realis-ing what Kelly has been doing she leaves angrily. The romanticised and seductive tone of the beginning of the scene is thus marked as a digression and a diversion from the emo-tional path of the episode as a whole, which is centred on the relationship between Kelly and Sipowicz and is about their different reactions to their physical, professional and emotional worlds. The audience's luring into this erotic and sensuously-shot sequence is parallel with Kelly's inappropriate choice of consolatory sex with Licalsi, and also Sipowicz's doomed consolatory sex with Lois. A moral issue about the detectives disengaging with the struggle to do their job and to connect with each other has been pointed out by the episode's stylistic and narrative disengagement from its established systems.

Characterisation, and the interweaving of workplace storylines with the precinct officers' personal lives was as important to the aesthetic of the series as its camerawork and editing. Sipowicz became involved with Sylvia Costas, who in the first episode he insulted after his blatant lying on the witness stand; Kelly had a relationship with Licalsi; the shy Detective Greg Medavoy (Gordon Clapp) became involved with the unit's glamorous secretary Abandando, and detectives James Martinez (Nicholas Turturro) and Adrienne Lesniak (Justine Micelli) paired up with each other. These pairings blurred the boundaries between workplace and domestic lives, demonstrating the importance of characterisation and the creation of evolving character arcs over episode-specific crime storylines. But working relationships between men – and especially between the central pair of detectives – rather than the romantic involvements, are the series' key focus. In this episode, for example, after Kelly meets Giardella's gangland boss Marino to turn down his offer to punish Giardella himself, Licalsi secretly meets Marino who arranges for her to kill Kelly. Her role is to be an instrument of a struggle between the two men.

Fig. 4.6

The most satisfying emotional encounter is between the two male detectives, in the closing scene of the episode in which Kelly visits Sipowicz in hospital. The camera is unusually still in the scene, with relatively long takes assembled in a conventional shot/reverse-shot sequence. Kelly tells Sipowicz that he is 'like a father to me', and the scene ends with a long close-up on Kelly's and Sipowicz's hands in which the apparently unconscious Sipowicz begins to clasp his partner's hand firmly, demonstrating that he is beginning a recovery (Fig. 4.6). The camera's unusual effacement of its own agency in this scene clearly serves to prioritise the relationship of the two men over any stylistic interest that the scene's direction might otherwise offer. This is especially true of the scene's long close-up on the hands, which is held for several seconds and centred in the frame.

The first episode of *NYPD Blue* is a bold statement of the series' interest in combining different kinds of visual style that respond in different ways to the generic components of the police series form. The use of fragments of the city environment, in close shots with little or no contextualisation by wide establishing shots, works alongside very prominent camera movement in the early parts of the episode to portray New York as a spatially confusing place for the viewer. As the drama begins to centre on the main characters, this tendency for unsteady camera and constant reframing becomes located more on character interaction than setting, and introduces the narrative motif of incomplete knowledge of these characters since the camera appears not to be able to anticipate the progress of character interactions. Framing characters harmoniously in conventional and stable shot compositions seems to be the ambition of the camera, but one that it cannot easily fulfill. Dramatic turning points like Sipowicz's shooting, Kelly's sexual encounter and his visit to Sipowicz in hospital are shot in ways that contrast with this because, respectively, they are characterised by slow motion, lengthy stable shots connected by dissolves rather than cuts and a long and stable sequence of shot/reverse-shots and the close-up on the men's hands. The choices made in visual style therefore work to centre narrative emphasis on the characters' feelings rather than their actions, by highlighting these moments where they suffer, make poor moral choices or momentarily experience emotional connection with each other. It is commonplace in the police genre to develop storylines about buddy relationships that enable the protagonists to survive a morally ambiguous fictional world, displacing certainty about how to make sense of that world onto the security of masculine friendship. The opening episode of *NYPD Blue* centres on this generic motif, but its visual style tends to hold the viewer at a distance from the fictional world by drawing attention to the camera's agency in presenting it. The effect of this is to give extreme weight to moments of emotional connection, such as the final close-up on the clasping of the men's hands, where the narrative significance of the moment is matched by its being fully accessible to the camera. For the viewer, these experiences of different kinds of access to the material and emotional world of the drama make the programme much more satisfying than a more conventional rendering of its generic components would be.

5. *CSI: Crime Scene Investigation*

The series *CSI: Crime Scene Investigation* has been the tent pole programme in the CBS network's schedule for the most significant weekday evening, Thursdays, screened in the one-hour slot beginning at 9.00pm. In the 2001–02 season (its second year), *CSI* achieved the second-best ratings of any programme and in the following year was the top-rated programme. It is currently still being made and broadcast, has spawned the spin-off series *CSI: Miami* and *CSI: NY*, and contributed significantly to the profile and audiences for Five when shown in the UK (see Bignell 2007b) as part of a strip of acquired US police series that were collectively labelled 'America's Finest'.

CSI was created by Anthony Zuicker who established its format, and is jointly produced by the Hollywood film production company run by Jerry Bruckheimer whose films (*Beverly Hills Cop* (1984), *Top Gun* (1986), *Days of Thunder* (1990)) share some of its interest in 'cool' masculinity. The writer/producer Danny Cannon was the most regularly employed director in the series, and had an important influence on its visual style of strong primary colours and frequent use of extreme close-ups of bodily injury (see Tait 2006). Though the series format is constructed around a 'work family' that develops the sense of a precinct community discussed in earlier chapters, *CSI* is primarily structured through paired buddy teams and dual storylines in each episode. In common with *Homicide*, it is much less about the commission of crimes than the process of solving them, in this case through forensic research using 'traditional' kinds of investigation like autopsy, but also high-tech computer simulations and complex scientific analyses. The focus on the technologies of forensic investigation leads to a preponderance of storylines about murder, missing persons, sexual crime and violent accidental death.

Visual style in *CSI* was consciously designed to ensure the differentiation of the series from competing programmes, drawing audiences to it because of its distinctiveness. Roy

Wagner, *CSI*'s first director of photography, recalled: 'Bruckheimer had demanded a show so stylistically different that a channel-surfing audience would be forced to stop and view the unusual looking images' (in Lury 2005: 38). Rapid zooms towards and inside body parts or items of evidence (often at extreme magnification; see Fig. 5.1) are integrated with computer-generated imagery to 'demonstrate' aspects of a crime. The main techniques used include ultra-close-up photography, 360-degree shooting using motion control cameras and ultra-high-speed

Fig. 5.1

cinematography for extreme slow motion, as well as the more conventional effects work of matte painting and construction of functioning ('practical') props representing body parts (see Feeny 2003). The resulting effects sequences are hybrids of in-camera and digital effects, which are blended as seamlessly as possible together and also blended with live-action footage that introduces and concludes them. This innovatively develops the notion of vision as an evidential-investigative-conclusive activity in the police genre, since it is by looking in specialised ways that the CSI team examine evidence, draw inferences and identify perpetrators.

Although the footage for *CSI*'s first season was shot in the cinematic 16:9 ratio, it was initially broadcast in the USA and also on Five in Britain in academy 4:3 ratio. Since on a television screen the width of the image is difficult to exploit for striking compositions because it is similar to the image's height, shots emphasise depth rather than breadth by zooms or camera movements that take the viewer closer into the image, as 'CSI shots' like Fig. 5.1 do. The interior studio sets of the programme extensively use glass, chrome and other reflective or metallic surfaces, so that one office area can be seen through another and background action can be seen while primary action takes place in the foreground. The effect is to layer spaces one in front of another, emphasising both depth of space and the activities of looking, reflecting and observing that are crucial to the processes of investigation carried out by the characters (see Lury 2005: 47). Within settings, there are often coloured lights in the background of shots which draw the eye from the foreground to the background action and back, enhancing the sense of depth. Film lights are equipped with gels that wash the action with colour, and post-production tinting is used to add a green, red or blue overlay, for example, to whole sequences as later analysis of scenes in 'Blood Drops' will discuss. Establishing shots emphasise colour saturation, for example by aerial shots of white residential housing, or the black night sky of Las Vegas with its brightly illuminated hotels and casinos.

A close analysis of sequences from the seventh first-season episode 'Blood Drops' (sometimes referred to by its alternative title, 'If These Walls Could Talk') develops the issues of looking, identifying and knowing that have been highlighted throughout this study. It has been chosen not because it is especially representative, but because its single main storyline reduces the need to explain plot complications, leaving space to discuss visual style in relation to format and *CSI*'s distinctive features. The storyline of the episode is based around the investigation of the murder of both parents and the two young male children of a suburban family. The two daughters, one a promiscuous teenager and the other a young girl, survive. Investigation reveals that the older daughter, Tina (Allison Lange), persuaded one of her boyfriends to stab the family members because she was abused by her father when much younger and neither her mother nor brothers protected her. Her motivation is not only to avenge this, but also to protect the younger daughter Brenda (Dakota Fanning) who is already becoming the object of her father's sexual attention. Furthermore, Brenda is actually Tina's daughter by her own father, as well as her sister. In subsidiary storylines, the CSI team's leader Gil Grissom (William Petersen) engages in a rivalry with the head of the day shift, Conrad Ecklie (Marc Vann), and Grissom's colleague Catherine Willows (Marg Helgenberger) is accused of neglecting her daughter by her estranged husband, Eddie (Timothy Carhart), and he also accuses her of having a relationship with Grissom. The CSI investigator Sara Sidle (Jorja

Fox) complains that she is being used simply as a childminder to look after Brenda but gradually establishes a quasi-maternal relationship with the girl.

It may already be evident from this brief summary that the narrative of the episode is held together by a few structural patterns. The CSI team is a 'work family' headed by the patriarchal figure of Grissom. His authority in this role is challenged by the chief of the day shift, but vindicated by the solving of the crime. Willows is accused of having an improper sexual relationship with Grissom which would transgress the conventions of this 'family', and this parallels the transgressive incestuous relationship between Tina (and Brenda) and her father. Willows struggles to maintain her maternal role, at one point arriving too late to collect her daughter from ballet class because of her absorption in tracing the position of blood drops at the crime scene. This questions the relationship between familial and work roles, and the scope for feminine activity alongside professional (in some ways masculine) responsibility. Sidle, too, begins by repudiating a maternal role, but gradually accepts one in relation to Brenda. Across the episode, the propriety of family relations and its ordering of gender roles is addressed both by the crime itself, which is motivated by improper sexual behaviour in a family, and in the familial hierarchy and inter-dependency of the CSI team.

This pattern of narrative strands centring on family, authority and sexuality is reinforced by a series of allusions by Grissom to *Macbeth*. *Macbeth* concerns a breach of hierarchy in which Macbeth murders his king, transgressing patriarchal and institutional structures. This reflects on both Grissom's rivalry with the day shift commander, and also the young murderer Jesse Overton (Eric Nenninger) and Tina's killing of the head of the family. Lady Macbeth encourages her husband to commit the crime, and is presented as an 'unnatural' woman who overreaches the conventional maternal or spousal roles set up in the drama. In 'Blood Drops', Tina persuades her boyfriend to commit the crimes, and is an 'unnatural' daughter who has 'unnaturally' become a mother, though this is because of her abuse by her father and her mother's and brothers' complicity in it. *Macbeth* is notable for its linguistic and (in performance) physical representation of blood, through verbal descriptions of King Duncan's body and the presence on stage of the bloody corpse of Macbeth's companion Banquo, for example. Several visual sequences and lines of dialogue in 'Blood Drops' make blood prominent. Grissom observes in the house that there is a strong smell of copper, indicating 'lots of blood'. He and Willows initially agree that first the mother was killed in her sleep, then the father was killed in the hallway as he ran to protect his children. The CSI team's narrative of the crime is incomplete and incorrect, however, because they agree there is 'not enough blood' to justify this theory. Grissom examines Tina's clothes and says, 'This is a Lady Macbeth', which he explains as a reference to the line in the play 'Out, out damned spot', about removing bloodstains. Searching the young killer's house, the bloody pair of jeans he wore are found in the rubbish bin. Grissom remarks, 'Who would have thought the old man had so much blood in him', quoting from *Macbeth* again. These linguistic allusions are supported by the many camera shots of blood drops, the family's bloody bodies, the killer's bloody jeans and photographs of bleeding bodies or blood-covered items of evidence.

The episode begins with three brief shots of Las Vegas at night, each separated by a white flash that recalls the camera flash of a crime scene photograph, seeing the city from overhead and showing the colourfully illuminated casinos and hotels of the downtown area. These minimal establishing shots are followed by a wide shot of the front lawn of a suburban house at night. The camera is positioned at ground level, shooting across the lawn towards the front door. A young woman (Tina) emerges screaming and there is a cut to a mobile shot following her running across the street to bang on her neighbours' door. Another cut, to the inside of Grissom's car, elides time and establishes his arrival at the crime scene. Grissom and the viewer are given initial information about the crime by the duty detective in a sequence of brief shot/reverse-shots. The episode's opening teaser has thus established place, time, Grissom's role as protagonist and the bloody killing of a suburban family. While the camera was present before Tina emerges into shot, suggesting its privileged access to the space of the action, the reason for her running towards the camera in panic is withheld from the viewer. As the episode develops, this pattern of introducing information and aligning the viewer with Grissom and the other CSI investigators as they try to understand it continues.

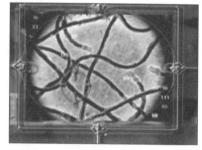

Fig. 5.2

The main title sequence follows, and introduces the central characters along with captions identifying the actors. Each performer is seen in role, undertaking an aspect of their CSI work. Grissom looks up from peering into a microscope, Sidle lifts a fingerprint using adhesive tape and the detective working with the CSI team, Captain Jim Brass (Paul Guilfoyle), holds up a personnel file, for example. Interspersed between these shots the screen shows metonymic examples of the scientific and physical work of the team, where the camera is not anchored to any character's point of view. Many of the shots illustrate scientific processes, such as an electronically enhanced visual scan of a piece of hair (Fig. 5.2), a microscopic investigation of two bullet fragments whose matching striated marks show that they came from the same gun (Fig. 5.3), and a magnified close-up of an entry wound on the grey skin of a dead body. The linkage between technology and the body is made by the juxtaposition of these enhanced modes of seeing, where actual

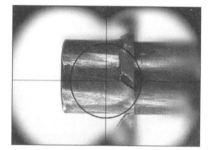

Fig. 5.3

Fig. 5.4

or simulated body parts are being investigated. The most lengthy sequence in the titles emphasises this, and is a montage in which Grissom raises a golf club over his head and brings it forward, cutting to a model of a human head which is impacted by the club and spurts artificial blood upwards into the frame (Fig. 5.4). The music that always accompanies the sequence (but is omitted from DVD sets of the first series) is the song 'Who Are You?' by The Who. The powerful guitar chords, contrasting with some quieter keyboard passages, and its insistent beat, provide a dramatic and exciting accompaniment to the images. The song's understated beginning and gradual escalation towards a crescendo of powerful guitar chords corresponds to the slow building-together of evidence and then climactic revelation that the CSI team's work can accomplish. The lyrics, whose refrain culminates in the line 'Who, who, who are you?', pick out a central premise of the series, which consists in the identification of dead bodies and the search for the identities of perpetrators of crime.

As the previous three illustrations show, the title sequence itself contains several images that set circular shapes within the rectilinear borders of the television screen. These reference the circular lenses of the microscopes and still cameras that the investigators use, as well as representations of the human eye. The lenses of microscopes are represented by circular iris shadows in Figs 5.2 and 5.3, and even the shape of the model head in Fig. 5.4 resembles a circle. The analysis of the episode discussed here argues for *CSI*'s reflexivity about seeing, and the uses of both careful optical observation and seeing that is enhanced by special investigative technologies. In this context, it can also be asserted that circular iris-like shapes in the title sequence and in the episode refer the viewer reflexively to these questions of seeing in relation to knowledge, by drawing attention to the activity of looking through or into a demarcated visual field. By adopting the same circular form for this frame and some of the objects that are framed by it, however, the motif also suggests that differentiating and discriminating between the things that can be seen might be problematic. For if many things are circular the significance of circularity diminishes, and this problem of reading evidence correctly continues through the visual motifs adopted specifically in the 'Blood Drops' episode.

As 'Blood Drops' continues, the camera is close to Grissom's point of view as he walks around illuminating parts of the interior of the house. The sequence aligns the viewer with Grissom, but emphasises his lack of knowledge about this space by surrounding him with darkness that contrasts strongly with the fragments of the visual field that his torch illuminates. Grissom's flashlight tilts up to a hand-enhanced photograph that shows the family in a generic pose emphasising their happiness and unity (Fig. 5.5). The small circle of light begins on the left of the photograph on the two male children, before panning right to dwell on the

Fig. 5.5

two parents and their two daughters. Again, a circular pattern represents Grissom's investigating gaze, contrasting it with the persistent darkness of the scene. Just as Grissom has to find his way through the house to the location of the bodies, the camera does too and the effect of very low lighting is to make the house labyrinthine, paralleling the viewer with both Grissom and the camera. The presence of the photograph capturing the appearance of the smiling family now destroyed by murder, and the fearful reactions of the policeman accompanying Grissom that contrast with his own calmness, all serve to generate a sense of the uncanny, of displacement and anxious expectation. Sidle arrives with her own torch, providing slightly more illumination in the scene, and they discover a swirling circular mark on the wall (and another is found later). Sidle wonders whether this is a calling-card left by a cult killer such as a member of the Manson 'family', recalling for some viewers a recurring storyline about a serial killer, Millander, who the CSI team have been unable to capture. The sense that something mysterious has yet to be seen and understood is conveyed in visual ways, as well as through dialogue and the intratextual reference to Millander.

The characteristic darkness of many sequences of *CSI* is demonstrated here, achieved in the first season by simulating the procedure of bleach bypass in the digital post-production phase of making *CSI*. The effect of bleach bypass is to exaggerate colour contrasts and shadows during film processing, by skipping the bleaching stage in the colour processing sequence, and thus to retain silver along with the film's chemical colour dyes. The result is in effect the superimposition of a monochrome image over the film's colour image, increasing contrast and darkening shadows, and sometimes bringing out the grain of the film's surface. This choice of technical process was part of the series creators' desire to evoke a mood of edginess by leaving areas of the frame so dark that parts of the action and setting cannot be seen. This restricts knowledge of the fictional world for the viewer and the protagonists, and suggests that such knowledge may be difficult or impossible to acquire. Grissom's and Sidle's movement through the house with the flashlight, providing very restricted visual access to the space for them and the camera, parallels the narrative's focus on a slow process of knowledge acquisition, creating and testing hypotheses as new evidence is gained.

Moving further into the bedroom, Grissom and Sidle discover the body of the mother, killed in her sleep. As well as a low undercurrent of synthesizer music during this scene, on the discovery of the mother's body there is the distinct noise of female exhalation on the soundtrack, signifying the last breath of the mother in non-diegetic sound. While this seems like an interpretive element added by the episode's narrating agency, providing a version of the mother's last moments of life, it is immediately marked by the dialogue as a representation of Grissom's and Sidle's shared experience. Asked by Grissom whether she feels something, Sidle replies that 'Her soul is still in the room', so the breath can be reinterpreted both as a sign of their emotions and also a narrative intervention which represents the death scene as they imagine it. However, Grissom's intuition and sensitivity is then harnessed as useful professionalism when he says, 'There's something else'. His instinct is confirmed as the duo push open Brenda's bedroom door, where they discover the bodies of the two boys. Outside the house, Grissom speaks to Brenda in a shot/reverse-shot exchange in which all she will say is that the sole person who came into her room was 'the buffalo', which sets up one of the key enigmas of the episode as a question about what or who 'the buffalo' might be. Since Brenda is a little girl who is too inarticulate and traumatised to communicate this, it is up to the CSI team to use their forensic skills to solve the mystery. While interviews and other dialogue-based investigative techniques are components of 'Blood Drops', what can be seen at the crime scene, then tested and analysed at the lab where the camera can see these processes, is much more central to its processes of narration.

The circle of Grissom's torch picks out footprints on the kitchen linoleum and he brings out his first piece of equipment, an electrostatic dust print lifter, prompting the accompanying detective to joke that 'You guys have all the best toys' and drawing attention to the importance of technology to investigatory processes in the series. A time ellipse finds the group back at the house in daytime, in a largely wordless scene accompanied by upbeat synthesized music. Here the camera is present as CSI team members discover in the garden the tyre print of a bicycle, a cigarette end and a used match. One of the three

Fig. 5.6

young men who share the bicycle whose tyre print was discovered is then interviewed by another CSI team member, Warrick Brown (Gary Dourdan). The youth has cigarettes with him that match the stub found at the crime scene, and also matches that resemble the one found there. This clue is visually established by another point-of-view shot through a microscope where a circular iris marks the borders of its visual field (Fig. 5.6). In his laboratory, Grissom retrieves a bloody pendant worn by the dead father, and removes the blood to reveal that it is a disc on which there is an image of a buffalo. Grissom then orders Sidle to take photographs of Brenda's body that can be enhanced to reveal signs of physical abuse.

While Grissom cleans and identifies the buffalo pendant, the camera provides close-ups of the object, making clear not only the process of gathering knowledge but also the similarity between the CSI team's methods of close visual examination and the episode's visual style. One of the functions of the close-up, and especially the zoom into an object or body in *CSI*, is to link the camera as narrating agency with the agency of the human characters. In fact, the relative paucity of conventional physical action in the series is related to this by parallelism and opposition. The stillness and reticence of the characters are parallel and opposite to the fluidity and revelation given to the camera and its narrative agency in the sequences representing forensic investigation. This also sets up a relationship between present and past. The present is characterised by its stillness, seen especially in the CSI operatives' absorption in their work and the literal stillness of dead bodies or evidential objects. But this stillness is made to reveal movement and passion that happened in the past. From the evidence of the buffalo pendant, Grissom and the rest of the team are able to hypothesise that the crime was in some way motivated by the pendant-wearer's relationship with Brenda, hence Grissom's order to Sidle to take photographs of the girl's body. In doing justice to the evidence, the forensic reconstruction of the process of the crime in *CSI* gives a body or an object back its story.

It is Willows who establishes the temporal and spatial sequence of the crime, in a scene where she maps out the directional lines of the killer's and victims' movements in the house on a large board. She makes notes by speaking into a Dictaphone, thus revealing her process of thought to the audience. Point-of-view close-ups follow the movement of her gaze as she looks concentratedly at the board, working out who must have been where according to the evidence of blood spatter that was gathered at the crime scene. The camera is closely aligned with Willows as she systematically examines the map of the crime scene to reveal its secrets, paralleling the activity of the forensic investigators with the activity of the camera.

Fig. 5.7

Willows telephones Grissom to tell him that a single blood drop found in the hall shows the direction of travel of the killer, and demonstrates that the father was not running to Brenda's room to protect her but was instead coming out of her bedroom when he was murdered. This dialogue information occurs at the point when the camera, again adopting Willows' optical point of view, closes up on a photograph of the blood drop (Fig. 5.7), emphasising the significance of the detail by shooting though an internal frame created by the circular magnifying glass that

Fig. 5.8

she holds. Here the vaguely elliptical blood drop is not a circle, and the lateral spread that deforms its otherwise circular shape is the key to the sequence of past events in the house because the spread indicates direction of movement. While Willows is talking on the phone, a reprise of her imagined reconstruction of the sequence of events shows the killer again attacking the father as he leaves Brenda's room and walks down the hallway (Fig. 5.8). Often in *CSI*, sequences like this restage a crime in the manner of a conventional flashback, or an injury to the victim's body is analytically re-enacted by means of digital effects, prosthetics and models so that the causal processes that gave rise to injuries become knowable. The present is therefore known by restoring a past that leads to it, or what is seen in the present is explained by reconstructing past events that the viewer is privileged to witness, although none of the CSI team could have seen them.

The process of thinking through the crime using her map thus leads Willows to mentally reconstruct the process of events as she imagines them, so one form of visualisation gives rise to another. Neither the map nor Willows' visualisation of the events are 'true', but are versions of the crime that move closer to what must have happened. The attribution of the reconstruction to Willows is indicated by adopting some different choices of visual style from the main body of the episode. In flashback reconstructions like this, camera movements in circles and tilts are much more common than in the slow and relatively stable camera movement of primary action. In the case of the visualisation being discussed here, the camera is positioned just above floor level, tilting sharply upward to witness the father, the killer behind him and the father's falling movement towards the camera. The new, but still partial and imagined access to knowledge of past events that Willows has is indicated by the unusual camera position and movement and the strong red colour of the component shots, since the camera position does not correspond to the physical position of any of the characters and the red colouring is not diegetically motivated.

When Grissom confronts Tina with Sidle's photographs, which reveal signs of bruising on Brenda's body, Tina sympathetically places her hand over the marks on the girl's chest. Tina reveals that she herself was abused much earlier as a child, and while she tells the story there is a reconstruction that must be understood as her retrospective visualisation of this. The sequence is accompanied by her voice-over narration, indicating that it represents her version of the events, and the shots are lit throughout with soft pink light. The camera shows Tina as a girl, with her mother closing Tina's bedroom door

to reveal the father hiding behind it. The scene then cuts to a point-of-view shot of the father's chest and open shirt bending towards Tina's body, with the circular buffalo pendant swinging down towards her face (Fig. 5.9). This final shot in the sequence is still strongly coloured pink, and signifies the emotional weight of the memory for Tina by suddenly filling the screen with this big close-up of the pendant and the male chest looming over her. The pink light of the mental reconstruction connects with the reconstructions of the multiple murders such as Fig.

Fig. 5.9

5.8 above, which are shot with a strong red light. It is as if the redness of those scenes has become greater as time passes, beginning with the soft pink light in the past and ending with the deep red, signifying both blood and the intensification of the effects of Tina's abuse. When considered together, it can be seen that the episode has established a systematic visual means to link the various reconstructed visualisations together.

Shades of red are not motivated by light sources in the episode's diegetic world, but are instead aspects of an expressive system within the narration.

CSI is distinctive in its use of long sequences showing the processes of autopsy and the scientific analysis of fragments from bodies or crime scenes, and this might suggest that the audience is expected to place confidence in the competence of the CSI team and their ability to reveal the truth of the fictional world. Referring to critical reaction to the series' beginning, and the principal characters of its Las Vegas, Miami and New York incarnations, *CSI*'s executive producer, Carol Mendelsohn, explained that 'because CSI was very black and white – the evidence never lies – it was comforting in a grey world. There is comfort when Gil Grissom or Horatio Caine or Mac Taylor are on the case. There aren't many people you can trust in the world today' (in McLean 2005: 12). Fluid but slow camera movements track around the dimly-lit spaces of the crime labs, discovering the characters conducting procedures observed in long, wordless sequences of alternating close-ups and medium shots. These procedures consist of what might seem tedious work such as examining clothing fibres or skin cells through microscopes, or painstakingly arranging the fragments of an object on a light-table. Pace and interest is created in these long sequences by the addition of non-diegetic music, contrast of lighting and the camera's often elegant and extended movement. All of this seems to indicate a world which is knowable by the characters and the camera. That knowledge is gained by their special kinds of visual access to events in the past, through specialised forms of looking such as the 'CSI shot' of a wound, technological examination of evidence in the lab or reconstructions of a crime that the camera can convey to the viewer.

But the victims' versions of events are reconstructed in memory, even though the camera has a privileged ability to see them. Similarly, the investigators' hypotheses are represented visually by the camera but are sometimes wrong and are very frequently repeated in modified form. Events in the past are reconstructed fragmentarily and inadequately, inasmuch as more evidence revises or disproves them, and thus the camera's ability to convey reliable information is put into question. Attention is drawn to the CSI team's processes of investigation, which are dominated by forms of forensic analysis that the camera can show or reconstruct visually for the viewer, but these too are only significant when assembled into a narrative and such narratives are open to modification and contradiction. The investigative looks of the camera and the characters are presented as processes of seeing that seem easy but are in fact problematically linked with knowing. These ways of seeing are made surprisingly active as processes and experiences rather than punctual moments of perception, in that the narrative gives time to the investigators' work on the evidence, to the movement of the camera into the interior space of a bodily wound, or the re-experienced duration of a crime during a reconstruction sequence. The role of seeing as an action, process or performance becomes significant in itself because of the prominence given to the ways that the fictional world is offered to audience through the programme's style. Visual style therefore highlights the conditional nature of seeing and the provisional nature of knowledge, because there are things that cannot be seen and things that can be only partially known. The technical processes of production of the images in *CSI*, and its systems for visually representing forensic investigation and detection more generally, are linked by their common effects of deferring and sometimes obscuring access to the truth of events. This occurs at the same time as these processes and systems of visualisation offer privileged kinds of look, deep within the human body or into a reconstructed past, for example, that appear to surpass the restrictions of sight and knowledge.

Conclusion

Two of the components that have been argued to characterise television as a medium are its possibility for intimacy and its potential for immediacy. Television is an intimate medium in the sense that it is broadcast into the private space of the home, and much of its output promises to reveal the detail of individual action through image and sound, with a special emphasis on the ability of the close-up to provide analytical observation of human behaviour. While this capacity is a resource for all television forms, it has been exploited particularly in police drama, where psychology, emotion and the expression of each of these has been facilitated by the patterning of dramatic forms to emphasise moments of character revelation. The immediacy of television derives historically from the fact that for the first twenty years or so after its invention it was very difficult to record television footage. This meant that in the USA and the UK television focused on the live broadcasting of both factual and fictional material, covering events such as sports fixtures or news events, and broadcasting drama that was shot live in the television studio and could not be repeated without assembling its cast of characters and performing the drama again. This expectation of immediacy, alongside intimacy, has a special relationship with realism in drama and the factual mode of television documentary, because of the claims of each to authenticity and witness. The police series is a programme type that has adopted hybrid blends of generic and modal resources from both fictional and factual programme forms, and necessarily addresses the meanings of seeing and knowing through these different forms.

Ultimately, this study argues for the significance of an evidence-based analysis of television aesthetics, which is particularly appropriate to the thematisation of pursuit, discovery, witness, explanation and justification that organises the visual and aural components of police series fiction. For police drama is always about what can be seen and evaluated, and how conclusions are drawn from evidence. This study has indicated that some police series reflexively meditate upon the activities of seeing and interpreting, to the extent that they become thoughtful and sometimes critical works about television itself.

Questions of authorship, 'quality', form, genre, historical development, institution and audience have conventionally been discussed in Television Studies as matters which require links to be established between programme texts, and this seems to militate against the kind of sustained attention to style adopted in this study. However, meta-arguments about these issues arise from and return to the style of programmes (see Bignell 2006), and the argument here is that the texture of individual texts needs to be at the heart of these apparently broader debates. The most significant challenge in planning and writing this study has been the relationship between detail and critical contexts, and the consequent problem of how to create coherent, free-standing chapters which at the same time relate to overall questions and themes. My answer to this was to discuss programme examples chronologically. This enabled concentration on episodes in their own terms, giving due weight to the sequence analysis that is at the heart of this project, but in the context of recurrent concerns, both critical and generic.

In the US television industry, writing has been valued over direction, cinematography or the other professions connected to visual style. But in the analyses of programmes considered here, information about the intentions of their creators, and the close relationships between writer/producers, episode directors and cinematographers has shown that this is a distorting emphasis. In a parallel way, academic attention to popular television drama has been concerned to relate programmes to the 'literate' components shared with canonical literature or written drama such as 'narrative, sequential, abstract, univocal, "consistent"' aesthetic features (Fiske & Hartley 1978: 125) in ways that seek to appropriate the characteristics that connote quality in forms outside of television, but this study has argued for the crucial place of visual style in discussion of such aesthetic features. However, the intention has not been to displace one approach by another: the emphasis on collaboration in the production process brings with it a corresponding need to place visual style within the networks of decision-making that underpin the experience of viewing and to understand the systematic relationships within the series and the individual episode that these produce.

In this context close analysis of visual style in popular television drama opens up a means of linking the aesthetics of television drama texts to the lived dialectics of sense and taste making, in ways that have the potential to enrich the emphasis Television Studies has placed on the inherent vitality of audiences as active interpreters of meaning. As fictions set in a contemporary world, the series discussed in this study each address their audiences' lived experiences, though in different ways. Their visual styles have been shown to be fully integrated into these modes of address, and in fact to be inseparable from them. Such a process of valuing the popular by analysing relationships between style and meaning motivated the procedures of mise-en-scène criticism in academic film studies from which many of the analytical techniques used in this study derive (see Gibbs & Pye, 2005). Further work about television could benefit from adopting the methodology of detailed analysis which derives from that tradition, to avoid some of the confusions around the valuation of television as a medium and valuations of one kind of television over another that were discussed in the Introduction to this study.

BIBLIOGRAPHY

Bignell, J. (2005) 'Exemplarity, pedagogy and television history', *New Review of Film and Television Studies*, 3, 1, 15–32.

_____ (2006) 'Programmes and canons', *Critical Studies in Television*, 1,1, 31–6.

_____ (2007a) 'Citing the classics: constructing British television drama history in publishing and pedagogy', in H. Wheatley (ed.) *Re-viewing Television History: Critical Issues in Television Historiography*. London and New York: I. B. Tauris, 27–39.

_____ (2007b) 'Seeing and knowing: reflexivity and quality', in J. McCabe and K. Akass (eds) *Quality TV Drama: Contemporary American Television and Beyond*. London: I. B. Tauris, 158–70.

Butler, J. (1985) '*Miami Vice*: the legacy of film noir', *Journal of Popular Film and Television*, 13, 3, 127–38.

Buxton, D. (1990) *The Police Series: From The Avengers to Miami Vice*. Manchester: Manchester University Press.

Curtin, M. (2003) 'From network to neo-network audiences', in M. Hilmes (ed.) *The Television History Book*. London: British Film Institute, 122–5.

D'Acci, J. (1994) *Defining Women: The Case of Cagney and Lacey*. Chapel Hill: University of South Carolina Press.

Ellis, J. (2000) *Seeing Things: Television in the Age of Uncertainty*. London and New York: I. B. Tauris.

Feeny, C. (2003) 'Stargate Digital: the best kept secret in TV', *VFX Pro*, 19 September, available at: http://www.uemedia.net/CPC/vfxpro/article_4684.shtml (accessed 10 June 2007).

Feuer, J. (1984) 'MTM Enterprises: an overview', in J. Feuer, P. Kerr and T. Vahimagi (eds) *MTM: 'Quality Television'*. London: British Film Institute, 1–31.

_____ (2003) 'Quality drama in the US: the new "golden age"?', in M. Hilmes (ed.) *The Television History Book*. London: British Film Institute, 98–102.

Fisher, B. (1996) 'Behind the scenes at *NYPD Blue* with Brian J. Reynolds', *International Cinematographers Guild*, available at: http://www.cameraguild.com/interviews/chat_reynolds/reynolds_NYPD.htm (accessed 7 June 2007).

Fiske, J. and J. Hartley (1978) *Reading Television*. London: Methuen.

Fretts, B. (1993) 'The Dead Beat', *Entertainment Weekly*, 156, 5 February, available at http://www.ew.com/ew/article0,,305491~7~0~,00.html (accessed 12 June 2007).

Friedman, J. (1985) *Miami Vice Scrapbook*. London: Columbus.

Frith, S. (2000) 'The black box: the value of television and the future of television research', *Screen*, 41, 1, 33–50.

Gibbs, J. and D. Pye (2005) 'Introduction', in J. Gibbs and D. Pye (eds) *Style and Meaning: Studies in the Detailed Analysis of Film*. Manchester: Manchester University Press, 1–15.

Gitlin, T. (1983) *Inside Prime Time*. New York: Pantheon.

Hillier, J. (1993) *The New Hollywood*. London: Studio Vista.

Jenkins, S. (1984) '*Hill Street Blues*', in J. Feuer, P. Kerr and T. Vahimagi (eds) *MTM: 'Quality Television'*. London: British Film Institute, 183–99.

Kerr, P. (1984) 'Drama at MTM: *Lou Grant* and *Hill Street Blues*', in J. Feuer, P. Kerr and T. Vahimagi (eds) *MTM: 'Quality Television'*. London: British Film Institute, 132–65.

King, S. (1990) 'Sonny's virtues: the gender negotiations of *Miami Vice*', *Screen*, 31, 3, 281–95.

Klein, P. (1975) 'The television audience and program mediocrity', in A. Wells (ed.) *Mass Media and Society*. Palo Alto, CA: Mayfield, 74–7.

Kozloff, S. (1992) 'Narrative theory and television', in R. Allen (ed.) *Channels of Discourse, Reassembled*. London: Routledge, 67–100.

Lury, K. (2005) *Interpreting Television*. London: Hodder Arnold.

Marc, D. and R. Thompson (1995) *Prime Time, Prime Movers: From I Love Lucy to L.A. Law – America's Greatest TV Shows and the People Who Created Them*. NY: Syracuse University Press.

McLean, G. (2005) 'CSI: Tarantino', *Guardian* (New Media section), 11 July, 12.

Milch, D. and B. Clark (1996) *True Blue: The Real Stories Behind NYPD Blue*. London: Boxtree.

Newcombe, H. (1974) *Television: The Most Popular Art*. New York: Anchor.

Ross, A. (1986) 'Masculinity and *Miami Vice*: selling in', *Oxford Literary Review*, 8, 1–2, 143–54.

Rutsky, R. L. (1988) 'Visible sins, vicarious pleasures: style and vice in *Miami Vice*', *SubStance*, 17, 1, 77–82.

Schwichtenberg, C. (1986) 'Sensual surfaces and stylistic excess: the pleasure and politics of *Miami Vice*', *Journal of Communication Inquiry*, 10, 45–65.

Stempel, T. (1996) *Storytellers to the Nation: A History of American Television Writing*. NY: Syracuse University Press.

Tait, S. (2006) 'Autoptic vision and the necrophilic imaginary in *CSI*', *International Journal of Cultural Studies*, 9, 1, 45–62.

Thompson, R. (1996) *Television's Second Golden Age: From Hill Street Blues to ER*. New York: Syracuse University Press.

Troy, P. (1997) 'Sixty-minute men and women: writing the hour drama', *Written By*, September.

Wang, O. (1988) '*Miami Vice*: sex and drugs and rock & roll in the TV market', *Jump Cut*, 33, 10–19.

Winston, B. (1995) *Claiming the Real: The Documentary Film Revisited*. London: British Film Institute.

3.2 WEIMAR CINEMA
Iris Luppa

ACKNOWLEDGEMENTS

I wish to express my gratitude to Douglas Pye, whose academic guidance and assurance over the years, from supervising my doctoral research to the completion of this study, has been invaluable. Thanks also to both Doug and John Gibbs: their editorial comments and suggestions greatly improved my writing. I would like to thank Christiane Elmanharawy, Toni-Lynn Frederick, Kathrina Glitre, Lorna Grounsell and Mike Stevenson for their advice and encouragement. A special thank you to Christina Adamou and Lisa Purse. I am grateful to the members of the close reading group, The Sewing Circle, in the Department of Film, Theatre & Television at the University of Reading for their insightful comments on several of the films discussed in this work and to Matthew Smith for help with the illustrations. I am indebted to Aubrey Thomas and Robbie for their support during the writing process.

For my grandmother Therese 'Resi' Spies.

Introduction

This study argues that accompanying Weimar cinema's self-conscious exploration of the aesthetic possibilities of film is a critical interest in ways of seeing and their consequences that is embedded in a range of films spanning the whole of the period from 1918 to 1933. Using a text-based approach, I shall argue that *Dr Mabuse, der Spieler/ Dr Mabuse, the Gambler* (Fritz Lang, 1922), *Menschen am Sonntag/People on Sunday* (Robert Siodmak/Edgar G Ulmer, 1929) and *Kuhle Wampe* (Slatan Dudow/Bertolt Brecht, 1931), though differing widely in terms of style and narrative concerns, employ methods of narration that challenge the spectator to become aware of the potentially treacherous relationships between what is seen, the rhetorical context in which perception takes place, and the forms of understanding or knowledge that can be derived from the seen. These are processes that George M. Wilson (1986) has explored in terms of the various 'epistemic' dimensions of film narration; Wilson and others have analysed their operation in some of Fritz Lang's films but little work in these terms has been done on other Weimar films.[1]

In the following chapters analysis will focus on each film's critical engagement with the relationship between seeing and knowing in a period when this relationship became increasingly ambivalent, not least because of cinema's impact on the audience's viewing habits. Each film, it will be argued, represents a critical engagement with particular ways of seeing but also sets its audience exercises in what Bertolt Brecht called 'complex seeing'.

In the essay, 'Notes to the *Threepenny Opera*' (first published in *Versuche 3*, 1931), Brecht discusses the use of theatrical devices such as titles and songs to force the audience into alert and critical ways of watching a play:

> The orthodox playwright's objection to the titles is that the dramatist ought to say everything that has to be said in the action, that the text must express everything within its own confines. The corresponding attitude for the spectator is that he should not think about a subject, but within the confines of the subject. But this way of subordinating everything to a single idea, this passion for propelling the spectator along a single track where he can look neither right nor left, up nor down, is something that the new school of playwriting must reject ... Some exercise in complex seeing is needed – though it is perhaps more important to be able to think above the stream than to think in the stream. (1992a: 44)

Several years prior to Brecht's experimentation with anti-illusionist methods (his first play making use of parable and other distanciation devices, *A Man's a Man*, premiered in 1926) the dramatist's impact on theatre was recognised by Herbert Ihering, who as early as 1922 observed, 'with Bert Brecht, there's a new tone, a new melody, a new vision in these times' (1958: 273). What is 'new', then, is above all – in the case of the young Brecht – dissatisfaction with existing conventions and subsequently a radical change in terms of audience address. Ihering's use of the words 'tone', 'melody' and 'vision' further suggests a degree of aesthetic experimentation in the artwork that is not as yet explicit or part of a coherent programme which could be articulated by the critic in terms of a fully-fledged concept. Instead, Ihering expresses the sense of a new threshold in the cultural output of the early 1920s, of which Brecht was one of the most articulate and outspoken advocates.

The young dramatist was not the only Weimar artist experiencing the discrepancy between existing modes of representation and rapid social and cultural developments: a range of films produced at the time raise similar kinds of questions. Thomas Elsaesser observes that 'the films usually indexed as Weimar cinema have one thing in common: they are invariably constructed as picture puzzles: consistently, if not systematically, they refuse to be "tied down" to a single meaning' (2000: 4). This study attempts to 'unpick' specific pieces of the 'picture puzzle' through its focus on the chosen films' concerns with issues of perception and knowledge, analysing the complex systems of looking – whether as aspects of point of view, or unexpected variations in tone or mode of address – through close attention to choices in the construction of the films' narration.

Studies of narration and point of view by George M Wilson (1986) and Douglas Pye (2000) provide frameworks for analysing the ways in which film positions the spectator in relation to the narrative. Pye's distinctions between various 'dimensions' of point of view, namely spatial, temporal, cognitive, evaluative and ideological (2000a: 8) facilitate detailed discussion of the means available to a film to both present its world and to guide the audience's attention to detail within it. In particular, the ideological axis of point of view serves to 'denote a film's implicit or explicit relationships to the systems of thought and representation on which it relies and which are drawn on, or find expression in, the film's world' (2000a: 11). This relationship between a given film, its material and the audience is of particular interest to this study and my analysis will draw on Pye's distinctions in order to explore its complexities.

Chapter one, 'Postwar: Dr Mabuse, der Spieler – The 'Suggestion' of Omniscience', questions the film's treatment of 'omniscient' ways of seeing both as a concern of the drama and a possible mode of narration. The film's spectacular images and fast-paced narrative initially offer the audience a seemingly unrestricted access to the world of the film and its protagonist Dr Mabuse (Rudolf Klein Rogge), who is himself presented as an apparently omniscient and omnipotent character. Through Mabuse, the spectator gains access to disparate locations across the city, including the stock market and illegal gambling clubs, which creates the impression of the city and its people tightly in Mabuse's grip and unaware of their manipulation by the doctor, whose real identity is only known to his henchmen and to the audience.

However, in part two of the film the police finally catch up with the self-proclaimed master criminal and any sense of the audience sharing a vision of omniscience is revealed to be illusory. Film's ability to present fragmented spaces as whole, to mislead the audience and to expose the spectator as unthinkingly participating in his or her own deception are respectively linked to the propagandistic function of cinema during World

War One, a matter that – as *Dr Mabuse* indicates – becomes more pressing as cinema technology and narrational methods become increasingly sophisticated.

Chapter two, 'Stabilisation Period: *Menschen am Sonntag.* 'Fleeting Days", examines a film that is generally regarded as a classic of the Neue Sachlichkeit (New Objectivity) movement which dominated Weimar arts and culture during the mid- to late 1920s. I shall argue that the film's representation of five young white-collar workers – the social class most influenced by this new and ostensibly liberating lifestyle – is far from uncritical, raising implicit questions about the ways in which objective ways of seeing, inextricably linked to the ever increasing rationalisation and commodification of modern life, impact on the individual. Focusing on the representation of the film's female characters, this chapter seeks to draw attention to the film's awareness of the discrepancy between expectations about the emancipated social role and liberated sexual status of the salaried female and the young women's more traditional romantic ideals and self-conscious, rather than self-assured, articulation of desire.

Chapter three, entitled 'Pre-Fascist Period: To Think and To Want: *Kuhle Wampe*', re-evaluates existing criticism and the claims that have been made about the film's use of Brechtian aesthetics. The chapter examines the tension between the film's political function of raising the political awareness of a proletarian audience and its sometimes negative representation of the working class, which critics noted at the time but which has since been overlooked. By focusing on moments in the film where its material is politically less explicit, the chapter seeks to draw attention to questions raised by the filmmaking collective about the potential and limitations of film in addressing the audience, changing consciousness and producing new ways of viewing the world.

A brief note on recent currents in Weimar scholarship

The title of a recent collection of articles on Weimar cinema, *Diesseits der 'Dämonischen Leinwand'/On This Side of the 'Haunted Screen'* (Koebner 2003) signals a generational shift in critical perspective on filmmaking in Germany between 1919 and 1933: *From Caligari to Hitler* (1947) and *L'Écran démonaique/The Haunted Screen* (1952) by Weimar contemporaries Siegfried Kracauer and Lotte Eisner have finally been relegated to 'the other side' of debates in Weimar scholarship. Since Barry Salt's polemic 'From Caligari to Who?' (1979), writers on Weimar cinema have repeatedly questioned Kracauer's post-World War Two thesis of a direct link between films produced in Germany in the early to mid-1920s and the rise of fascism in the late 1920s. In current debates, critical attention is increasingly drawn to the various facets of Weimar modernism with a focus on cinematic representations of the city itself, as well as the impact of new technologies and the various phenomena of Berlin's mass communication culture. Yet despite the 'post'-Kracauer surge of fresh perspectives in recent years, there are still too few close readings of Weimar films outside the canon of 'classics' by Fritz Lang, Ernst Lubitsch, F. W. Murnau and G. W. Pabst. Notwithstanding the attention to textual detail in *Weimar Cinema and After: Germany's Historical Imaginary*, Thomas Elsaesser himself observes that 'a study of Weimar cinema easily becomes a meta-critical discourse' (2000: 5). Holding the magnifying lens of the *Close-Up* rationale to the finer details of a small selection of Weimar films, this study seeks to contribute to the current broader revaluation of this unique period in film history with three detailed readings, falling back onto 'meta-critical discourse' only where the historical remove necessitates broader elaboration.

1. Postwar: *Dr Mabuse, der Spieler* – The 'Suggestion' of Omniscience

War of ideals and illusions

It is generally acknowledged that prior to the events of World War One (1914–18), Germany's film industry was dominated by French, American and Danish imports. The outbreak of the war led to increased domestic production and, in 1916, to the founding of the 'Bild- und Filmamt' (Bufa), a military film board responsible, amongst other things, for the provision of frontline footage for Germany's weekly newsreels. In his seminal world war 'documentary drama' (an insufficient term to describe the opus), *Die letzten Tage der Menschheit/The Last Days of Mankind* (1926), Karl Kraus caustically documents the tone and ideological function of these 'frontline' productions. A scene in Act IV vividly portrays cinema's role in actively shaping public opinion about the war:

> Movie Theatre Manager (*stepping forward*): There will now follow the first showing of the great film made of the Battle of the Somme. In this film you will get to see the heroes of the Somme, the flower of youth running forward, side by side with grey-haired men, weather-beaten and steeled in battle, falling to the ground yet attacking fiercely, fighting between licking flames and the hail of bullets; over shaking ground pulverised by mines, in the all-crushing forge of this howling war ... In three parts, scenes of that fearsome battle of fall 1916 unroll before your eyes, that battle with which the enemy's great hope sank into its grave ... And then, thanks to the unique courage of brave cameramen, four of whom met a hero's death while loyally carrying out their duty during filming of this sequence, you shall behold in flickering moving pictures a sublime example of purposeful, precise efficiency ... Over mine fields and obstacles, through byways of death pregnant with explosives, onward into the heat of close combat! Hand grenades are cutting them down! From trench to trench, onward into the enemy position! Our own artillery draws breath and sprays horror into the enemy reserves; trench after trench is taken. This film ranks with the most beautiful, among the most impressive of the present war.
> FEMALE VOICE: Emil, keep your hands to yourself! (In Kraus 1974: 151–2)

The rhetoric of victoriously storming enemy trenches of course belies the reality of these trench offensives, in which the war 'assumed its murderous character and men were slaughtered in their tens of thousands' and young men 'could look forward to a high probability of being killed or wounded shortly after their eighteenth birthday' (Bessel 1993: 6). Although Kraus's scene indicates that the audience may not have paid too much attention to this crass attempt at ideological positioning (having their eyes and hands elsewhere), the medium's potential for influencing public opinion at home was welcomed by the military. In a letter to the war ministry in Berlin in July 1917 General Erich Ludendorff emphasises that 'the war has shown the phenomenal power of photography and film as a means for explanation and persuasion' (1977: 68). Yet the looked-for 'political and military manipulation' (ibid.) of films such as *Unsere Helden an der Somme/ Our Heroes at the Somme* (1917), could not conceal the mounting number of deaths and casualties in a conflict that, far from being glorious and short-lived, had turned into a long drawn-out battle which left hardly a family in Germany unaffected. The nation's war of ideals, of soldiers 'fighting in the spirit of Goethe's *Faust*, of Nietzsche's *Zarathustra*, even of Beethoven's *Eroica* symphony' (Timms 1986: 307) had turned into a war of illusions, with lies and distorted views about the front propagated and reproduced by weekly newsreels and the printed press.

In *The Cinema's Third Machine* Sabine Hake comments on how the first German newsreels, Eiko-Woche and Messter-Woche, sought to capture the audience's attention by turning news about the war into a cinematic spectacle:

> Initially less than successful, these newsreels soon adopted a more narrative style, re-placing monotonous long shots with dynamic editing and including comic episodes. One of their functions was to disperse rumours about the horrors of the war and to highlight the soldiers' discipline and morale. (1993: 17)

Increasingly elaborate systems of narration and the powerful grip of narrative thus turn footage of human carnage into stories about a 'hero's death'. The medium's potential to present a picture which, though ostensibly the most authentic representation of actual events, could nonetheless be distorted using the visual rhetoric of camera angle, move-ment and framing, as well as early and emerging editing techniques, comes to the fore.

The following analysis seeks to show that Fritz Lang's mastery of narrational tech-niques in the cinema of the early 1920s is matched by the director's awareness of the implications of film's impact on the audience's perception. I shall argue that elements of Lang's early films which, taken on their own, could be read as no more than a play with generic signifiers to produce responses of shock and surprise is revealed, in the wider context of his oeuvre, to offer a critical awareness of the impact of modes of visual representation on ways of seeing in a postwar society undergoing rapid modernisation and radical social and political change.

Analysis will focus on how systems of narration initially offer the audience a privi-leged access to the events and characters of the filmic world. Yet by the end our 'cogni-tive' point of view, which derives 'not from what the film spells out but from inferences we draw from the rhetoric of performance and from the image and sound context in which performance is presented' (Pye 2000a: 10), is exposed as surprisingly restricted, pointing to a gap between what we see and what we may claim to know. This thematic and conceptual movement from an 'all-seeing' perspective to moments of miscompre-hension and 'blindness' points to the increasingly problematic relationship between see-ing and knowing brought about by the emerging mass media in the early twentieth century, and to Lang's sophisticated grasp of what this might imply. In the context of postwar Germany's unstable social and political situation, Lang's play on the audience's perception develops into a serious exercise in complex seeing at a time when people were coming to terms with the disillusionment and harrowing consequences of the 'war of ideals' and simultaneously experiencing, especially in the cities, rapid modernisation in all areas of life.

'With your permission: Dr Mabuse'

There's a moment one hour into part two of Fritz Lang's *Dr Mabuse, the Gambler* where, in the course of his investigation into suspected gambling fraud, State Attorney von Wenk (Bernhard Goetzke) returns to chambers and is told by his assistants that nothing of importance has happened in his absence. The men are on full alert given that a recent attempt to blow up the attorney's office was very nearly successful, resulting in the death of one of von Wenk's men. Sitting at his desk amidst the devastation, von Wenk is alerted by a noise and, to his and the audience's surprise, discovers that he has an unannounced visitor: rising from an armchair in the far corner of the office, the stranger politely introduces himself as 'Dr Mabuse'. In fact, Mabuse is the man behind the gambling scam as well as other criminal activities, though this is unknown to von Wenk at this point. The doctor, by profession a psychoanalyst, invites von Wenk to attend a public demonstration of mass hypnosis by a certain 'Sandor Weltmann' (subsequently revealed to be none other than Mabuse in disguise), then leaves. After Mabuse's departure a furious von Wenk reprimands his dumbfounded colleagues for letting a stranger walk into his office unnoticed.

Visual strategies of misperception

This brief moment in the film, consisting of seven shots and one intertitle, is characteristic of what has since become a recognised Langian 'trademark' – the director's devious delight in setting the audience 'traps for the mind and eye' (Elsaesser 1997: 28). Moreover, a closer look at this scene links the moment of von Wenk's and the audience's surprise to a wider system of calculated narrative and narrational strategies employed to (mis)guide the audience's attention. The spectator's experience of simultaneous seeing and blindness, of knowing but not knowing, not only plays a key part in the narrative, it also becomes central to our understanding of the film's wider concerns with the function of cinema as an apparatus for perception and misperception.

There are several systems that guide our attention in this short scene. We also need to place this moment in the film in the context of the action which precedes it in order to shed light on Lang's cognitive play. Arguably, one could accuse Lang of cheating; after all, von Wenk's assistants reassure him – and by implication the audience – that nothing of significance has happened in his absence. We therefore do not expect Mabuse to be sitting in the office armchair. Indeed, the previous scene shows the doctor's nervous-looking servant Spoerri (Robert Forster-Larrinaga) preventing von Wenk's entrance to Mabuse's house and the inference that can be drawn from Forster-Larrinaga's performance (he actively blocks the entrance and fiddles with a handkerchief in his breast

Fig. 1.1

Fig. 1.2

Fig. 1.3

Fig. 1.4

pocket) is that Spoerri is preventing access to his master. We have no reason to question the reliability of the attorney's assistants, but every reason to mistrust the doctor's cocaine-addicted manservant when he assures von Wenk that 'the doctor is out'.

But Lang does not cheat. He could manipulate the editing to produce Mabuse like a rabbit out of a hat. Instead, he relies not on the selective revelation of space through editing but on the spectator's selective attention. As von Wenk enters his study, the establishing shot (Fig. 1.1) gives us the 'full picture' of the space in which the action is played out and close scrutiny reveals somebody sitting in the armchair holding a book: it is all there in front of our eyes. However, Lang can depend on the logic of narrative attention and the attractions of movement within the image. He works to keep our focus on the action – von Wenk traversing the space to his desk, sitting, then turning over the letter in his hands (Fig. 1.2) – evidently of more interest to him than the other messages – and then placing it back on the table. A letter at this moment could well imply a narrative development of a kind characteristic of the detective film – new information to propel the investigation forward. In addition, we may take note of the beam that dangles precariously from the ceiling not far from von Wenk's head. Both the desk area and the beams are well lit, ensuring that none of this detail escapes our attention, but we have no immediate reason to scan the rest of the set for hidden visitors.

At this stage the two opponents literally sit back to back across a diagonal line and yet our gaze will almost certainly be directed to the front left of the frame. When the film cuts to him, Mabuse's actions are magnificently staged: we do not need sound to imagine the thud of a book snapped shut (Fig. 1.3). The element of surprise is entirely in the hands of the doctor: startled by the noise, von Wenk turns to look over his shoulder (Fig. 1.4); Mabuse rises from his chair (Fig. 1.5). The cut on action and the eyeline match along a diagonal line suggest that Mabuse and von Wenk share the same space; Mabuse's greeting is directed offscreen in what we conclude is the direction of von Wenk. Yet because we have not noticed Mabuse in the establishing shot, the spatial relationship between the two men retains a degree of ambiguity.

The brief scene mirrors strategies employed in the opening shots of part one, *The Great Gambler – A Picture of the Times*. Noël Burch draws attention to a dialogue between Dr Mabuse and Spoerri, which is depicted 'in a series of cross-cut close shots which isolate each of the men in turn *in a setting we do not see*' (1980: 585; emphasis in original). Burch continues:

Fig. 1.5

> As an opening gambit this was a dangerous move at the time; yet thanks to the perfect angular articulation between the direction of the secretary's eyes and the glances Mabuse casts at him over his shoulder, the spectator can be in no doubt as to the relative position of the two men in the surrounding – and as yet hypothetical – space of Mabuse's salon. (Ibid.)

"With your permission: Dr. Mabuse!"

Fig. 1.6

For the opening shots of part one this means that *despite* the fragmentation of the space the spectator is able to place the two characters in relation to each other and make sense of what could potentially be a disorientating viewing experience. Burch identifies the perfect use of camera angle as the method that enables the viewer to place the men, though spatially separated, in relation to each other. We might, however, understand Lang's demonstration of the power of editing to articulate apparently coherent space as the first move in systems which across the film will unpick the security of spatial orientations (as well as wider securities of viewpoint) that the continuity system seems to provide. In the series of shots Burch describes, Lang withholds the establishing shot which would make the position of the two men plain in favour of an isolating treatment. In the sequence from part two, *despite* the establishing shot of the office space and the equally

Fig. 1.7

Fig. 1.8

Fig. 1.9

'perfect angular articulation' between the direction of von Wenk's glance over his shoulder and Mabuse's gaze, it is momentarily difficult to make sense of the relative position of the characters. As a result, we are as astonished as von Wenk to find ourselves face to face with Mabuse (Figs 1.6–1.9).

There is, of course, a generic context here. The film belongs to a well-established tradition of serialised novels and serial films popular at the time. Audiences would have been familiar with master criminals such as Feuillade's Fantômas (from the series of films named after the character) or the enigmatic Lio Shah in Lang's *Die Spinnen/The Spiders* (1919; 1920). Mabuse's undetected entrance to the office can be associated with the uncanny powers of such figures. Based on the character in Norbert Jacques' serialised novel, Dr Mabuse is a skilled hypnotist and thus capable of manipulating his victims to see things that do not exist.[2] Looked at in isolation, the sequence could thus be taken for a moment of shock and surprise characteristic of the genre.

Yet this moment of perceptual and cognitive manipulation anticipates Mabuse exercising an act of mass hypnosis on a theatre audience in the following sequence, suggesting that hoodwinking von Wenk's assistants is just one in a series of acts of 'mass suggestion and sleepless hypnosis' (as the placard advertising 'Sandor Weltmann's' performance promises).

I will argue that Lang appropriates the crime serial's staples of shock and surprise to question the generally held idea that seeing equals knowing and to undermine the apparent security of the spectator's viewing position. Drawing on Douglas Pye's (2000b) observation that epistemic privilege and restriction are central to an understanding of Lang's concerns, the following sections will examine the careful choices that place the spectator in privileged as well as epistemically restricted positions in relation to the action.[3] In the discussion of both parts of the 1922 Mabuse series (*The Great Gambler: A Picture of the Times* and *Inferno: A Play about People of our Times*) particular attention will be drawn to moments where the audience's experience of 'omniscience' is deconstructed and revealed to be a mere 'suggestion', a way of influencing the audience to accept uncritically what they are shown.

Opening images – introducing the 'Great Unknown'

Part one, *The Great Gambler: A Picture of the Times*, opens with an intertitle ('HE and his day'), then cuts to a close-up of a set of portrait photographs being spread like playing cards in the hands of a person as yet unknown. The image then slowly dissolves to a medium shot of Dr Mabuse. Shuffling the cards and picking one, Mabuse chooses his first mask and costume. The act of selecting his first disguise – that of an elderly stockbroker – has led critics to identify Mabuse as the quasi-dramaturge of the unfolding narrative. Tom Gunning notes that the 'image of a hand "holding all the cards" is, of course, an image of control and power' and that 'Mabuse's character as master of appearances and role playing, as controller of other people's destinies, works out an analogy with the film director or author' (2000: 100). Joachim Paech suggests that the film's opening moments 'present more than the exposition of a character or a plot, it is the film itself joining in the game' (1988: 132). Although the analogy of Mabuse with Lang is enticing, an examination of the opening moments in the context of the film as a whole undermines the view of Mabuse and Lang as equal 'metteurs en scène' and instead supports the possibility of a different understanding: namely of Lang's subtle play on the audience's susceptibility to visual rhetoric and the exaggerated sense of Mabuse's status that this kind of rhetoric powerfully – but falsely – evokes.

Significantly, in the serialised novel on which Thea von Harbou's screenplay is based, the true identity of Mabuse – a doctor of psychoanalysis and hypnotist – is not revealed to the reader until chapter five. By 1922 the Mabuse series had gained great national popularity, however, and audiences would have been familiar with Mabuse from both the serial published in the *Berliner Illustrierte Zeitung* and the novel published by Ullstein.[4] To introduce us to Mabuse and his facility for disguise in the opening shots could, therefore, be regarded as a directorial choice borne out of necessity. Whereas the novel greatly depends on the mystery surrounding its enigmatic protagonist ('he was always someone different, but fantasy collated the various pictures and made it into one' (Jacques 1996: 22)), Lang chooses to open the film with a collation of the 'various pictures' that make up the character of Mabuse by superimposing the second onto the first shot in the film (Fig. 1.10).

Fig. 1.10

The audience is privileged in seeing the 'Great Unknown' in the totality of his disguises, and therefore will have a good chance of seeing the true identity hiding behind the mask, whereas this vision of Mabuse holding the cards is denied to the characters in the film. For instance, von Wenk does not recognise Mabuse until the Sandor Weltmann sequence in part two (and even at that stage von Wenk's point of recognition only occurs moments before he is rendered helpless under the spell of the hypnotic gaze).

In short, for the duration of the opening moments we share Mabuse's vision of himself 'holding the cards' and are party to the secret of his many disguises. Our powerful epistemic position is maintained in the following sequences through directorial choices that construct a sense of the audience's unrestricted access to a series of fast paced and spectacular events. The film creates the experience of spectatorial omniscience by firmly aligning our point of view with that of Mabuse.

Master of (narrational) techniques: the 'theft of commercial treaty' sequence

The sequence depicts four strands of simultaneous action: the theft of the treaty from a train compartment; a getaway car racing down a track to take away the stolen briefcase; a messenger on top of a telegraph pole relaying messages to Mabuse; and the doctor himself, 'overseeing' the operation from his headquarters with the help of a telephone. The sequence opens with Mabuse in his study with his manservant Spoerri busy changing the doctor's appearance into his first disguise. During this process Mabuse keeps a close eye on his pocket watch. A cut takes us to the image of a train travelling at great speed. The shot of the train begins with an iris-out, linking the circle of the watch with the circular framing of the iris-out and creating the impression that, by looking at his watch, Mabuse can 'see' the carefully planned action unfolding. The audience shares the doctor's ostensibly omniscient point of view through the film's use of crosscutting.

The combination of sophisticated editing methods and the use of the camera conveying the rapidly unfolding events offers the audience both an immediate access to the world of the film and a powerful encounter with modernity: we are invited to share the sense of Mabuse's control over his environment and modern technologies.[5] A review in *Das Tage-Buch* (1922) by Kurt Pinthus (one of Lang's most ardent critics), entitled 'The World of Dr Mabuse', highlights the spectator's experience of a quasi-omniscient access to the fictional reality and draws parallels between Lang's portrait of the time and the world outside the cinema:

> In our atomistically fragmented social order each individual secures only a shred of the fabric which now encloses us all on every side … yet each and every one of us wants to claim it all for himself. Unreeling temporally and spatially remote phenomena and events in rapid succession, the movie can restore the sense of community we have lost and yet continue to crave. (2001: 78)

Aligned with Mabuse, we are drawn into the spaces he frequents and are able to observe him claim them all for himself – from controlling the stock market to gaining entrance to exclusive gentlemen's clubs and an invitation to the villa of Count Told (Alfred Abel), Mabuse asserts his power. As Pinthus comments:

> Firstly, he [the spectator] sees an exciting tale of crime, the fanatic gangster of awesome format with a vital urge to play with human beings and fates, whose superb cunning and powers of suggestion shake off all attempts at prosecution and win anyone he wants over to his side. Secondly, the eye is charmed and enchanted by the highly skilled, exquisitely mature (I'll risk saying it) extremely artistic photography of Carl Hoffmann. The film's use of light and shadow; the lights of the city train racing, wavering and smoldering along the dark night street; the distorted blurred image of

the group assuming clear contours as the wheel of the opera glasses is turned; the looming shadow of the villain captured on screen as an omen of dark deeds – these are photographic innovations never seen before. Thirdly, director Fritz Lang has fervently sought to capture the suicidal madness of our time in typical characters and milieus [sic]. (2001: 74)

When Mabuse's scheming causes a drastic slump on the stock market, the audience is firmly 'in the know' about the gang's plan: news of the theft of the commercial treaty causes a panic amongst the traders, which Mabuse uses to his own advantage. In scenes set at the 'Folies Bergères' variety theatre and the '17+4' gambling club we gain access to Berlin's postwar *demi-monde*. As Mabuse casts his eyes on a new victim – millionaire's son Edgar Hull (Paul Richter) – we share the doctor's optical point of view. As the narrative progresses, it clearly is Mabuse who is holding the cards.

At this stage, our apparently unrestricted access to the character of Mabuse enables us to observe his *modus operandi* as well as the 'milieu' in which he operates. The slow-paced and exhaustive depiction of the card game in the club sequence and Hull's subsequent loss of a large sum of money establishes Mabuse's control over his victims and indicates his interest in 'playing with people and their destinies' (as he phrases it to Countess Told (Gertrude Welcker) during a séance they both attend). Significantly, Mabuse is presented not so much as part of the decadence surrounding him but as a 'stranger' and, at most, a 'guest' at the exclusive '17+4' club.

Once again, it is worth drawing attention to the combination of the elements at work and to highlight their effect on the viewer. Our unrestricted access to Mabuse is paired with a quasi-limitless access to the spaces depicted in the world of the film. On one level, the film's powerful images and speedy pace entice us into Mabuse's world, a world that – despite its fragmentation – Mabuse is seemingly able to control. This in turn gives the audience the experience of a 'totality' that – according to Pinthus – was no longer part of the audience's experience of the world outside the cinema. Lang's 'portrait of the times' effortlessly pieces the fragments together, offering the audience a glimpse of omniscience in the (fragmented) spaces of modernity.

The sophisticated use of narrational techniques in part one of *Dr Mabuse, the Gambler* can thus be regarded as the perfect example of what Sabine Hake describes as cinema's aesthetic function in the reproduction of the perceptual and cognitive experience of modern mass society 'within its own parameters' (1993: 90). The multifaceted opening sequence challenges the audience's perception and understanding of the events presented onscreen, yet at the same time signals the film's mastery in offering the audience images 'never seen before', safe in the knowledge that the spectator will be able to make sense of what is shown. The audience's visual and cognitive pleasure in experiencing both the sensational images and the narrative's racy pace is inextricably linked to the rhetoric surrounding Dr Mabuse's powers – his hypnotic skill as well as his apparent omniscience and omnipotence.

'Übermensch' rhetoric and 'zeitgeist': the 'Great Game' sequence

Part one draws to a close with an event at a social gathering in the house of aristocrat Count Told (Alfred Abel). During the party we observe Mabuse, now in his identity as psychoanalyst (which requires no make-up, wigs and false moustaches), standing by himself by a fireplace in the count's home. The room is dominated by a large painting on

display above the fireplace; it depicts a demon with glaring eyes emitting light rays. The picture dwarfs the man, and belongs to the count rather than the doctor, but can be regarded as a reference to the doctor's powerful hypnotic gaze (Fig. 1.11).

Subsequently, in a conversation with Countess Told, Mabuse reveals his conviction that 'there is no happiness – there is only the will for power'. Mabuse then 'wills' Count Told to cheat in a game of cards and snatches the countess. The abduction of the countess and Mabuse's raucous celebration

Fig. 1.11

with his gang completes the first part of the film.

Friedrich Nietzsche's philosophy of the 'will to power' and ideas surrounding the 'superhuman' qualities of Mabuse are expressed implicitly and – at this point – explicitly in the narrative. The concept of Mabuse's many disguises is reminiscent of the Nietzschean thought that truth consists only of metaphors and that 'truths are only illusions of which we have forgotten that they are illusions' (Kunzmann *et al.* 1993: 177). As spectators, we are consistently presented with the different layers of illusion and deception that govern the world of the film. Falsehood, not truths, are the order of the day in Lang's portrait of the time. Thomas Elsaesser argues:

> One of the most extended commentaries on these Nietzschean deconstructive impulses is *Dr Mabuse, der Spieler*, where more than anything, one is introduced, right in the heart of the modern metropolis, to several worlds that already look false even before they become real. (2000: 152)

A particularly cynical example depicts the rise of Emil Schramm (Julius E. Hermann) in a self-contained episode (a narrational device not repeated in the film) entitled 'Schramm's World'. It depicts the character's 'career' from street trader and incarceration during the Great War to his subsequent success as a war profiteer. Schramm's 'Grill' restaurant is merely a shop front for a hidden casino. Later on in the narrative, the opening of another gambling hall – the 'Petit Casino' – manifests the view of a world ruled by deceit and decadence hidden behind virtuous façades: in the 'Petit Casino' sequence, the drab entrance to the house at 11, Haydn Street conceals the glamour hidden inside; the casino is disguised as a cabaret promoting self-indulgent entertainment, governed by the maxim that 'Everything that pleases is allowed'. Aligned with the master criminal, we gain entrance to these exclusive and secret places whose promise of indulgence and debauchery holds no interest for Mabuse. His rejection of all moral values, true or false, as well as his crimes, seems motivated not by a desire for money or luxury (like Schramm's) but solely by his lust for power.

Mabuse's vitality and ruthlessness stand in stark contrast to the feebleness and slavish adherence to the latest trend embodied by the count and the bored bourgeoisie frequenting the city's clubs and gambling halls. Mabuse's will to power sets him apart from the sluggish decadence around him, his gamble with materialist and moral values that have become relative and unstable is, in a nihilist sense, 'beyond good and evil'. Celebrating his capture of the countess, Mabuse is intoxicated by the idea of being all-powerful, a modern-day Zarathustra pitilessly leaving behind all that is weak and cowardly.

In post-World War One Germany, the indefatigable and invincible figure of Mabuse stands out, seemingly wholly unaffected by both the humiliation of defeat in the Great War and the oppressive economic conditions imposed by the Versailles Treaty. At a time of economic paralysis the figure of Mabuse taking control of the stock market and robbing the wealthy at the casino table takes on a role that exceeds that of the master criminal of the crime serial tradition. In a review of the film in *Das Blaue Heft* (1922), critic Max Moritz (Roland Schacht) describes Mabuse as a 'superior' being in all aspects: 'There, in Thea von Harbou's script: psychological and mental collapse of a super-human, super-criminal, super-hypnotist' (Schacht 2001: 24). The film's engagement with ideas of the 'super human' further corresponds to a post-World War One Nietzsche revival in the popular culture of the Weimar Republic.[6] However, the Nietzschean rhetoric surrounding Mabuse is not employed uncritically by the film. Instead, it functions to 'bait' the spectator. Narrative and narrational choices invite us to regard the doctor as 'Übermensch', gradually turning our initial spatio-temporal alignment into a moral allegiance with the victorious Mabuse by the end of part one.

In the light of Pinthus's suggestion that *Dr Mabuse, the Gambler* both acknowledges the 'atomistically fragmented social order' of a postwar society in the process of radical change and modernisation but simultaneously 'synthesises' that fragmentation in order to recreate a 'whole' through specifically cinematic means, it is possible to argue that the film offers the spectator a seductive glimpse of the apparent omniscience enjoyed by its protagonist. In addition, the film initially encourages readings of Mabuse as a kind of metteur en scène with an all-powerful status within the narrative. Yet a closer look at part two, *Inferno: A Play about People of Our Time*, will demonstrate how specific choices drastically qualify some of the ideas about Mabuse's omniscience and omnipotence and can lead us to review our responses to and understanding of Lang's methods.

No longer 'in the know': moments of epistemic restriction

In the second part of the film the narrative focus gradually shifts from Mabuse to State Attorney von Wenk and his various attempts to track down the 'Great Unknown'. This shift has implications for the audience and our access to the world of the film changes from a privileged point of view in part one to a more restricted access to actions and characters in part two. Visual strategies employed in part one to give the audience a sense of omniscience in relation to action and characters are now increasingly problematised.

I have already discussed the film's use of eyeline match as one example of its ability to construct and deconstruct the spectator's coherent access to the world of the film. Another reversal of our epistemic position from omniscient to restricted occurs in a scene depicting Mabuse's assassination of his own henchman Pesch (Georg John) following Pesch's arrest.

In this scene, Mabuse takes on the role of a political *agent provocateur* who incites a crowd of workers in a bar to interfere with Pesch's transport from police station to prison. In the ensuing chaos (stirred by Mabuse dressed as a worker, the crowd believe the prisoner to be 'Johannes Gutter' – though who Gutter is remains unclear) Pesch is killed by a bullet. Significantly, although we recognise Mabuse's right-hand man Georg (Hans Adalbert Schlettow), we may not immediately recognise Mabuse in his proletarian disguise. As Mabuse incites the crowd, the camera remains at a distance and at the level of the mob in the bar. We only get the 'full picture' at the moment where Pesch – not the man called Gutter – emerges from the prison car and is instantly shot. Above all, the sequence signals that we are no longer complicit witnesses of Mabuse's plans.

Our cognitive ties with Mabuse thus severed, we increasingly share the restricted perspective of Mabuse's adversary. Our alignment (a perceptual process described by Murray Smith as 'two interlocking functions, *spatio-temporal attachment* and *subjective access*' (1995: 83; emphasis in original)) with van Wenk not only carries the loss of the 'all-seeing' perspective we shared with the doctor; in terms of characterisation, von Wenk is a much less charismatic figure than Mabuse. The introduction of von Wenk early on in the film is juxtaposed with images of Mabuse extracting poison from a snake. Whereas the snake-handling scenario portrays Mabuse as fearless and daring, von Wenk is presented as a formal and rigid character whose investigation has so far not yielded any satisfactory results. However, as the narrative progresses, von Wenk is getting closer to Mabuse, which forces the doctor to act, resulting in his aforementioned visit to von Wenk's office. The subsequent sequence of Mabuse in the disguise of hypnotist 'Sandor Weltmann' signals the film's most explicit engagement with seeing and blindness.

Sandor Weltmann: experiments in mass suggestion

The Sandor Weltmann sequence lasts nearly 14 minutes and portrays Mabuse's mesmeric skills, including the illusion of a North African desert and a caravan of travellers and horses emerging from the stage into the auditorium of the hall where the experiment is taking place. During the caravan illusion the camera is in a slightly elevated position at the back of the auditorium, placing our view higher than that of the audience in the world of the film (Fig. 1.13). We are therefore able simultaneously to enjoy the illusion, created through the employment of cross fades and use of the theatrical space, and to observe the audience's response. Mabuse then proceeds to coerce von Wenk, who is in the audience with several of his men, into participating in a number of experiments, which eventually lead to von Wenk's complete hypnosis and near death in a car accident.

The sequence could thus be regarded as a self-conscious demonstration of film's ability to create images and visions, to blur the demarcation line between reality and illusion for both the audiences in the world of the film and in the cinema. The poster (Fig. 1.12) advertising the Weltmann experiments with 'Mass Suggestion, Sleepless Hypnosis, Trance' and other exotic and psychological phenomena draws attention to what Anton Kaes describes as the 'uncanny effect' (1994: 618) of the medium itself.

Yet despite this repeated demonstration of Mabuse's power of hypnosis and the calculated plan to eliminate his enemy, the sequence simultaneously questions the apparent 'suggestive' or 'hypnotic' powers of both Mabuse and the filmic medium by raising questions concerning the spectator's *own* role in relation to Weltmann's or, on a wider level, the film's 'experiment'.

Today! Today! Today!

An Evening of Experiments
Sandor Weltmann

Experiments in Mass Suggestion, Sleepless Hypnosis, Trance, Natural Magnetism, The Secrets of the Indian Fakirs. The Secrets of the Psyche. The Subconscious in Man and Animal.

In the Main Auditorium of Philharmonic Hall

Fig. 1.12

Fig. 1.13

In the Sandor Weltmann sequence the 'theatrical' character of the spectacle, complete with the participation of a sensation-hungry urban audience, is foregrounded: Mabuse's 'mad professor' disguise and exaggerated gestures on stage, the proscenium arch and the 'planting' of Spoerri in the auditorium to 'assist' in the 'experiments', highlight the theatrical and fabricated quality of Mabuse's powers. This focus on the artificiality of the scenario has implications for the spectator, not least in guiding our attention to the obvious constructedness of the spectacle, from opening the sequence with a poster advertising the show as an example of 'Mass Suggestion', to the emphasis on the theatrical space and the presence of an audience to whose reactions the film returns throughout the scene.

This recognition in turn complicates our alignment with Mabuse, suggesting, arguably for the first time, that his 'omniscience' might in fact be partly rooted in our own partial perception of what is happening in the world of the film. In contrast to previous demonstrations of his hypnotic skills, the machinations behind Mabuse's powers are actively foregrounded during the Sandor Weltmann scene. Whereas earlier demonstrations of hypnosis turned us into immediate witnesses of Mabuse's powers, even at times sharing his optical point of view, we are now observing the reactions of an audience as stunned and delighted by what they see – or think they can see – as we may have been ourselves during such visually striking scenes as the initial hypnosis of von Wenk in the 'Andalusia' club, a scene I shall discuss in greater detail below. Following Pesch's assassination and Mabuse's surprise entrance to von Wenk's office, the Weltmann sequence continues to question the status of our perception, implying that we, like the audience of Sandor Weltmann's 'experiments', may in earlier scenes have fallen victim to a set of magic tricks, a sophisticated optical – and cognitive – illusion.

In his analysis of the relationship between the film's narrative methods and Mabuse's controlling power Douglas Pye argues that although it 'is tempting, for instance, to say that the narrative strategies *express* Mabuse's power, as if they could be identified with the control he exerts ... the opening sequences make clear that the film's narration and our access to the fictional world are developed in quite complex relationships to Mabuse's control' (Pye 2000b; emphasis in original). Drawing attention to moments early on in the film in which Mabuse cannot control the human weaknesses of his gang (Spoerri's cocaine addiction, Pesch's lateness) Pye argues that 'human failings begin, in other words, to qualify, however trivially in the early parts of the film, Mabuse's assertions of omnipotence and omniscience' (2000b). In part two of the film, the human weaknesses of Mabuse's gang become more obvious: for instance, Pesch fails to kill the state attorney by planting the bomb in his office and is captured by von Wenk's men.

Pye draws attention to the first appearances of von Wenk and Countess Told, two characters who initially 'are outside Mabuse's controlling web and the evolving narrative patterns which centre on him; their entrances are therefore *contingent* events which escape the apparent necessity of Mabuse's schemes and the narration mimes this contingency by their unannounced entrances' (2000b; emphasis in original). The characters' 'unexpected entrances challenge the idea that "omniscient" might be an appropriate way of describing the spectator's view of the film's world and simultaneously suggest that the film's interests include questions of perceptual and cognitive restriction' (2000b).

There are other moments in the narrative which indicate that Mabuse's powers are in fact not limitless. As he hypnotises von Wenk on stage in the Weltmann sequence, Mabuse uses the phrase 'Tsi Nan Fu', which triggers von Wenk's – and arguably the audience's – memory of his first encounter with Mabuse, in part one, during a card game in the Andalusia club. In the Andalusia episode von Wenk, also dressed in disguise, refused to be willed by Mabuse into taking another card during a game at the gambling table. This moment is the first instance in the narrative where von Wenk is on an 'equal footing' with Mabuse, as neither opponent recognises the other. However, the significance of von Wenk's achievement in refusing to succumb to Mabuse's powers of suggestion is overshadowed by a series of visually stunning special effects throughout the Andalusia scene, including dissolves, superimpositions and the use of trick photography, which creates the sudden appearance of the letters 'Tsi Nan Fu' flashing up and vanishing on the surface of the gambling table. The surreal quality of the images in this scene (at one point, Mabuse's head appears to dislodge from his body and fills a blacked-out screen) diverts our attention from the narrative significance of von Wenk's first serious challenge of Mabuse's hypnotic powers to the enjoyment of its various optical illusions.

Although von Wenk does not yield to Mabuse's powers of suggestion during the Andalusia sequence, he fails to identify and catch the criminal. In the Weltmann sequence of part two, von Wenk is finally able to see Mabuse as the sum of his various parts and disguises: in a short montage sequence, the grotesque masks of 'Sandor Weltmann' and the sinister figure in the Andalusia club dissolve to reveal the doctor's face. Thus unmasked, Mabuse can no longer hide from von Wenk and his men. A second attempt to kill von Wenk is unsuccessful and the state attorney's ability to see clearly spells the end of Mabuse's powers.

Finale: seeing bracketed by blindness

The final sequences of part two comprise a car chase and a lengthy shoot-out in which Mabuse's men are either killed or captured and the countess is released from captivity. Mabuse escapes but becomes trapped in a cellar used by Hawasch (Karl Huszar), a gang member now dead, to produce counterfeit notes with the aid of a printing press and a group of blind slave workers. Mabuse loses his mind and is plagued by visions of his dead victims, who force him to play a game of cards. The thrill of 'playing with people and their destinies' is stripped of its 'Übermensch' rhetoric to reveal the underlying disregard for human life and its loss.

Fig. 1.14

The final images depict von Wenk and his colleagues leading the blind slave workers up the stairs (Figs 1.14 –1.15). Heide Schönemann points out that this image is reminiscent of a painting entitled 'The Parable of the Blind' by Pieter Bruegel the Older. Schönemann argues that, whereas the painting shows the blind tumbling into a ditch, the film's final image shows them being led out of the cellar, thus presenting the audience with an image of hope amidst the despair (see 1992: 94–5). Significantly in this respect, the film's closing moments emphasise less von Wenk's victory over Mabuse than his part in releasing the blind from their prison. In addition, though, the decision to return to the blind slave workers at the end of the whole film brackets the narrative with the theme of blindness.

Fig. 1.15

Mabuse's first visit to the cellar occurred shortly after his successful assault on the stock market near the beginning of part one, depicting the printing of forged banknotes (one more play on deceit and authenticity) as another part of the 'world of Dr Mabuse'. The question I have wanted to probe is to what extent we have ourselves been 'deceived' by appearances and held 'captive' by the film's visual and narrative rhetoric, whether perhaps our enjoyment of fast-paced action and visual spectacle was not unlike the audience's enthusiastic response to Mabuse's 'mass suggestion' in the Sandor Weltmann scene.

The experience of omniscience, in the end, is reduced to a mere delusion of grandeur. The apparition of Mabuse's victims and the framing presence of the blind can thus be related to our own misguided spectatorial position. The blind prisoners are released but of course they will still be unable to see. We have to be careful of drawing too exact a parallel with the spectator but Lang's use of blind characters across his work was rarely without implicit reference to the less literal 'blindness' that the rhetoric of film can induce.[7] As we, too, escape from Mabuse's world – our glimpse of 'omniscience' bracketed by the narrative presence of blindness – do we remain partially-sighted witnesses?

In *The Material Ghost: Films and their Medium*, Gilberto Perez observes that 'In *Spies* as in *Dr Mabuse, the Gambler*, Lang associates omniscience with villainy, the commanding manifolds of the film's plot with the will to power of a criminal plot to take over the world' (1998: 132). The notion of linking omniscience to villainy has implications for the audience and their placing in an apparently omniscient position for large parts of the film.

Sharing a point of view with Mabuse need not, of course, imply that we share his (im)moral values – we are witnesses of, not partners in, the crimes he commits. What seems at stake, though, is our ability to maintain a critical distance and not be enticed to see the world merely through Mabuse's seductively all-seeing eyes. To see the 'whole of the fabric' (to use Pinthus's metaphor) in 'atomistically fragmented' times may seem enticing, but is – as the film seeks to demonstrate – less a sign of omniscience than a complacent or even deluded point of view.

Conclusion

Looked at historically, *Dr Mabuse, the Gambler*, with its references to lawlessness, war profiteering and social instability, seems to be above all a commentary on the social and political chaos of Germany's immediate postwar years. At the same time, there are no direct references to actual political events. Lang's own description of the film, 45 years after it was made, as 'a documentary of the postwar period' (2003: 93) should be read with caution. Frieda Grafe, in her cornerstone essay 'Fritz Lang: A Place, Not a Monument', points out that throughout his career Lang never sought a purely mimetic representation of reality:

> Lang's films are not realistic. They never reflect their immediate environment. They proceed from a recognisable abstract form of reality, created by specifically cinematic means, a method whose claim for truth is based on the fact that it does better justice to the artificial, fabricated, historical character of social reality than any ideas about a simple reflection of reality. (1987: 22–3)

What Lang's 'document of the time' records and examines is less the social reality outside the cinema than the medium's own part in creating, in Pinthus's words, 'photographic innovations never seen before' for an audience that had already been deceived once by spectacular images that appeared to promise victory but had only covered up defeat a few years earlier. After the 'Great War', which turned out to be but a war of illusions, spectators were now experiencing to an even greater extent the sensation of 'photographic innovations' provided by a rapidly expanding mass culture with only their senses and reason available to them to tell fact from fiction, the actual from the impossible.[8]

In *Dr Mabuse, the Gambler* 'the eye is charmed' (as Pinthus said) by a quasi-'authentic' visual experience of modernity, only to reveal the medium's ability to deceive the eye. Lang's mastery of film, and his invitation to the audience to master modern ways of seeing – speedy, fragmented, simultaneous – is informed by his awareness of the implications of film's ability to guide the spectator's attention. The film's critical engagement with its own rhetoric can be understood in this context as an exercise in complex seeing, inviting us, as spectators, to be aware of film's potential to offer partial and misguided perceptions in the guise of 'totality'. As his movies opened in Berlin's splendid picture palaces, Lang, never openly didactic, would leave it up to the spectator to pay attention or be tricked.

2. Stabilisation Period: *Menschen am Sonntag*: 'Fleeting Days'

In einer kleinen Konditorei, da sassen wir zwei bei Kuchen und Tee. Du sprachst kein Wort, kein einziges Wort und wusstest sofort, dass ich dich versteh! Und das elektrische Klavier, das klimpert leise eine Weise von Liebesleid und Weh! In einer kleinen Konditorei, da sassen wir zwei bei Kuchen und Tee.

(In a small pastry shop, we both sat with cakes and tea. You did not say a word, not a single word, but you immediately knew that I understood you! And the electric piano quietly played a song of heartache and sorrow. In a small pastry shop, we both sat with cakes and tea.) ('In a Small Pastry Shop', composed by Fred Raymond, a popular tune in Germany 1929)

'A group of unknowns'

Menschen am Sonntag, a late silent film, was shot during the rainy summer of 1929. Its directors, Robert Siodmak and Edgar Ulmer, belonged to 'Film-Studio 1929', a production team that included Siodmak's brother Kurt as well as Billy Wilder, Fred Zinnemann, Moritz Seeler and Eugen Schüfftan.[9] Founded in June 1929, the group sought to produce experimental films in a collaborative manner. Reviewing the film a day after its premiere in February 1930, Herbert Ihering describes 'Film-Studio 1929' as a group of 'unknowns' (1961: 300), with the exception of Schüfftan, already a well-known expert in trick cinematography. Based on an idea by Kurt Siodmak, *Menschen am Sonntag* was conceived as a 'reportage', or 'querschnittsfilm', a non-fiction mode conceptually similar to a newspaper report in terms of its factual style, objective narration and focus on the everyday. The term 'querschnitt' (cross-section) refers to the genre's objective of investigating particular strata (a 'slice') of society and its role and function in the working life of the city.[10] Stylistically, 'querschnitt' films are often linked to the aesthetics and themes of New Objectivity, which peaked in the visual arts, literature, theatre and cinema during Weimar Germany's economic and social 'stabilisation' period between the implementation of the Dawes plan in 1924 and the stock market crash in October 1929.

In the absence of a programme or unifying theory of New Objectivity's artistic intentions, various writers have attempted definitions encompassing its manifestations in 1920s literature and visual arts. Wieland Schmied argues that New Objectivity is:

> not so much a new style as a new way of seeing, corresponding to a changed attitude to the phenomena of life; it reflects a radical commitment to the modern environment and everyday life. (1979: 13)

Schmied lists 'visual sobriety and acuity, an unsentimental, largely emotionless way of seeing ... concentration on everyday things, on banal, insignificant and unpretentious subjects ... a new mental relationship with the world of objects' (ibid.) as amongst New Objectivity's key characteristics.

With its sober and impersonal focus on the everyday life of the city and the leisure activities of five ordinary young people, *Menschen am Sonntag* ostensibly adheres to New Objectivity's approach and the conceptual parameters of the cross-section film. Thematically, the film's focus on five people employed at the lower scale of the city's service industry – respectively a taxi driver, a shop assistant, a salesman, a film extra and a shop model – demonstrates its awareness of the emerging class of 'Angestellten' ('salaried', or 'white collar' workers), whose lifestyle and leisure activities reflect processes of increasing commodification and consumption during the mid- to late 1920s period in Weimar Germany. *Menschen am Sonntag* could thus be regarded as firmly 'neusachlich' both stylistically and thematically.

The purpose of the following close reading of selected moments, however, is to reveal the film's surprisingly ambivalent relationship to the style it so demonstrably employs. The analysis will focus on subtle shifts in the film's processes of narration, changing from a detached and sober observational style at the beginning to an increasingly subjective, gently ironic and empathetic depiction of the young people, particularly its female characters, as the narrative progresses.

The focus on the film's narrational nuances seeks to show its subtle critique of New Objectivity's 'largely emotionless ways of seeing' and the effects of the 'new way of seeing' (Schmied 1979: 13) on those sections of society most eager to embrace them – in the world of the film and, by implication, its audience. The film's exercise in complex seeing lies in its invitation to the spectator to balance the detached observation of the social transformation brought about by the modern, urban, but also increasingly isolating and consumerist lifestyle, with a more subjective grasp of the subtle imagery hinting at the emotional vulnerability of the young women and, ultimately, their confinement to insignificant, largely passive gender roles, despite their growing financial independence.

Saturday

The film's opening sequence introduces the 'cross-section' of five young people representative of the city's salaried class, whose lifestyle and leisure pursuits are at the centre of the film's inquiry. The last of the opening titles promises, 'These five people appeared before a camera for the first time in their lives. Today they are all back in their own jobs.' The first image we see is a close-up of a car registration number on the back of a vehicle. We are then introduced in a series of seven shots, to Erwin Splettstösser, who, an intertitle informs us, 'drives taxi 1A 10088'. The next intertitle reads: 'Last month Brigitte Borchert sold 150 copies of the record "In a Small Pastry Shop"' and we observe the shop assistant outside an Electrola record store in the city. Subsequently Wolfgang von Waltershausen, whose line of work includes 'officer, farmer, antique dealer, gigolo, [currently] wine trader'[11] and Christl Ehlers, a film extra, are introduced in the same manner: with an intertitle and several shots of each character in their day job. Annie Schreyer, a 'model', is encountered in the crammed tenement flat she shares with Splettstösser. The sequence concludes with an introduction to the city of Berlin itself with mobile shots capturing the capital's traffic and pedestrians on their way home from work on a Saturday afternoon.

This sequence lasts just under three minutes. Its emphasis is on the authenticity of the five young people presented: 'Today they are all back in their own jobs', signals the film's apparent adherence to a documentary mode of representation, albeit one that involves 'experimentation'. From the start, the boundaries between fiction and non-fiction modes are blurred: the film employs real people to play 'themselves' in a 'matter-of-fact' romantic sketch written by Billy Wilder in the functional style of 'neusachliche' prose and poetry.[12]

Opening image: IA-10088

Our epistemic access to the world of the film is tightly controlled in the first shot (Fig. 2.1): the framing dictates that we gain narrative information only from the code on the plate, as its immediate surroundings are excluded. Stylistically, the image is characteristic of New Objectivity's focus on everyday objects and attention to detail. At the same time, it

Fig. 2.1

presents an image reduced to a sign system that is either instantly recognisable, or wholly inaccessible to the onlooker unfamiliar with the symbolic code.

We are historically at one remove from the image, but it can be assumed that the Berlin audience at the time would have been familiar with the code: according to Ludwig Bauer (1988) the Roman number I stands for the county of Prussia and the letter A signals that the car is registered in the district of greater Berlin. The numbers after the hyphen give the individual registration of the vehicle. Later in the film other objects, such as historical buildings, geographical landmarks and monuments in a park will become emblematic of the city, but none will be as *abstract* as the emblem depicted in the opening shot. Considering that the film could have opened with a range of images that would unmistakably – and perhaps more dramatically – disclose the location for viewers outside the capital (Reichstag, Brandenburg Gate, for example) this unusual choice by the filmmakers invites further deliberation.

What is on 'display' for the audience to take note of in this 'establishing' shot is not so much an evocative location that summons up the city but a *style*: the shot of the number plate propagates a kind of visual representation that is factual, dispassionate and unambiguous. The number plate conjures up no sense of patriotic sentiment, historical knowledge or political association. Instead, it encourages – even prescribes – a wholly rational way of seeing: the obvious – and only – inference the primary audience could draw from this image is that this is a number plate for a vehicle registered in the city of Berlin. The cognitive process would be automatic, the answer precise and accurate: the Roman I reads 'Prussia', the letter A stands in for 'Berlin'. It is a purely mechanical way of making sense of what we see onscreen, an instruction to apply a sober and non-subjective approach to reading the image. We are encouraged to take up the position of an objective, knowledgeable and analytical observer of events. In short, perceptual and cognitive processes initiated by the opening shot mirror a form of rationalisation commonly associated with the 'rapid industrial modernisation' (Durst 2004: xxx) between 1924 and 1929.[13]

The number plate represents not only a specific place, but also a specific time: not Berlin's historical past but the infrastructure of a modern city with its asphalt streets, tramlines and busy boulevards. The wording of the intertitle introducing Erwin Splettstösser is factual in tone, and the detail, 'drives taxi 1A 10088' is characteristic of New Objectivity prose: the use of non-literary elements, such as numbers, statistics or advertisement slogans, typified the movement's striving for authenticity and its focus on present-day life. In the opening seconds we are faced with a familiar facet of modern city life, a taxi pulling off a curb, 'pulled' into sharp focus by the camera, whose mechanical look firmly guides and enhances the viewer's attention to technical detail.

Little shop girls...

The prose of the intertitle introducing Brigitte Borchert continues in the factual style and attention to detail of the previous intertitle. In contrast to Erwin, we do not actually see Brigitte selling a copy of the record 'In a Small Pastry Shop'; instead, a long take of the imposing glass fronted façade of the Electrola gramophone record shop foregrounds not the sales assistant, but the elaborately decorated shop windows of the company that employs Brigitte (Fig. 2.2). Her introduction emphasises not only the young woman's marginal position in the company

Fig. 2.2

and her limited involvement with the product she sells but also points to processes of commodification and cultural consumption – in this instance, of human experience and feelings captured in popular tunes like the one Brigitte has sold to over a hundred customers.

In the film's Sunday section, Brigitte takes a portable gramophone to a rendezvous at the lake. Though love songs, such as 'In a Small Pastry Shop', or the popular tune 'On Sunday My Sweetheart Wants to Take Me Sailing' (which were played on a gramophone in the cinema auditorium during screenings; see 'E. L.' 1930: 5), can to some extent be expressive of Brigitte's feelings and desires, they simultaneously 'compartmentalise' notions of love and romance, stressing not the uniqueness of Brigitte's experience but the clearly defined rituals of the 'boy meets girl' scenario. Significantly, it is after Brigitte's hurried sexual intercourse with Wolfgang adjacent to a rubbish tip that one of the records gets broken and Brigitte is left – literally and figuratively – to pick up the pieces of her brittle romantic aspirations.

Wolfgang

Von Waltershausen is introduced by a mobile camera, which depicts an advertisement for wine (Fig. 2.3) and subsequently pans right to reframe on Wolfgang standing out-

Fig. 2.3

Fig. 2.4

side Lehmann's, a wine trading company (Fig. 2.4). The movement draws attention to the character's itinerant occupational status as well as once again foregrounding processes of commodification and consumption. The advert, which depicts an idyllic rustic setting with a wine drinker composing the poetic slogan 'What is wine? Sunshine caught [in a glass] … it certainly will do no harm', stands in contrast to the urban environment and 'Lehmann's wines' wholesale business's interest in wine and its large-scale consumption.

Yet von Waltershausen not only trades in wine: his work as 'Eintänzer' ('paid dancer'/gigolo) refers to another novel phenomenon of modern urban living, whereby Berlin's Grand Hotels hired male dancing partners for the surplus of female guests attending the capital's popular 5 o'clock tea dances (see Haustedt 1999).[14] Wolfgang's looks, charm and skills as a dancer become commodities that can be purchased, for a small fee, by (salaried) single women. All these considerations are made possible by the pan, introducing Wolfgang *after* the adver-

tisement and enabling us to take a swift glance at two types of realism – one romantic/ nostalgic, one sober/detached. Yet both are present in one shot, capturing the fabric of a zeitgeist Ernst Bloch referred to as 'ungleichzeitig' (non-simultaneous): the process of capitalist modernisation in a society in transition from old to new (see Durst 2004: 1).

Christl and Annie

The occupations of Christl Ehlers and Annie Schreyer as film extra and model introduce notions of role-play and image construction to the socio-economic discourses discussed so far. There are various implicit parallels between the two characters, which are played out in the narrative. Both Christl and Annie are fashionable, young, independent women; crucially though, whereas the well-dressed Christl is depicted on the streets waiting

(Fig. 2.5), respectively, for an audition and shortly afterwards for a date (though the man she claims to be waiting for never appears), Annie is presented as dishevelled in appearance and confined to the flat she shares with her boyfriend Erwin (Fig. 2.6). The introductory images emphasise the overt differences between the two women, juxtaposing Christl's zeal in gaining a part in a film with Annie's lethargy, Christl's groomed appearance with Annie's neglect of her beauty and Christl's élan in meeting young men for a date with Annie's preference to savour romance (a film with Greta Garbo) at the movies.

Fig. 2.5

As the narrative progresses it becomes apparent that Christl and Annie are at different stages of the transformed social roles occupied by 'modern' urban women. Christl is presented as a young woman enjoying the city's streets and cafés for her own pleasure. Yet streets and cafés, rather than being the romantic spaces serenaded in 'In a Small Pastry Shop', will be exposed as sites of potential deception and exploitation by the end of the film, inviting a surprising revaluation of Annie's self-elected confinement to, and isolation in, the fraught domestic space of the tenement flat.

Fig. 2.6

Although ostensibly designed as random 'snapshots' of the five young men and women chosen to represent the 'people on Sunday', the detail of the shots of the opening sequence reveals that they are, in fact, tightly controlled and significantly organised. Narrational processes analysed so far foreground a number of characteristics that can be summarised as follows: first and foremost, the film stresses that the people we see are 'real', that they exist outside the world of the film, that they have real names and indeed work as taxi driver, shop assistant, wine dealer, film extra and model. As a 'cross-section' of Berlin's citizens, all five are salaried workers, carrying out tasks brought about by the rationalisation and specialisation of modernist capitalist production. All five belong to the lower spectrum of this socio-economic group, working in the service and culture industries. They serve the city's growing consumer society, themselves human commodities in a market where low-skill workers can easily be substituted. The emphasis in the opening (their 'first time' in front of a camera, now all back in their own jobs) on the supposed 'normality' of the chosen five is thus accompanied by an implicit commentary about the limited scope of the professional roles they perform on a day-to-day basis. As the sequence continues it becomes apparent that processes of commodification and consumption experienced in their work extend into the realms of their private lives.

Yet another intertitle introduces a sixth 'character': the city of Berlin itself (Fig. 2.7). A series of shots filmed around the central Bahnhof Zoo area presents the city as a

Fig. 2.7

space dominated by movement and vision. Neither following nor anticipating any action in the conventional sense, the camera assumes the role of observer, with no fixed object of study, and images of traffic, pedestrians and a busy intersection are edited in a loose montage style. Another montage depicts trains leaving Zoo station and shows various advertisements posted on a railway arch. The representation of the city in terms of disconnected movements of people and traffic emphasises the mechanisation and fragmentation of the contemporary urban environment.

Jost Hermand argues that 'the central space for the *Neue Sachlichkeit* was the city, because city-dwellers had already achieved a positive alienation: the atomisation of an anonymous and impersonal society based on the homogenisation and standardisation of all forms of life' (1994: 61). From presenting Berlin as the definitive visual expression of New Objectivity, the film progresses to scrutinise the modern, rational and pragmatic lifestyle associated with the movement.

In the sequence following the introduction of the characters and the city of Berlin, the narrative's focus on the social environment of the city is replaced by the study of the social behaviour of its citizens. The camerawork continues in the same observational style employed to depict the city, linking the modern environment to emerging forms of transformed social behaviour. The passing of trams and the passing of strangers is depicted from the now familiar perspective of the detached, high-angle camera.

Instead of witnessing the beginning of a romantic encounter, we are presented with a dispassionate dissection of social behaviour in the sequence depicting Christl's encounter with von Waltershausen on the forecourt of Zoo station. Framed by other familiar Saturday afternoon activities, such as finishing work and cleaning the city in readiness for the collective day off, Christl's and Wolfgang's attempts to find someone to spend their Sunday with are presented as merely another ritual in the wider social phenomenon of increasingly secular leisure pursuits on Sundays.

Cruising

The sequence depicts Wolfgang approaching Christl, who appears to be waiting for someone near a small kiosk outside the station. Eventually, they go to a café, flirt and arrange to meet up at Nikolaussee, a lake on the western outskirts of the city, on Sunday. At the beginning of this sequence, the considerable distance between camera and characters signals the camera's apparent non-intervention in the action, which on the surface is just one of the many things happening in this scene. Frequently, passing traffic obscures our view of the two young people at this busy traffic intersection.

Though the interaction between the two characters is by no means privileged by the camera, it is nonetheless a tightly choreographed piece of performance. What could be perceived as a casual encounter between two strangers is revealed, by the high-angle, observational distance of the camera, as a calculated, almost predatory circling of the young woman by Wolfgang (Fig. 2.8). Eventually, the camera follows both characters as they cross the busy street between the traffic island and the pavement (Fig. 2.9).

By mixing documentary modes with elements of fiction, the film creates a tension between the representative (documentary) and exceptional (fictional) character of what is shown. Because the camera observes from a distance, there is little sense of an active intervention into a chance event, which, it seems, would unfold regardless of the presence of the camera, in the same way that other events unfold – from people boarding trams to trains leaving the station on the overhead track. The camera purposefully blends the individual story into the wider social fabric of the city.

Before dissolving to a more conventional two-shot of the couple in a café, the vantage of the camera shows Christl and Wolfgang crossing the tramlines: narrational strategies situate the negotiation of sexual attraction in the context of the city's modern infrastructure, juxtaposing strangers standing and walking side by side, with modern rites of courtship that have to negotiate the urban phenomenon of the increasing anonymity of individuals amongst the masses.

Fig. 2.8

In the café, Christl's confident assertion that she was not stood up by another man suggests that she may not simply be the passive victim of Wolfgang's advances but that she may have chosen to stand outside the kiosk of her own volition with the intention of attracting a suitor on a Saturday evening. During their conversation a caterpillar falls onto the coffee tray and we observe Wolfgang dripping water on the young insect. Briefly, the camera's focus on the couple's flirtation is replaced by a close-up of the caterpillar on the metal tray (Fig. 2.10). Stylistically, the sudden focus on the insect amidst the quasi-still life of everyday objects – the tray, water glasses and cups on the table – is in line with the visual art of New Objectivity. The striking sharpness and precision of the image signals the camera's equal interest in the larva and the characters – they

Fig. 2.9

Fig. 2.10

Fig. 2.11

are all placed under the scrutiny of the photographic lens for the audience to study, like organisms under a microscope.

Additionally, by placing the courting ritual (Fig. 2.11) and the inspection of the insect side by side, the film introduces a motif of juxtaposing romance with objects that may produce a physical response of distaste (such as the caterpillar) and which is repeated later on in the film where lovemaking takes place near discarded rubbish. The tone of both scenes is distinctly unsentimental; instead, the film's interest in the flirting couple only lasts as long as the couple's interest in the caterpillar.

Comparing the opening of *Menschen am Sonntag* to Irmgard Keun's novel *Das kunstseidene Mädchen/The Artificial Silk Girl* (1932), Richard W. McCormick notes that in both film and novel similar social processes take place: a young woman allows a man to speak to her on the street and then goes out with him. In both cases, the encounter turns out to be unsatisfactory for the woman. McCormick argues that both texts cite 'a common behaviour that alludes to other broader social and cultural discourses in late Weimar Germany about the supposedly emancipated sexual morals of young people, especially young single women of the white-collar work force' (2001: 10).

However, in contrast to the novel, which is told in a first-person narration, *Menschen am Sonntag* consistently emphasises its observational, non-subjective stance and the film's unwillingness to prioritise the characters over their surroundings (great or small) complicates conventional methods of alignment. Instead of being invited to focus on the characters' subjectivity we are asked to place them in relation to their environment, from station forecourts to street cafés. These decisions thus firmly position the spectator at a distance to the characters, stressing the representative, or 'cross-section', nature of what is shown and the role of the spectator-as-observer. Soon after recording Christl's encounter with Wolfgang, the camera returns to capturing non-fiction images of road sweepers cleaning the city streets in preparation for Sunday.

Images and role play

The final Saturday section takes place at the flat Erwin shares with Annie in one of Berlin's working- class district tenement blocks. It depicts the couple's volatile relationship and less than harmonious home life, qualifying more traditional notions of the home as a safe haven from the dangers of the street. In the scene, Erwin returns home from work and before long he and Annie start arguing. As a result, instead of going to the movies, the couple stays in, where they are joined by Wolfgang. The men start playing cards and Annie retreats to bed.

As in the opening, the sequence opens with a close-up, this time of several postcard-sized pictures of actors Willy Fritsch and Greta Garbo attached to the wall of the flat (Fig.

2.12). During their spat, Erwin intentionally splat-
ters shaving foam onto the photo of Willy Fritsch,
and Annie 'retaliates' by burning a picture of Greta
Garbo. The narrative's foregrounding of the photos
raises questions about the relationship between the
pictures of the movie stars and the couple. They
ironically illustrate the discrepancy between the actual and the fictional; the couple's home life differs
greatly from the star vehicles and romantic com-
edies featuring the actors. The selective destruction
of the images suggests a considerable degree of
sexual investment in the stars, which leads to Erwin and Annie acting on a jealous impulse. Dissatisfied with each other, it seems that Erwin and Annie project dreams and
desires onto their favourite movie stars, whose pictures (plastered over the walls of their
flat) they tear down and rip up at the climax of their quarrel.

Fig. 2.12

However, the focus on the images also draws attention to the film's own devices and
its objective of portraying the lives of five young people *through* the camera. The contrast
between the non-professional status of Erwin, Annie and the others and the star status
of Fritsch and Garbo only adds to the narration's self-conscious practice: it firmly propagates its objective of offering a snapshot of everyday 'people', not stars. Significantly, the
film's modernist practice of making its own devices clear draws attention to the social
function of cinema in Weimar Germany's visual culture.

Sabine Hake draws attention to the 'tremendous impact cinema had in constructing
the uniform, seemingly classless subject of consumer society' (1987: 152), which Erwin,
Annie and the others exemplify. The narration thus hints at its own status in constructing
the kinds of images that influence the perception and social roles the young people in
turn strive to adopt. Whereas on a narrative level the film claims merely to show what
already exists outside the studio, specific choices of what to show foreground the medium's social function, which far exceeds its own claim of being merely the facilitator of a
purely observational experience of reality, or, in this case, of a cross-section of society.

Sunday

In the second part of the film, the Sunday section, the narration shifts from presenting
the five as a cross-section sample and begins to engage with the implications of new
objective ways of seeing and with the New Objectivity lifestyle.

The Sunday section forms the main body of the film, focusing on the activities of
Berlin's citizens on their day off. As in the opening sequences, there is an alternation
between narrative strands involving the five young protagonists and extensive non-
fiction material depicting different parts of the city and its outskirts on a Sunday in
the summer of 1929. The non-fiction sequences omit more traditional Sunday pursuits
such as Sunday service or lunch with the family; instead, families are depicted in parks,

Fig. 2.13

Fig. 2.14

lidos and the city's Strandbäder, the public beaches along the shores of Berlin's lakes.

An extended montage sequence depicts a range of activities, including a hockey match (Fig. 2.13), families playing and sunbathing in a park and a crowded lido (Fig. 2.14). Other shots capture those remaining in the city enjoying the sun on balconies and benches placed along the city's tree-lined boulevards. Hausvogteiplatz, a usually busy square in the heart of the city centre, lies deserted as people rest in the afternoon sun. The flow of documentary images is ruptured by a shot of Annie in the flat, and the narrative then briefly turns to the other protagonists, depicting Brigitte and Christl snoozing in Wolfgang's arms by the lake, before reverting to views of shop windows advertising manicures and near deserted city streets and squares. By foregrounding various leisure activities and emphasising their mass appeal, the film portrays the modern, democratic lifestyle propagated by New Objectivity values. Jost Hermand argues:

> From the beginning of the 1920s on, proponents of *Neue Sachlichkeit* believed that the most important of these new leisure-time opportunities were those offered by the rapidly expanding entertainment industry: sport such as soccer, boxing, cycling and auto rallies, new technological accomplishments such as automobiles, radio, film and records; advertisements, shop windows and household implements; the feeling of being constantly up-to-date and informed by newspapers and illustrated magazines; and the largely free satisfaction of sexual needs in the homosexual and lesbian scene, or in open and uncommitted heterosexual relationships. (1994:61)

Hybrid forms

The blending of factual cross-section with methods of the avant-garde – such as the episodic, non-linear structure of the montage sections – is similar in style to the 'city symphony' mode produced across Europe in the mid- to late 1920s. Discussing the film which epitomises this sub genre, Walter Ruttmann's *Berlin – Die Sinfonie der Großstadt/ Symphony of a Big City* (1927), Sabine Hake notes

> The principles of cross-section facilitate the displacement of social experience into spectatorial relations, thereby accomplishing the mixture of visual stimulation and critical detachment that is so typical of *Neue Sachlichkeit* and its conceptualisation of mass culture

... Cross-section, it seems, involves an investigation of forms and structures, of appearances and essences. Yet both interests are articulated without regard for the object under investigation. (1994: 127–8)

Although the extended montage sequence of parks, lidos and deserted city streets sweltering in the heat adheres in many ways to the cross-section ideal, the insert shot of Annie in the flat breaks the convention by developing a different kind of relationship to the character: more subjective than the disregarded 'object under investigation', as I shall argue below.

'Fleeting Days'

The shot begins with a close-up of a newspaper, displaying on its open page a serialised novel by Carl Bulcke entitled *Und so verbringst du deine kurzen Tage*, then pans left to reveal Annie still asleep in bed (Fig. 2.15). Her passivity stands in sharp contrast to the sports and leisure activities depicted up to this point and the title of the novel, *And This is How You Spend Your Fleeting Days*, implies a gentle admonishment of Annie for not making the most of a warm and sunny Sunday afternoon. This shift has implications for the position of the spectator in relation to the world of the film: framing decisions concerning Annie no longer keep us at an 'arm's length' from action and character, but bring us – both perceptively and cognitively – closer to the object of study.

Fig. 2.15

Of all the 'people on Sunday', Annie's behaviour is the most distinct in its opposition to the uniform activities of her peers, which raises our interest in the character and her motivation (or, more precisely, lack of it). However, as the camera returns to the four other characters at the lake snoozing in the sun, it soon becomes apparent that the ways in which they spend their fleeting days may be equally at odds with certain expectations propagated by New Objectivity's lifestyle.

Christl

The shot of Wolfgang holding both Christl and Brigitte in his arms is tightly controlled. It pans from Erwin snoring on his back to Christl lying in Wolfgang's arms and stroking his hand. Despite their physical proximity, Christl's and Wolfgang's bodies never share a frame. The pan continues left to reveal Wolfgang playing with Brigitte's hair. The camera pauses as Wolfgang looks from one girl to the other, only to start playing with the torn shoulder strap of Brigitte's swimsuit. The camera reframes to include Brigitte with Wolfgang. After several attempts to gain her attention, Brigitte eventually responds to

Fig. 2.16

Wolfgang's advances by turning her face to him in a smile (Fig. 2.16). Then follows a cut to a close-up of Christl with eyes closed and resting her head in Wolfgang's hand (Fig. 2.17).

The mobile framing in the first shot firmly guides the spectator's attention to reveal, step-by-step, Christl's unrequited fondness for Wolfgang, the man's spurned, then successful, advances to Brigitte and her hesitant complicity in the flirtation, then the return to Christl on her own. The composition of this triangle of fickle emotions and erotic pangs has an awkward relationship to the modern liberated lifestyle associated with New Objectivity. As Hermand comments:

> In all these activities, participants were supposed to develop an attitude toward life based no longer on values like love of other human beings, time-consuming higher education, the capacity for intellectual criticism, high culture, and comradely solidarity – values increasingly seen as obsolete and therefore threatening the achievement of a completely free and open lifestyle – but rather on selfishness, entertainment, change, mobility, the avoidance of frustration, and the release of sexual and psychic pressure … Even in the realm of love, the future lay not in spiritual union but in a sober eroticism carried out with sportsmanlike fairness. (1994: 61)

Whereas the pan can be read as the visual expression of these forms of social interaction, the close-up of Christl conveys a different meaning. Conceptually, it differs from the sharpness of the preceding images: our view is slightly obscured by grass blades casting partial shadows across Christl's arm and face. In contrast to the depiction of Brigitte and Wolfgang in the harsh glare of the afternoon sun, the use of shade in the close-up of Christl gives the image a sense of depth and emotional resonance.

Fig. 2.17

The image is both observational and expressive, revealing Christl's longing for tenderness as she moves Wolfgang's open palm closer to her face. Yet as she nestles her head more resolutely in his hand, she lies with her back to Wolfgang, who is fondling Brigitte's breasts with his other hand. The thin lines of shade on Christl's arms express the ephemeral quality of the moment, as she is holding on to Wolfgang before he will pull his hand away and reject her for Brigitte. Through all this, Christl's eyes are closed, shutting out her surroundings and – consciously or subconsciously – the activities behind her back.

Our view is privileged over Christl's in relation to Wolfgang's actions, which elicits our sympathy for the young woman, whose longing is so cruelly at odds with the actual situation. The image thus invites a kind of empathetic contemplation that differs from the more sober ways of seeing the film has – with the exception of the insert shot of Annie – encouraged us to adopt so far. The respective shots of Annie cooped up inside (when everyone else is not), and of Christl 'dreaming' of an intimacy with Wolfgang reserved for Brigitte, elicit curiosity and sympathy for their behaviours, with Annie oblivious and Christl vulnerable to their surroundings.

Nonetheless, this moment of expressiveness is only brief and the film reverts to non-fiction sections, once again depicting public spaces in the city and various leisure activities enjoyed by sunbathers on the sandy shores of Nikolaussee. When the narrative returns to the protagonists we observe them meandering through the woods surrounding the lake. A chase ensues, which separates Brigitte and Wolfgang from the others and they end up making love in a clearing.

Brigitte

During the couple's lovemaking the camera performs an extended pan, which traverses the surrounding ground and skyline of treetops. As mentioned earlier, it is at this point that the camera takes in the sight of discarded rubbish in the clearing. The camera breaks away from the story of the romance to consider other aspects of human activity, and to provide another kind of view. The decision to include the rubbish tip alters the tone of the scene, suggesting that the setting is not as idyllic as it appears to be, and inviting us to view the budding romance in a different context to that which a simple evocation of nature would have provided.

When the camera returns to the couple Brigitte is still on the ground, her head turned away from Wolfgang and the camera. A close-up reveals that Brigitte's eyes are closed and the branches of overhanging pine trees cast a subtle layer of light and shade on her face. The bowtie fastening her dress around the neck has been ruffled, leaving us in no doubt about what happened to Brigitte while the camera 'looked away'.

Akin to the shot of Christl earlier (Fig. 2.17) the subtle pattern of light and shade of overhanging branches is reflected on Brigitte's face (Fig. 2.18). Lying motionless, with eyes still closed, Brigitte, like Christl previously, wishes to prolong the moment. The tone is impressionistic, a composition of Brigitte's youth and vulnerability as well as a reflection on her introvert nature, preferring to linger in a state of contemplation instead of getting ready to leave; in contrast, Wolfgang can be seen fastening his tie (Fig. 2.19).

The camera rests on Brigitte's face and after a short while she opens her eyes. As she rises, Brigitte becomes aware of a pinecone digging into her torso. As the couple inspect the cone in Brigitte's hand, the movement from two-shot to a close-up of the cone mirrors the earlier shot of Wolfgang and Christl studying the caterpillar in the café (Figs 2.20–2. 21). Whereas for Brigitte the cone becomes a unique token of their lovemaking, it becomes apparent that Wolfgang seems less inclined to marvel at the beauty of nature.

Fig. 2.18

Fig. 2.19

Fig. 2.20

Fig. 2.21

Moreover, the repeated use of the composition suggests that for Wolfgang locations, objects and girls are exchangeable, moments of intimacy replicable.

The strong sense of Brigitte and Wolfgang's opposed perceptions of the significance of their sexual encounter is strengthened in the scenes immediately following. Brigitte returns to the group to find that one of her records has been broken and others left carelessly scattered on the grass; as she picks up the pieces, the sense of a greater loss than that of a prized commodity becomes palpable.

Reunited, the group returns to the lake shore to hire a paddling boat. As they cross the lake, the camera once more rests on Brigitte's face. As in the previous shot of Brigitte lying under the pine trees, the use of light and shade adds expressiveness to the image as the pattern of the boat safety net is visible across her face (Fig. 2.22). We are invited to observe the young woman as she tenses and stretches her body across the edge of the boat, fervently enjoying the sensation of the water and the physical experience of her sexuality that afternoon. Yet despite this demonstration of Brigitte's vitality, the pattern of the net acts as a reminder that Brigitte is unwittingly caught in a tacit agreement stipulating that the lovemaking will mean nothing more than a brief sexual encounter without any promise of an emotional commitment. The latter becomes obvious when Erwin and Wolfgang eagerly exchange contact details with two different young women in another vessel (Fig. 2.23).

'Such a thing as desire ' – a Berlin *Reigen*[15]

This impressionistic representation of Christl and Brigitte differs perceptibly from the cross-section mode employed in previous sequences. This gradual shift from encouraging initially detached to subsequently more empathetic ways of seeing continues for the remainder of the film, and includes moments of social commentary: on their return to the city, Brigitte arranges to meet up with Wolfgang the following Sunday. After Brigitte has left, the camera stays with the men and we witness them planning to go to a football match instead. In the end, it becomes clear that it is Brigitte who will be stood up the following weekend, taking over the role Christl occupied the week before.

The narrative structure thus alters from sober cross-section mode to a quasi-Berlin *Reigen* scenario, with Billy Wilder's script echoing the circular movement and theme of Arthur Schnitzler's rondo of unfulfilled desire. Although shots of Wolfgang and Brigitte back at work book-end the narrative, the last image before the final intertitles depicts the traffic island outside Bahnhof Zoo and more precisely the newsagent stall where Christl first stood awaiting a rendezvous that never materialised. Our last sight of Brigitte is once again outside the Electrola record shop, inviting us to wonder at what point the 'little shop girl' will realise that longing to spend Sunday afternoons sailing with sweethearts is a sentiment which may be in tension with the ways relationships are conducted in the modern city and which might be best confined to the kinds of records she sells.

Fig. 2.22

Fig. 2.23

Conclusion: 'Horror vacui'

Back in the city Erwin returns to the flat to find that Annie has slept through most of the day. Whereas the young man despairs at such seemingly decadent behaviour, a waste of youth's 'fleeting days', the audience has gained greater understanding of Annie's refusal to take part in modern weekend leisure activities and courting rituals. However, Annie's rejection of the limited options for expression available to a young woman of her social group confines her to the status of a sleeping beauty, unlikely ever to be woken by a kiss. Christl, in turn, will continue to chase after roles as a film extra during the week only to be similarly auditioned, cast and sidelined on Sundays. Similarly, it seems that Brigitte is unlikely to do anything too drastic in response to being stood up by Wolfgang. Rapture, passion and despair fit uncomfortably with the sober rationale – and rationalisation – governing all areas of modern city life.

The film thus begins to establish a link between New Objectivity's 'largely emotionless' ways of seeing and soulless human relationships rooted in the capitalist logic of means and interest. Though perhaps not as radical a critique of the petit bourgeoisie as a Franz Kafka novel, *Menschen am Sonntag* exposes the cross-section ideal of turning people into objects of inquiry as alienating and, essentially, inhumane. Significantly, the sober tone of early sequences and the use of techniques such as montage and freeze-frame, hint at the film's awareness of its own role in constructing mechanical ways of seeing. Close-ups of stylised photos of movie stars and the humorous juxtaposition of picture postcards with actual footage of sunbathers strengthens the inextricable link between seeing and perceiving – but also understanding and interpreting – the world through images.

The film's non-judgemental stance on the social processes it presents was heavily criticised by the left-wing press at the time of its release, who accused it of lacking the 'revolutionary ideology of the Russian films' and displaying 'petit bourgeois tendencies':

> Should Film-Studio 1929 remain attached to this petit bourgeois 'neutrality' and disregard the social reality of the revolutionary working class, this studio, destined for something better, will without fail end in a cul-de-sac, stranded in the inertia of bourgeois art. (Review in *Die Rote Fahne*, reprinted in NGBK 1977: 181)

Menschen am Sonntag certainly does not offer a political critique of New Objectivity comparable to other cultural outputs, such as Brecht's parable *A Man's a Man*, in which the kindly packer Galy Gay is transformed, like a car, into the callous and cold-hearted fighting machine Jeraiah Jip. Whereas *A Man's a Man* relied on the use of props and masks to distance the audience from the action on stage, *Menschen am Sonntag* sets the spectator a different exercise in complex seeing. It invites the audience to refrain from adopting 'mechanical' ways of seeing, and to engage with action and characters compassionately, exceeding the purely observational experience of watching 'people on Sunday'. However, this is not to suggest that the film encourages sentiment, or a nostalgic romanticism for traditional social mores and morals; on the contrary, the everyday life of the city and its modernity are at the centre of the narrative.

The film's subtle critique of the social implications of alienated and alienating paradigms and the increased rationalisation of public as well as personal aspects of city life corresponds to Siegfried Kracauer's notion of the 'horror vacui' (1995: 132) of modern city life, the 'emptying out of people's spiritual/intellectual space' (1995: 129). Drawing attention to the emotional void in the lives of its characters, *Menschen am Sonntag* challenges the audience to engage with the everyday with reason *and* compassion. At a time when the left idealistically urged people to adopt ways of seeing rooted in reason and the scientific study of social relations, and the right sought to fill the 'horror vacui' with reactionary nostalgic rhetoric, finding a middle ground became increasingly difficult and opting for 'objective' perspectives progressively confined the onlooker to a state of inertia. For Film-Studio 1929's 'group of unknowns', the journey eventually led not into political concession and an artistic cul-de-sac, but into exile.

3. Pre-Fascist Period: To Think and To Want: *Kuhle Wampe*

They weren't just paid workers, who did the work for the employers – those still exist today – but amongst these people there was a shared perception of their collective materialist conditions, and a desire to radically change those conditions. (Decker & Hecker 2002: 1)

Introduction: Breaking with traditions ... realist and real

On 4 May 1932, the German Communist Party paper, *Die Rote Fahne*, printed an invitation by Fichte, the umbrella organisation of Berlin's workers' athletics clubs, which read:

Fichte's rambler section is breaking with the traditional men's outing on Ascension Day! Because Fichte's rambler section, the only revolutionary organisation of all working class ramblers, week-enders and excursionists, is organising a mass meeting at Kuhle Wampe under the motto 'Red Weekend in Kuhle Wampe'. No class conscious young worker, no class conscious proletarian, no employee should go on a traditional men's outing but should instead, on Thursday, 5th May, join the Fichte rambler's section for an outing to Kuhle Wampe. (In Gersch & Hecht 1973: 191)[16]

The last third of the film *Kuhle Wampe* depicts just such a mass sports day organised by Berlin's communist athletic clubs, which brings together the city's young proletariat for a day of comradely sparring and political agitation. Due to financial difficulties at the time of production, the filmmakers even had to rely on the voluntary co-operation of 3000 Fichte sports club members when shooting the film's (fictional) sports day section. That events depicted in the film should so closely mirror the leisure pursuits of Berlin's class-conscious workers is hardly surprising considering the political stance of the production company and the collective of artists responsible for its creation.

Prometheus Film, the film's production company until its bankruptcy in January 1932, was founded by Willi Münzenberg, a publisher, whose pamphlet 'Let Us Conquer Film!' (1925) propagated a strong proletarian film culture in Germany to mount a left-wing opposition to the reactionary tendencies of several of the republic's powerful media conglomerates. Münzenberg's initiative brought together like-minded distribution and production companies in order to counteract the increased censorship of so-called 'Russenfilme' (Soviet montage films) and to meet the requirements of the 1925 'contingency' law, which stipulated that for every film imported into the country, a German film had to be exported to the country of the import's origin. Prometheus Film initially specialised in the production of these 'contingency films', mostly political documentaries intended for Soviet audiences in exchange for Russian imports, but produced its first fiction film, *Mutter Krausens Fahrt ins Glück/Mother Krause's Journey to Happiness* (directed by Piel

Jutzi) in 1929, followed by its first and only sound film production, *Kuhle Wampe*, two years later.[17]

The artistic collaboration between Slatan Dudow, Bertolt Brecht, Hanns Eisler and Ernst Ottwald equally ensured that *Kuhle Wampe* was firmly rooted in the revolutionary programme of communist cultural activity. Similar in theme to previous Prometheus productions, the film focuses on the representation of Berlin's proletariat in the face of growing unemployment and increased poverty in the city's working-class districts. Despite the convergence in content – both *Mother Krause* and *Kuhle Wampe* depict unemployment affecting two working-class families, leading to despair and suicide, as well as increased political activism amongst individual family members – they differ greatly in style. Whereas the form of realism employed in *Mother Krause* owes more to the overtly dramatic conventions of Weimar cinema's 'street film' genre than communist agitational propaganda ('agitprop') methods, *Kuhle Wampe* is for the most part constructed around Brecht's emerging criticism of conventional realist aesthetics and his search for new realist models.

Rooted in theatrical practice, Brecht's concept of political realism developed during the 1930s and led to various definitions:

> *Realist* means: laying bare society's causal network/showing up the dominant viewpoint as the viewpoint of the dominators/writing from the standpoint of the class which has prepared the broadest solutions for the most pressing problems afflicting human society/emphasising the dynamics of development/concrete and so as to encourage abstraction. (1992d: 109)

Brecht's concern with the social function of art needs to be placed in the context of the political situation at the time of the film's production. Against the background of an economic crisis and the political instability brought on by a democratically elected parliament unable to govern, the film's revolutionary intention was instantly recognised by the censor. This led to two complete bans and several cuts before the film's eventual release barely a year before the German National Socialist Workers' Party finally gained the majority in the republic's parliament and all communist political activity was henceforth banned.

Retrospective readings of *Kuhle Wampe* generally prioritise the film's social and political meaning, not least because its powerful appeal to solidarity resonates with the contemporary historical perspective that whereas reactionary wings joined forces, the left ultimately failed to unite. Brecht's own writing on the film and the communist spirit of the Kuhle Wampe collective also support explicitly political interpretations. Discussions, therefore, tend to locate the relationship between film and audience in the framework of Brecht's political theatre, particularly the epic model, which defined the spectator as an active observer of the events happening on stage. As a result, readings of *Kuhle Wampe* frequently discuss moments where the filmic style is at its most innovatively 'Brechtian', engaging its audience in progressive political dialogue by means of distanciation.

The following reading will refer to established analyses of certain 'key' scenes in order to proceed to moments in the narrative which have, on the whole, been afforded less critical attention. Examination of these less 'telling', at times even puzzling, moments will suggest that they could be regarded as instances where the film momentarily suspends its didactic role in order to reflect self-consciously on the impact of its chosen style.[18] Detailed study of certain decisions will illustrate the ways in which the film simultaneously creates and scrutinises the tightly controlled relationship between film and audience. The chapter further explores the tension between the film's didactic function as an explicitly political address to a proletarian audience and certain decisions made concerning the actual representation of the working class in the world of the film. Comments made by reviewers at the time of the film's release, especially left-wing writers, about its noticeably negative representation of some sections of the proletariat, suggest that *Kuhle Wampe*'s engagement with the class it sought to address was possibly more complex than standard political readings would suggest. Discussion will focus on the ways in which the film seeks both to address a class and critically reflect on the extent to which art could affect ways of seeing and create political consciousness, especially when, as will be demonstrated, the characters in the world of the film repeatedly fail to ask questions about their situation. Stylistic decisions taken by the filmmakers can be seen as linked to the film's awareness that ways of seeing the world are neither natural nor simply available to be learned but are intimately bound with ways of life and with inferences characters draw from and about their situations. The film's incorporation of varied forms of rhetoric in its address to the audience (including the conventionally realist as well as overt agitprop) suggests that its interest is not simply in making promises about a revolution but in stimulating this cognitive process: to think and to want.

Opening: 'One unemployed less'

Following the first chapter heading, 'One unemployed less', the opening shots of *Kuhle Wampe* depict a series of buildings: the Brandenburg Gate, instantly establishing Berlin as the film's location, factories and industrial areas in and around the city, as well as the façades and courtyards of tenement blocks in Berlin's working-class districts. Another series of shots comprises a montage of newspaper headlines charting the relentless rise in mass unemployment in the country; the final headline informs us that there are now over five million unemployed in Germany with 315,000 unemployed in Berlin, of which 100,000 do not receive benefits.

The first images we see are authentic, documentary shots of the city. The collage of statistics and newspaper headlines is presented in the detailed factual mode of the New Objectivity style. James Pettifer criticises the scene's mimetic style and collage method for producing an effect he describes as 'basically synthetic rather than analytic' (1974: 57). He proceeds: 'The conventional response – banal – would be horror at the mechanisms of capitalism – basically a liberal response that is exploited every week by the popular Sunday press' (ibid.). Pettifer further notes that there 'is no real *gest*

[sic] or social attitude found here, by any criteria drawn from Brecht's writing' (ibid.). Pettifer attributes the absence of 'gest' (now generally referred to as 'gestus', an epic theatre method, which emphasises the social and economic processes between people by means of parody, distanciation or demonstrational acting) to the collaborative working method of the group, whereby Dudow, Brecht, Eisler and Oswald each were able to contribute to individual sections, with Oswald responsible for the opening.

For the purpose of this analysis, it is important to note that Pettifer's critique of the opening suggests that there are various, at times quasi-cognitively opposed, styles in play from the very beginning of the film. A closer look at this section reveals that not only does the style differ from subsequent scenes, but that individual elements within the scene are juxtaposed in conscious opposition.

Polyphonic styles and meanings

The stylistic 'clash' becomes apparent when taking into account the music accompanying the opening images. The fast staccato rhythm of Eisler's polyphonic prelude is set against sober images devoid of any such vitality. Eisler himself comments on the function of the music:

> The contrast of the music – in terms of form and tone – in relation to the mere montage of images achieves a kind of shock, with the intention of evoking resistance rather than empathetic sentimentality. (In Adank 1976: 35)

Eisler's suggestion that the intention is to 'shock' the audience, in order to stir opposition to the images of a Berlin 'slum district in all its despair and dirt' (ibid.) seems overstated, since the opening images of the city contain no visible evidence of 'despair and dirt'. But the lively tone of the composition clearly clashes with the drab images of industrial areas and tenement blocks and thus brings into question the relationship between images and sound. The images are bland and contain little additional narrative detail beyond establishing a location – Berlin's proletarian north. Where the opening sequence of *Mother Krause*, set in the same Wedding district, incorporates actual footage of people living in impoverished conditions in overcrowded tenement blocks, *Kuhle Wampe* denies the audience access to such images of want and neglect. In contrast to the music, which instantly seeks to address the audience, rousing the listener into critical opposition, the images refrain from drawing the audience into the social milieu in which the action will be played out.

This discrepancy between images and sound draws attention to the status of the image: whereas Eisler's music fits in with the wider programme of producing films for and about the working class, the images convey no such impetus and could, on the contrary, be grouped with the apolitical optical experience propagated by New Objectivity. This 'lack' of agitational enthusiasm in the opening minute suggests that the film's relationship to its imagery is complex. Indeed, what seems at stake is the image itself, in particular its status as representative of the socio-economic reality outside the studio. In essays and notes written between 1930–32 (as a response to a failed lawsuit against Nero-Film productions) Brecht discusses the verisimilitude of the photographic image in a short paragraph entitled 'No insight through photography':

> You don't have to doubt whether the cinema is up-to-date! Photography is the possibility of a reproduction that masks the context ... from the (carefully taken) photograph of a Ford factory no opinion about this factory can be deduced. (2000a: 144)

I want to argue that this issue of the spectator's process of cognitive 'deduction' informs wider questions of *how* to construct the film's (fictional) reality in opposition to forms of realism that strive towards authenticity and verisimilitude. Visually, the film opens with a representational approach, which is then gradually juxtaposed with methods of rupture and distanciation in subsequent sequences. The opening can thus be regarded as the first instance of the film's interest in how stylistic decisions position the audience in relation to the narrative in more or less habitual ways by juxtaposing conventional documentary-style footage with the avant-garde sound of Eisler's composition. The following sections continue to examine the cognitive positioning of the audience in relation to the narrative by focusing on the ways of seeing displayed by the characters in the world of the film.

Epic methods and meanings: the 'job hunt' sequence and young Bönike's return home

The abrupt ending of the overture music over the last headline, '315,000 unemployed in Berlin', concludes the prologue section. In contrast to the previous headlines, the following shot of the vacancy page in a local Berlin paper is without sound, signalling a temporary 'halt' – musically and cognitively – prior to the next section, in which another sharp and driven orchestral piece accompanies shots of a large group of unemployed workers 'chasing' after the few available vacancies advertised in the paper.

The fast pace of the music initially stands in contrast to the images, which depict workers gradually gathering in a street waiting to pick up a copy of the local advertiser. Amongst the crowd, though not foregrounded, is the son of the Bönike family. At this stage, the pace of the editing is slow and the mode observational. The editing pace gradually increases as the workers ride their bikes across the city in search of work and repeated shots of the front wheels and of legs pushing pedals foreground the 'race' that now develops between the men (Figs 3.1–3.2). Although Bönike is the first to arrive at one building, the receptionist rebuffs

Fig. 3.1

Fig. 3.2

Fig. 3.3

Fig. 3.4

him. When two more cyclists follow in close succession the receptionist places a sign in the window. A close-up depicts the sign, which reads, 'Workers not needed'. The scene continues in this mode, alternating abruptly between shots of the legs and the upper bodies of the cyclists racing along the streets (Figs 3.3–3.4).

The rhythmic montage pattern is broken by a longer take of another factory building. As the cyclists pass the entrance, the camera tilts up and down the height of the building, catching the men as they reappear, already back on their bikes. Another brief montage section focusing on the wheels racing along the asphalt and a final unsuccessful bid for work at a glazing company concludes the section (Figs 3.5–3.6). The music rises to a crescendo and then stops abruptly.

In this sequence, the familiar process of looking for work is made unfamiliar by the use of camerawork, montage-style editing and sound. Several writers stress the desperation and competitive character conveyed by the combination of the disharmonious music, accelerated editing pace and the repetition of images (see Happel 1978; Silberman 1995). Frequently, these techniques are linked to Brechtian theatre methods: Yvonne Leonard notes that the scene contains three layers of epic distanciation, 'musically, through montage and structurally' (1977: 59) and Pettifer identifies the act of 'riding bicycles' as the scene's 'gest' (1974: 57), though he stops short of defining *Kuhle Wampe* as an epic film. Mark Silberman argues:

In contrast to the Epic Theatre, gestus in *Kuhle Wampe* shifts from the actor of the performance to the camera and editing, in particular to their functions of interrupting and citing reality. Breaking the illusion of total visibility, montage becomes a means of deconstructing everyday actions and expressions into their social determinants and inscribing in them the conditions of their construction ... For Brecht reality is not what the spectator sees but what the spectator re-cognises [sic], that which is behind the visible. The 'epic cinema', then, results precisely from the control of vision and seeing produced by the montage. (1995: 43)

This use of cinematic means of deconstruction, drawing attention to the economic conditions which, for Brecht, essentially determine human behaviour, thus mirrors the function of distanciation and gestus in the epic theatre. The repetition of images firmly guides the spectator to perceive and become more critically aware of the process of competition and growing desperation amongst the work force. Although the audience would of course have been familiar with the situation, the aim of the distanciation is to bring to the fore the actual materialist position in which the proletariat finds itself in capitalism – their dependency on a weekly pay-cheque, the constant threat of poverty and homelessness when their labour is not needed, and the unresponsiveness of capitalist institutions. The shot taking in the whole of the factory front in an upward and downward tilt of the camera seems to suggest that whereas the workers are competing and growing desperate, entering and exiting factory gates and forecourts, the foundations of private

Fig. 3.5

Fig. 3.6

property and paid work are rock-solid, impervious to the needs and in opposition to the interests of the people who do the work.

Epic methods in Brecht's theatrical practice are closely linked to instruction and knowledge – processes which in turn are rooted in observation: '[Epic theatre's] aim was less to moralise than to observe. That is to say it observed, and then the thick end of the wedge followed: the story's moral' (1992c: 75). Yet despite the scene's use of epic methods and its strong didactic tone, there is no 'moral' at the end of the unsuccessful job hunt, no explanation as to the causes that foster competition, not solidarity, amongst the workers. The call for solidarity remains suspended until the final section of the film; meanwhile, the narrative focus shifts from the wider socio-economic complex to the particular situation of one family.

From addressing the audience as a class, the film now proceeds to examine the class it seeks to address, starting with the Bönike family. The sequence following the job hunt centres on the ways in which individual family members perceive their financial situation. Critical analysis will focus on the juxtaposition between the ways in which the social and economic situation has been presented to the audience in the cinema and views held and expressed by the Bönikes. The young man's return home links the job hunt episode to the subsequent section of the family dinner.

The scene begins in silence: after the prolonged and harried race around the city, a group of cyclists now pushing their bikes comes to a halt outside the entrance of a tenement block. As the young man (uncredited) parts from the group and heads for

Fig. 3.7

Fig. 3.8

Fig. 3.9

the entrance, a piece of music becomes audible. In contrast to the disjointed previous piece, this music is melodic and jolly in tone. A cut takes us inside the courtyard, displaying the façade of a wing facing the inner courtyard. The shot is taken from a low angle, pointing up the façade displaying rows of windows facing the courtyard (Fig. 3.7). The music gradually swells and the following shot reveals two street musicians sitting in the courtyard as the diegetic source of the sound, with one man playing the saw, the other a harmonium. The saw's swinging metal blade produces an unusual high pitch vibrating sound. The piece, 'In Rixdorf ist Musike' ('Music in Rixdorf'), is a polka rooted in the folk music tradition. The musicians sit with their backs to the camera. Young Bönike enters the frame right and pauses to listen to the music (Fig. 3.8). After a while, he moves on.

The shot continues for a few seconds after his exit and then there follows a cut to the family's living room. The music can still be heard from the courtyard below, repeating the lively chorus of the tune. Bönike's father (Max Sablotzki) reads the paper, while the mother (Lili Schoenborn) is laying the table for the family meal.

Father: The boy won't get any more dole from now on.

When his wife fails to respond, he continues:

Father: You don't care any more, do you?

A cut to the entrance hall of the flat shows the bike suspended from the ceiling with the young man fastening the rope holding the bike in place to the doorframe (Fig. 3.9). The camera is positioned behind the wheel and the action is filmed through the spokes of the front wheel. The polka piece comes to an end.

The scene depicts the passage from street level to the private sphere of the Bönike household. The low-angle shot of the rows of windows facing the inner courtyard on one level confirms the typicality of the setting (tenement blocks built around small inner courtyards). The musicians are situated opposite the dilapidated façade of a basement flat, emphasising the very basic and utilitarian conditions of proletarian living quarters. The run-down courtyard environment stands in contrast to the tempo and vivacious melody of the polka music, which evokes associations of the merriment of communal dance in the more traditional setting of a Bohemian village fair. The presence of street musicians 'busking' in the inner courtyard is not too dissimilar from a scene following the documentary-style opening section of *Mother Krause*, in which the tenants of Mother Krause's flat merrily dance along to the 'sound' of an organ-grinder (implied by cross-cutting between the musician and the characters in the flat) in the courtyard of their tenement block. However, whereas the organ grinder in Piel Jutzi's film is woven into the narrative to add to the proletarian 'milieu' of Berlin's 'Red' Wedding district, I want to argue that the musicians in *Kuhle Wampe* carry a more complex narrative function.

The music is the first instance of diegetic sound in the film. The unusual swinging and gliding sound of the saw, produced by running a bow across a metal blade, works against the familiar polka sound and its more traditional instrumentation of a clarinet or fiddle. In contrast to the characters in *Mother Krause*, young Bönike's response to the music is impassive; whilst clearly listening to it he shows no obvious response to the dynamics of the polka, such as a tap of the foot, or a nod of the head. His reaction could be read as an expression of his disillusionment with the unsuccessful job hunt, yet as the film cuts to the Bönike family's flat, it becomes apparent that Father and Mother Bönike also ignore the music, which can be heard from outside their window. I want to argue that the music creates a noticeable disjunction between sound and spoken word.

The first lines of dialogue ('The boy won't get any more dole from now on') sixty shots into the film is significant in several ways: firstly, it introduces the topic that will dominate the dinner conversation and which will, ultimately, lead to the son's decision to commit suicide. Secondly, it presents the film's overriding theme – the effects of a capitalist economy on its working class. Despite the gravity of the consequences of this piece of 'news' the actor articulates the line in a factual and bland manner. The jolly music underlining the dialogue opens a 'gap' between the joyful spirit evoked by the polka piece and the gravity of the situation, and creates a moment of cruel irony: the musicians may wish to earn a penny by playing a cheerful tune, but it clashes with the stark reality faced by thousands of men like Bönike. The initial low-angle shot of identical rows of windows indeed suggests that the Bönikes may not be the only ones in the tenements affected by the latest government decree.[19]

Significantly, the scene illustrates the first instance of the characters' reluctance to respond to what is happening around them: the son appears to be listening but remains unresponsive to the music and withdraws even further during the subsequent discussion at the dinner table; the father reads the latest news, but seems unaware of what is happening outside the window; the mother shows only indifference to the worsening situation. The final shot in this scene (also shot through the spokes of Bönike's bike) briefly but succinctly evokes a sense of the young man being 'trapped' by the economic situation the wheel of a bicycle (an object extensively utilised in the earlier montage sequence) represents. The choice of camera position thus provides a visual clue of the role economic conditions play in determining a character's behaviour; in the young man's case, the daily repetition of the unsuccessful job hunt has led to dejection and almost a sense of institutionalisation, represented by Bönike's unresponsiveness to the 'outside' world, and, in his parents' case, the world 'outside the window'.

Conversation over dinner

In this section the family gathers around the dining table for the main meal of the day, during which both parents accuse the son of not trying hard enough in his efforts to find work. The sister (Herta Thiele) defends her brother and an argument ensues between father and daughter. The son remains silent throughout. The conversation evolves around the concepts of 'Tüchtigkeit' (efficiency) and 'Höflichkeit' (good manners), which the parents regard as essential qualities in finding employment. In their view, the son is lacking in both and therefore to blame for being out of work.

Singled out by the camera, the mother recites a proverb, 'Initiative always brings its rewards', which the actor delivers in a stylised speech pattern which lacks expression, accent and intonation. The mother then turns to the son and continues speaking in a more conversational manner, with her noticeable Berlin accent now breaking through again. Her comments are followed by a cut to a previous shot of the unemployed workers riding their bikes. This method of inserting an unrelated image is repeated when the daughter's exclamation, 'There is no work', is juxtaposed with a previous shot of the workers pushing their pedals. The father's comments are noticeably generalised, sug-

Fig. 3.10

gesting that '*one* can be poor, *one* can be unlucky' rather than addressing the son directly. The section ends on a close-up of a tapestry hanging over the kitchen stove. Bordered by flowers, the inscription on the tapestry reads: 'Don't worry about tomorrow and its troubles/it is a joy to care for those we love' (Fig. 3.10).

Truisms and proverbs thus dominate the conversation, but specific choices by the filmmakers, namely the use of stylisation, the juxtaposition of word and image and the camera's focus on the embroidered tapestry, invite us to scrutinise the taken for granted meaning of what has been said. Bourgeois mannerisms and the parents' comments are presented as questionable beliefs in the present situation: the inserted shots of the unemployed looking for work challenge notions of 'efficiency' and 'good will'. Following the mother's recital of the proverb about the rewards of initiative, the insert shot of men on their bikes emphatically draws attention to the inherent contradictions in the parents' perception of the situation, demonstrating the discrepancy between what the parents think and believe to be true and the situation previously portrayed.

The earlier moment of the disjunction between the diegetic music and dialogue is followed by a clear contradiction between the parents' perception of the reasons for their son's unemployment and the economic causes presented in the earlier sequence.

In *Brecht on Theatre* John Willett notes that this emphasis on contradictions, 'the conflicting elements in any person or situation' (in Brecht 1992b: 51) gained importance in Brecht's writing in the early 1930s (parallel to his study of Marxism). The reassuring inscription on the tapestry ('Don't worry about tomorrow and its troubles/it is a joy to care for those we love') offers a first glimpse at the various contradictions to which the characters are exposed: the inference which can be drawn from the inscription is that the family (those we care for and love) is regarded as a safe haven from the competition and strife ('troubles') of the world outside. The ideological function of the inscription is to suggest that the private sphere is unaffected by the outside world. As the film progresses, the shortcoming of this flawed rationale is rendered visible as the family are forced out of their flat due to non-payment of rent.

Fig. 3.11

After depicting the tapestry, the film's attention returns to the son. Still seated at the table he turns his head and looks to the left – the opposite direction of the kitchen and the tapestry (Fig. 3.11). In addition to the lack of motivation in looking this way (rather than, for example, at the window, if the thought of jumping is already on his mind), the act of looking itself constitutes a conscious look at the camera, particularly in comparison with the young man's blank stare in previous scenes. He then averts his gaze and, after a brief moment, leaves the chair and walks over to the window.

The effect of the look on the spectator momentarily creates a sense of being 'looked at' by the character. I want to argue that this is less an instance of the character stepping out of role, and more one of direct address: of us being confronted by Bönike with his predicament. The rest of the family are busying themselves in different activities; we are the only ones witness to Bönike's moment of decision.

The son's suicide

This scene is carefully choreographed: after leaving his seat by the table, Bönike walks over to the window, opens the right pane and looks out. Initially at a slight distance, the camera now pointedly tracks in to show him taking off his watch and carefully placing it on a sideboard. We then observe Bönike as he moves a pot plant out of the way and climbs onto the windowsill. Then follows an insert shot of the mother ascending the stairwell and a close-up of Bönike's hand letting go of the window pane. This moment signals the jump, confirmed by the sound of a scream echoing from the courtyard. A brief montage section follows and contains these shots (Figs 3.12–3.15):

Shot 90: The windowsill with the flowerpot.
Shot 91: The wrist watch.
Shot 92: Previous shot of workers riding their bikes.

Fig. 3.12

Fig. 3.13

Fig. 3.14

Fig. 3.15

Shot 93: Bönike's bike suspended from the ceiling.

The narrative proceeds with a shot of Bönike's body, which is covered up with a sheet. The neighbours' reactions to the suicide and a brief conversation between the young man's father and another worker in a pub conclude part one of the film.

Alongside the job hunt sequence, the suicide scene is one of the most frequently analysed parts of the film and there appears to be little disagreement about the meaning it conveys; readings (see Happel & Michaelis 1978; Leonard 1977) most commonly suggest that the scene strongly implies that social conditions, rather than personal reasons, are the cause of the son's suicide. In his own analysis of the scene in 'A Small Contribution to the Theme of Realism' (written during the 1930s), Brecht argues that rather than merely portraying an individual tragedy, the son's suicide represents the desperate situation of a class driven to extremes by bleak economic conditions. Brecht notes that the 'acute censor', whose argument he records as follows, instantly picked up on this important political point:

You have not depicted a human being, but rather, let us admit it, a type. Your unemployed worker is not a real individual ... He is superficially portrayed, as artists pardon me this strong expression for the fact that [sic] *we learn too little about him*, but the consequences are of a *political* nature ... Your film has the tendency to present suicide as typical, as a matter not of this or that (morbidly inclined) individual, but as the fate of a whole class. (1974: 46; emphasis in original)

Brecht further stresses the censor's awareness of the scene's 'decidedly demonstrative character' and his likening of the lack of emotion conveyed by the actor's performance to a demonstration of 'how to peel cucumbers'. Brecht describes his encounter with the censor as 'a little lecture on realism. From the standpoint of the police' (ibid.), indicating that to link the worker's desperate act to the social situation of a whole class introduces a political argument which the state has to suppress. Ironically, Brecht's analysis amounts to a rather un-Brechtian 'preferred' reading of this scene.

Despite this authoritative analysis, some writers have questioned the methods employed to convey the scene's politically explicit meaning. For instance, James Pettifer argues that there is no clear evidence in the scene that the suicide has social causes:

> His [the son's] silence is anyway symbolic, and as such the social causes of his action become unrelated to the effect they created ... What is at issue is not the simple fact of watch ownership, as some bourgeois critics have suggested, but that it is a token surrounded with mystery when the main *gest* of the young Bönike is in relation to it, not to any social being. The weakness of the pure montage method in concentrating on the reproduction and juxtaposition of appearances of objects is clear here. (1974: 58)

Pettifer's observation raises questions surrounding the construction of meaning in this scene. Above all, it suggests that there is a greater degree of ambivalence than is generally acknowledged. Perhaps, indeed, the very use of montage, with its focus here on objects – flowerpot, watch and bike – brings with it the possibility of variant readings. Pettifer himself draws attention to 'the puzzlement of the first Soviet audiences of *Kuhle Wampe*, many of whom could not understand the suicide of a worker who owned a watch' (ibid.).

Yet it seems important to ask whether other answers are available to the questions raised by the filmmakers' decisions in this scene. In particular, the choices made take on fresh significance if, rather than being interpreted as confusing the supposed political point, they are understood as attempting something more nuanced – an engagement with various methods through which the spectator's habitual ways of making sense of what they see onscreen can be challenged.

Same reality, different ways of seeing: the suicide scene in *Mother Krause*

An approach can begin by returning to Brecht's interest at this time in realism and discourses surrounding realism. In his essay 'The *Threepenny* Lawsuit' (written 1931 and published in *Versuche* in 1932) Brecht examines the status of art and the culture industry under capitalism. Whilst discussing the lawsuit in detail and the role of the film industry in more general terms, the essay consistently returns to questions of the representation of reality. 'The *Threepenny* Lawsuit' begins with the observation that 'Everything said about culture from a more remote, general point of view that does not take account of practice can only be an idea and therefore must be tested in practice' (2000b: 148).

The question of *how* to represent the reality of the working class in Weimar cinema's first proletarian sound film was of course paramount in relation to the debates about the artistic and social function of Weimar's proletarian film culture. Though *Kuhle Wampe* was Prometheus's first sound production, it was not the first film made for and about the republic's working class. Despite the convergence in themes mentioned above, *Mother Krause's Journey to Happiness* sought to address the audience's political consciousness through the use of a conventional mimetic realist style, a climactic dramatic structure and Aristotelian catharsis. The film emphasises the 'authenticity' of the social milieu and its characters, including the depiction of Berlin's 'Lumpenproletariat', a social underclass of pimps, prostitutes, thieves and alcoholics.

Mother Krause is broadly divided into two narrative strands, one depicting the mother's increasingly ineffectual struggle to support her grown up but unemployed children by delivering newspapers, the other focusing on the daughter's emerging relationship with a young class-conscious worker. The film includes scenarios which are also played out in *Kuhle Wampe*, including a wedding depicting the guests' insatiable appetites and, of particular interest here, a character's suicide as a way out of a financially desperate situation.

Mother Krause (Alexandra Schmidt) returns home from a socialist workers' garden party (during which her daughter (Ilse Trautschold) announces her engagement to worker Max (Friedrich Gnass)), to find her wayward son (Holmes Zimmermann) has unexpectedly returned home. The arrival of two police officers and the young man's arrest for theft and the killing of a security guard thwart the happy reunion between mother and son. Alone again in her kitchen, Mother Krause looks confused. A point-of-view shot depicts her gazing around the room, then resting on a tapestry with the slogan, 'Don't despair. Every new day brings happiness.'

A series of shots depict Mother Krause making a pot of coffee, a ritual that involves several steps, from putting money in the gas meter, to boiling the water and measuring the exact amount of coffee for the pot. After ladling two spoons of coffee into the pot, she hesitates, adds two more scoops, then unexpectedly tips the whole jar of coffee into the pot. This action is depicted in medium shot, enabling the audience to study the mother's impassive face, devoid of emotion. A dissolve shows Mother Krause putting on her headscarf and taking a seat at the kitchen table, where a cup, saucer, spoon, milk and sugar are neatly laid out. Several close-ups depict her drinking the cup of coffee. Mother Krause then carries her pet, a caged bird, outside of the flat, returns and disconnects the gas lead from the cooker: she and her lodger's young daughter (Fee Wachsmuth) are killed by the toxic fumes.

The scene is unbearably sad to watch even on repeated viewings with the mother's confusion, helplessness and loneliness at this moment made palpable not through tears, or the mother expressively lamenting her woes, but in her actions. A series of shots early on in the scene, which depict the kettle and the cooker and also a shot of the gas mains, provoke our concern about what she might be about to do. When we see her boil the water, our worries subside, but they return when she pours all the coffee into the pot on the table. As we observe the mother drinking the coffee the focus is on her impassive face framed by the headscarf she put on while the kettle boiled. The scene plays on the tension between the normality of putting money into the gas meter, boiling water and brewing the coffee and the extremity of the act of disconnecting the gas lead. Pouring the whole tin of coffee into the pot marked a point of recognition for Mother Krause, namely that all her prudence and efforts to make ends meet have not prevented her family's spiralling descent into destitution.

The intention to portray accurately the living conditions in the working-class districts enables the *Mother Krause* filmmaking collective (which included, among others, prominent socialist artists Otto Nagel and Käthe Kollwitz) to address the audience in a very immediate manner, arousing feelings of pity and anger. At the same time, the character of Max (Fritz Gnass, an actor from Berlin's Piscator Stage ensemble) offers an idealised portrayal of a class-conscious and politicised proletariat ready to demand social change. Yet although both this film and *Kuhle Wampe* share the intention to affect change, *Mother Krause* does not raise questions about the economic causes of the family's hardship; the mother's situation is presented not as the inevitable logic of capitalism, but as an individual tragedy. The gesture with the coffee could be framed as a powerful comment about the conditions of the working class under capitalism, though the film never makes explicit this link between the personal and the wider political perspective.

Kuhle Wampe rejects this kind of subjectivity in favour of montage and distanciation devices. According to Brecht, 'the means must be asked what the end is': even the most accurate description of the workers' inhumane social conditions under capitalism is in danger of perpetuating dominant ideologies if the causes behind the conditions are not exposed and adequately explained (1992d: 110). Brecht's observation in relation to questions of realist aesthetics, that 'there are many ways of suppressing truth and many ways of stating it', can in that sense be applied to *Mother Krause* (ibid.).

Methods employed in the representation of young Bönike's suicide can thus be considered as in conscious opposition to the ways in which the parallel scene in *Mother Krause* addresses the audience. The focus on objects rather than character places the audience at one remove from the action but emphasises the familiarity of the individual objects. The ordinariness of the windowsill and pot plant stands in sharp contrast to the extraordinary character of the event, downplaying any expectation of spectacle, or any attempt to bring us close to Bönike's experience.

The close-up of the watch could be explained contextually, mirroring the actual case of a young unemployed man who, before committing suicide, left his watch on the kitchen table (see Leonard 1977: 58). Yet the montage works against any kind of subjectivity. In *Mother Krause*, the cup of coffee carries a symbolic function: to have the means to *afford* to offer visitors coffee (or have a cup oneself on special occasions) is understood to give Mother Krause a sense of pride and self-worth. The luxury of brewing a pot of (strong) coffee in *Mother Krause* is therefore presented as both representative of a class and specific to the mother (with detailed accounts of her counting an exact number of spoons for the pot). In contrast, the narrative texture linking Bönike to his watch is more sketchy. Though we can assume that the young man wants to preserve the watch (which would otherwise be damaged by the fall), it is not clear what – or whether – the watch means anything to him beyond its 'market value'.

Focus on the neighbours' reactions

Although Bönike's sister and her boyfriend Fritz (Ernst Busch) arrive at the scene shortly after, the narrative focuses on portraying the neighbours' responses to the death, rather than the family's. The first three shots of the following sequence depict neighbours talking about the event:

> Shot 97: (Two women chatting on a staircase with a third ascending the stairs)
> Woman one: He put the wristwatch on the table first.
> Woman two: Of course, it would have been smashed falling off the fourth floor.

> Shot 98: (Three children in the courtyard pointing upwards at a row of windows)
> Child left: Which window was it?
> Child right: (pointing) This one!
> Child middle: (also pointing) No, not this one, that one!

> Shot 99: (Close-up of a woman on a staircase)
> Woman: One unemployed less.

The camera positions differ greatly between the shots, varying from long shots 'capturing' snippets of dialogue from a distance to interview-style talking heads. This, coupled with the decision to focus on the public rather than the private reaction to the death, gives the section a documentary feel. In shot 97, one woman's observation that a fall from the fourth floor would have naturally ('natürlich') smashed the watch acknowledges the impact of the fall but avoids talking about the suicide in a more direct manner. The tenor of the conversation, that it somehow stands to reason that a watch (a flowerpot/a person) falling from this height would be damaged, seems like a clumsy attempt to talk about the event in confined but safe terms, without having to address the question whether it, too, somehow stood to reason.

The dialogue of the three children in shot 98, concerned with the actual window, enhances the prevailing sense of 'childlike' incomprehension amongst the community. The woman's comment 'One unemployed less' in the following shot conveys an air of resignation, aligned with a certain acceptance of the inevitability of the event.

In his analysis of the same section James Pettifer argues:

> When another woman says, 'One fewer unemployed' she only sketches a relation of young Bönike's death to the external conjuncture. Comment is weighted towards recognition of natural necessity, rather than clarification of the historical situation, as would be found in the mature Brecht. Young Bönike's death is a defeat for everyone present and living nearby. The bearing-witness at the scene of the martyr's death has many antecedents, perhaps the earliest being on a hill in Palestine. In few of them is there implied the possibility of the transformation of the social order that caused the death to take place. (1974: 59)

Whereas I agree with Pettifer that the scene lacks any suggestion that there could have been an alternative to Bönike's desperate act, I want to argue that the resigned tone of this scene is wholly deliberate (and not a flaw in its politics as Pettifer seems to suggest). What the film precisely conveys is a continuation, from the dinner sequence, of certain ways of seeing amongst the community which naturalise, rather than question, incongruous actions and events affecting the tenants' lives. The film's sharp focus on the characters' ways of looking at events as given and determined continues in the shot depicting Bönike, as yet unaware of his son's death discussing politics with another man in the pub:

Shot 101: Father Bönike: There are now seven million unemployed in America.
Another man: Yes, they used to drive to work and now they are demonstrating against unemployment.
Father Bönike: Yes, but on foot.

Once again, the topic of unemployment is raised and addressed by the characters in the world of the film. Father Bönike's observation could, at first sight, be regarded as a thoughtful observation on the fact that American workers – cars or no cars – are as much subject to the requirements of the market as their Berlin comrades. However, it is doubtful that the comment could be read as a sign of the father's awareness of the subjugation of a whole class to the requirements of the political economy of capitalism, as he certainly did not show this level of political insight with regards to his son's situation in the earlier scene.

On the contrary, the self-contained episodes in shots 97 to 101 give an insight into the characters' rather sketchy awareness of the economic conditions that affect their lives. The dinner table and suicide scenes equally draw attention to the gap between the actual situation and the kinds of inferences the Bönikes and their neighbours draw about their circumstances. Whereas the job hunt sequence illustrated the wider conflict of interest of a class with no other option than to partake in the competition for paid work, individual members of this class are shown to meekly accept the given conditions even though they are clearly not in their own interests.

Setting epic methods utilised in the job hunt sequence – which invite the spectator to ask what all this racing across the city is good for, whose benefit it really serves – against the representation of people in the world of the film who do *not* ask questions but tacitly accept dominant ideological viewpoints, a tension between the audience's and the characters' perception and understanding of events begins to emerge. This strategy is developed further in part two and brought to a conclusion in part three.

Part Two: 'The best years…': adjustment and compensation

In part two, 'The best years of a young person's life', the narrative continues to examine the family's behaviour in the light of their deteriorating financial situation. Being forced to leave their flat as a result of non-payment of rent, the family moves to Kuhle Wampe tent colony to reside with daughter Annie's boyfriend, Fritz. A major strand of the narrative deals with Annie's pregnancy, her engagement to Fritz and, subsequently, Annie's decision to leave Fritz and seek an abortion. The problems both Annie and Fritz face due to the unwanted pregnancy stand in sharp contrast to the assumption that youth represents the 'best years of a ... person's life', as the chapter title proposes.

Narrationally, the section is dominated by self-contained episodes, as well as the use of songs and montage sections. Whereas the couple's courtship and the sexual act leading to Annie falling pregnant are presented in a detached and rather abstract manner through the use of non-diegetic music (a song performed by Helene Weigel) and nature photography, the focus on the parents' adjustment to their new surroundings is studied meticulously in an extended sequence (the so-called 'Mata Hari' sequence).

Don't worry about tomorrow...

The scene juxtaposes the mother's calculation of the household expenditure with the father reading aloud a lurid article about the trial of Mata Hari, the Dutch dancer accused of espionage for Germany and executed in France in 1917. The article contains titillating descriptions of Hari's figure and sexual affairs; a close-up of the calculation lists basic groceries, cigars and talcum powder. A series of insert shots depicts the goods on the list, ranging from liver sausage to bread and cheese; for each item, the cost is displayed. Between inserts, the camera depicts the mother's anxious expression as she adds up the cost of living whilst the father struggles to decipher more difficult words in the article.

The juxtaposition of the intimate details of the dancer's extravagant lifestyle with everyday goods such as fat and herring creates humour. The article's insinuation regarding a former Berlin police commissioner's 'visit to the dancer's changing rooms to ensure that the nude dance routine was in order' escapes the father, but is not lost on the audience. Yet despite these elements of comic relief the sequence does not show the parents' behaviour in an uncritical light. Sitting with her back to the tapestry which previously adorned the kitchen, we are encouraged to observe not the mother's joy but her increasing burden in 'caring for those' she 'loves' (Fig. 3.16). The father still reads the paper but has swapped current affairs for the distraction of the *feuilleton*. Both characters are seen to compensate for the stark reality of their descent into homelessness by adjusting to, rather than challenging, the circumstances of their existence.

Cleanliness and listening to military marches played on the radio dominate the day-to-day routines at Kuhle Wampe tent colony, not protest against the lack of housing for workers living on the breadline. The colony's romantic setting amidst forests and fields loses its appeal when Fritz is forced into proposing to Annie due to petit bourgeois soci-

Fig. 3.16

etal pressure. Part two ends with Annie leaving the tent colony after the couple's engagement party, determinedly abandoning her parents and Fritz.

In his review in the *Berliner Börsen-Courier* Herbert Ihering comments on the film's unflinching look at some sections of the proletariat:

> The workers are not idealised. On the contrary: it also shows the philistine sides, the petit bourgeois leanings (during an engagement party and in reading matters). It doesn't show the sentimentality, but the nasty bigotry of their crammed insularity. (1973: 143)

Whereas Ihering welcomes the film's 'unsentimental, therefore just' (ibid.) approach, Heinz Lüdecke in *Die Rote Fahne* criticises the 'at times unjust representation of the proletariat'. He comments:

> The producers themselves will have to admit the film's sharp focus on petit bourgeois mannerisms and yet the fighting proletariat is presented in a bland, sweeping and idealised manner. (1973: 155)

The film's critical engagement with various sections of the working class raises several issues. Considering the film's prominence as Weimar's first proletarian sound film, the presentation of workers so decidedly not embodying the socialist ideal of a class-conscious working class at first seems puzzling. Yet taking into account the film's interest in *how* to address its proletarian audience, the 'sharp focus' on class-unconscious workers seems apt. Throughout part two, systems established in the first part of the film continue to foreground the influence of commonly held beliefs surrounding work ethics and family values, typified by the enduring presence of the tapestry. Privileged over the characters, the spectator is encouraged to view critically the parents' actual and intellectual 'adjustment' to their circumstances.

Part Three: 'To whom does the world belong?' – reason over rhetoric

The film's final chapter, 'To whom does the world belong?', presents the workers as a class united by shared materialist conditions and interests. As already mentioned, it depicts a mass sports day organised by Berlin's communist athletics clubs. In clear contrast to the job hunt sequence, however, we are invited to observe workers racing on this occasion *not* in competition but in the name of solidarity, as a motorbike rally (part of the sports day) from Berlin to Müggelsee gets underway. A series of shots depicts different groups of young communist athletes gathering in the city, singing and whistling Hanns Eisler's 'Solidarity Song' as they march out of town on their way to the event.[20] The song's forceful lyrics and dynamic melody celebrate the strength of a united body of workers no longer willing to accept their forced exclusion from the wealth they create, as the second verse ('Forward and don't forget/Our street and our field/Forward and don't forget: whose street is this street?/To whom does this world belong?') makes clear.

Fig. 3.17

Fig. 3.18

Annie can be seen amongst a group of young people marching and singing the song.

The following section illustrates the variety of disciplines taking place on the day, and shots of the motorbike rally, rowing and swimming events are collated in a montage section (Figs 3.17–3.18). The show of speed and physical strength of both men and women is accompanied by Ernst Busch's rendition of the 'Sports Song' on the soundtrack. The song is an appeal to the working class to 'fight together and learn to win'. The pace of the montage gradually accelerates and concludes with motorcyclists, rowers and swimmers crossing respective finish lines.

Marc Silberman comments that these 'scenes of mass enthusiasm (marches, competitive sports, steaming crowds), which for the filmmakers represented a political aesthetics, became in just a few years the dominant aesthetics of fascist politics' (1995: 48), in essence suggesting that the filmmakers were somehow unaware of the unfortunate convergence in communist and fascist styles, or that, in the least, their use of this aesthetics of the masses was in some ways employed uncritically. Based on my analysis of earlier sequences, in which the film's relationship to its material and the strategies it employs to convey meaning is perhaps less clear-cut than one would expect of such a political piece of filmmaking, I want to argue that the various sections of part three might carry an additional function to that of politicising its audience.

The images of the marching athletes and the various competitions undeniably convey a strong sense of the workers as a physically powerful and united body. At the same time, Busch's recital of the 'Sports Song' which accompanies shots of athletes crossing the finish line, rather than taking victory for granted, emphasises the daily struggle of the workers to unite as a collective body: 'From the pennies of deprivation you have bought your boats/And the fares have been saved from your dinners.' Busch's recital of the chorus 'Learn to win!/Learn to win!' is sung with a sense of urgency which results in a pleading, rather than confident, tone.

In fact, the film seems as its most confident in conveying an unambiguous political message as it records another medium – the informal space and impromptu performance of agitprop theatre. The sporting competitions are followed by an afternoon of political activities, including an agitprop theatre performance by 'Das Rote Sprachrohr' ensemble. The ensemble's opening line 'We are the "Red Megaphone", the megaphone of the masses/We tell what oppresses you', delivered through big megaphones, grabs the crowd's attention. The theme of the performance is the eviction of a family in a Wedding district tenement block and an insert shot shows Annie and Fritz watching the action with interest. The focus is on the actual performance and the audience watching in equal measure (Fig. 3.19) so that even after the performance has finished the camera stays in place. Surrounding the now empty stage the workers start up the 'Solidarity Song' once again (Fig. 3.20). An extended sequence shows workers joining in the song in a thousand-strong chorus.

Fig. 3.19

(It is worth noting that this sequence was censored in parts: the final verse of the 'Song of the Red United Front' – sung by the actors on stage as part of their performance – which appeals to neighbours to unite and 'stand as one' against landlords, bailiffs and the police in order to prevent the eviction of families from their homes, had to be cut as a condition of the film's release (see Gersch & Hecht 1973: 79).)

Fig. 3.20

The agitprop play's impact on the audience assembled around the stage is illustrated by the apparent unwillingness of the crowd to simply disperse after the performance has ended. The relevance of the topic presented and the vivid and easy-to-grasp methods of agitprop have addressed the audience in a direct and unambiguous manner, advancing the kind of heightened political awareness (resulting in the rendition of the 'Solidarity Song') the film is concerned with. Political dialogue permeates the remaining activities of the day: a group of young men is trying to get to grips with a passage from Hegel and a man offers brochures on topics ranging from contraception to union rights.

Despite the explicit and imposing use of political rhetoric in part three, *Kuhle Wampe*, unlike its predecessor *Mother Krause*, does not end with shots of workers marching the city streets in a much needed demonstration of mass unity. As the workers make their way back to the city the 'Solidarity Song' can be heard on the soundtrack, but it is less amplified than in previous scenes. Instead of presenting the audience with a rousing finish, the final episode depicts a discussion between workers and other passengers on a train.

Talking, not marching – the S-Bahn debate

The burning of coffee in Brazil and the capitalist logic of a free market economy are at the centre of a heated debate between several passengers in a train compartment. A man's casual comment about the burning of 24 million pounds of coffee in a Brazilian port is initially met with incredulity by those standing within earshot: one passenger 'simply can't believe' the news, another dismisses the headline as 'lying propaganda' and a third passenger interjects that 'ordinary common sense tells you it can't be true'. None of these passengers are part of the group of communist athletes who have just boarded the train, but soon a debate ensues between them and the athletes, until, gradually, the discussion spreads and produces a range of opposed responses in the crowded space. Stylistically, the scene differs from the temporal ellipsis and episodic character of previous sequences: close-ups and continuity editing, as well as attention to detail in the performances (some bordering on parody, especially the more bourgeois characters) create an unusually conventional realist representation of the action compared to the rest of the film. The camera is positioned in close proximity to the actors, creating a sense of being amongst the passengers as they argue.

Although the film appears to present random snippets of conversations, including a small group of female passengers discussing the intricacies of brewing coffee, the overall development of the argument is tightly controlled: the topic of the world economy is introduced into the debate early on, which leads to the passenger with the most reactionary viewpoints to comment on what he believes to be Germany's disadvantaged position in world politics:

Passenger (standing):   If we had a fleet, we'd have colonies, too. If we had colonies, we'd have coffee. And if we had coffee…

Passenger (seated):   Then what? Would prices go down?

Passenger (standing):   Maybe not. But *we'd* make the profit.

It is at this point that Kurt (Adolf Fischer), the politically conscious worker, joins the debate (Fig. 3.21).

Kurt: You keep saying we. Who is this we? You and I? That gentleman, these ladies, that old man? We would make the profit? You don't even believe that yourself.

The film then cuts to another group of passengers trying to calculate the monetary loss of burning so much coffee and a debate about the price of a pound of coffee ensues. This scene is humorous in tone, but also draws attention to the difference in financial means, with some passengers being able to afford more expensive brands than others. As the argument between Kurt and the reactionary passenger is becoming increasingly heated, another passenger asks them to calm down: 'Gentlemen, you are not the only people in the carriage.' The debate ends with an extended speech by Kurt about the kinds of people in the carriage who will

Fig. 3.21

not attempt to do something about the economic crisis and who will not 'change the world'. To the provocative question by the reactionary character: 'And who will change it?' Gerda (Martha Wolter), Annie's friend, replies: 'Those who don't like it'.

On this cue the film cuts to the workers walking down a foot tunnel; on the soundtrack, Ernst Busch sings the 'Solidarity Song' with renewed vigour (Fig. 3.22). The lyrics allude to the discrepancy between the actual and the possible, the world as it is and the world as it could be: 'We've seen the sun shin-

Yet we never did believe
this was our true world

Fig. 3.22

ing/on the street, in the fields/Yet we never did believe/this was our true world', and the film finishes on the song's final stanza: 'Whose street is the street?/To whom does the world belong?'

The film's focus in the final episode is on discussion as a way to create political consciousness. It shows the multifaceted responses one topic – the world economy and its impact on people – can evoke in those from different classes and with different levels of political awareness. It presents progressive and reactionary perspectives, but also draws attention to those who remain 'apolitical' (in the scene one character continually switches between the viewpoints put forward and ends up shaking hands with the reactionary passenger). It soon becomes apparent that the final episode presents a political microcosm in which different class interests come to the fore.

However, the focus is on the social and the thought processes that happen between the characters, rather than on providing the audience in the cinema with an explicit answer to the question to 'whom the world belongs' (though implicitly the answer is clear). The episode thus differs in tone from the agitprop of the previous scene and only imitates agitational techniques in Gerda's final declaration that the world will be changed by those 'who don't like it'. Nonetheless, discussion replaces megaphones, and images of young communist workers give way to wider sections of society. The people in the carriage may be sharing the same space but they are far from united. For change to occur, people's thinking has to change drastically.

The film's final episode, with its focus on most people's limited grasp of political issues, once more engages with the question of how to address the audience as members of a social class, something previous proletarian film productions, such as *Mother Krause*, mostly took for granted or never raised. The episode illustrates that the very 'reasons' the passengers find to explain the actual causes of their economic circumstances are also the main obstacle in re-thinking and possibly transforming an economic system which so fundamentally works against the interests of a whole class.

A major change between parts one and three, however, is the move from characters' silence to talking. The eloquent worker Kurt replaces voiceless young Bönike, but people unable to comprehend their thoughts, actions and behaviour surround both. Marc Silberman argues that *Kuhle Wampe* 'does not aim at providing an answer for the spectator but at the spectator's recognition of the possibility of change' (1995: 46), thus centring the film's attention on its impact on the viewer. In this chapter I have attempted to show the film's interest in experimenting with different modes of address, exploring the use of diverse techniques to find different ways of producing meaning and to explore ways of enabling the spectator to draw inferences based not on habitual but on new ways of seeing.

If the film's curiosity in how ideas are formed and articulated is as important as their actual content it is inevitable that it cannot, like *Mother Krause's Journey to Happiness*, end on a kind of semiotic closure of workers, all differences resolved (and all questions presumably answered by Hegel and the 'Red Megaphone'), marching as a uniform and united body. As *Kuhle Wampe* draws to a close the lyrics of the 'Solidarity Song' on the soundtrack call for workers to unite, but the imagery is understated, with workers back in the city walking down a foot tunnel, not marching in the streets.

Refusing to end Weimar's first (and only) proletarian sound film by resorting to em-phatic agitational rhetoric, the filmmakers invite the audience to gain pleasure from its politically unambiguous scenes but also to engage with the complex relationship between image and sound. That *how* to address the audience as a class became pivotal at a time when paid workers were also targeted by another type of political rhetoric which, though diametrically opposed to Marxist principles, was nonetheless deceptively similar in its appeal to the republic's proletariat to join a national revolution, seem sadly self-evident in retrospect.

Conclusion

This study has examined the relationship between seeing and understanding in Weimar cinema, from the self-conscious use of visual rhetoric in Fritz Lang's postwar film *Dr Mabuse, the Gambler*, to Film-Studio 1929's sceptical engagement with detached ways of seeing in *Menschen am Sonntag* and, finally, *Kuhle Wampe*'s explicitly political focus on ways of seeing as a means to create political consciousness. Each film, I have argued, encourages the spectator to adopt a critical perspective in relation to what is shown and how it is presented onscreen, so that not only a film's content, but its systems of narration come under scrutiny.

The complex relationship between ways of seeing and the spectator's ability to reason has been the dominant theme in each chapter. In *Dr Mabuse, the Gambler*, stunning images deceive the eye, and the narrative drive offers few opportunities to pause and think about the implications of our ambivalent alignment with the doctor. In *Menschen am Sonntag*, the initially detached perspectives on New Objectivity's modern urban lifestyle may fail to register the contradictions and constraints manifested in its assertion of social and personal liberation. It is only through a more attentive look at the young women of this new class of salaried workers that the limitations of 'neusachliche' ways of seeing, resulting from reducing people to the status of a simple object, becomes apparent. *Kuhle Wampe* examines the impact of preconceived and unquestioned ideas on people's understanding of the social and economic processes affecting their lives, and experiments with new forms of audience address to stimulate moments of recognition and more politicised ways of seeing.

Why do these issues of seeing clearly, of seeing for oneself and of making sense of what is shown, play such a significant role in films spanning the period? Henri R. Paucker identifies a significant 'tension between rationalism and irrationalism' (1991: 11) as representative of the Weimar era, which culminated in increasingly violent clashes between reactionary and progressive forces in the republic's unstable political arena. According to Paucker, opponents of National Socialism 'all sought to counteract the irrational, the intoxicating mythical, by applying reason and ... to continue in the spirit of the European enlightenment, rather than the German romantic tradition' (ibid.). With nationalist factions intent on holding on to nostalgic and determinist paradigms and Marxist thinkers understanding history as a process which could and would be radically altered by the proletariat, the question of what to think and believe when faced with irreconcilable world views becomes a process of complex and potentially confusing negotiation between perception and knowledge.

Each film's engagement with different systems of looking can thus be regarded as an implicit or explicit response to radically different perspectives, vehemently vying for the public's attention in an age increasingly dominated by visual and mass culture. Where *Dr Mabuse, the Gambler* draws attention to the influencing power of visual rhetoric as a dangerous shortcut to more elaborate (and laborious) thought processes, *Menschen am*

Sonntag warns of the danger of a depersonalised perception without an eye for the complexity of human experience, even at times of drastic rationalisation in all areas of public and private life. In *Kuhle Wampe*, Slatan Dudow and Bertolt Brecht juxtapose irrational and rational thought in the critical awareness of how difficult it is to alter habitual ways of seeing and, crucially, conventional modes of audience address.

When the unpredictable circumstances of exile brought some of the artists discussed in this study together in Hollywood, collaboration between them (most famously Lang's and Brecht's joint effort on *Hangmen also Die* (directed by Lang; 1942)) was both rare and fraught. Nonetheless, their concerns with the visual rhetoric of film and the ideological positioning of the audience would continue during and beyond exile.

NOTES

1 See Douglas Pye (1988; 1992) for writings on point of view and epistemic dimensions in American Fritz Lang films.

2 *Dr Mabuse, der Spieler* was published in the *Berliner Illustrierte Zeitung* between 25 September 1921 and 29 January 1922.

3 See 'Demonstration and Disguise: Observations on Lang's Style', unpublished manuscript. This is from a collection of critical essays on Fritz Lang, edited by Douglas Pye, originally intended for publication in 2000, which has regrettably not yet appeared. The essay is cited with the kind permission of Douglas Pye.

4 Following its serialisation in the newspaper, sales of the novel by the Ullstein publishing house topped the 100,000 mark in 1922. See Scholdt (1996: 372) and Kreimeier (1992: 105–7) for accounts on the popularity of the Mabuse series and the film release as an early example of a carefully crafted modern multi-media event.

5 See Tom Gunning (2000: 94–8) for an in-depth analysis of the use of modern technologies in the film.

6 In his essay, 'Der Schlafwandler', Klaus Kreimeier draws attention to the novels of several Weimar authors whose stories were occupied by 'broken, addicted, fed up with civilisation, Nietzsche-obsessed heroes' (1987: 92).

7 See, for example, the significance of blind characters, or characters faking blindness, in other Lang films of the Weimar period, *Kämpfende Herzen/Four Men and a Woman* (1920), *Spione/Spies* (1927) and *M* (1931), as well as Lang's American films and the (fake) 'blind seer' Jordan (Wolfgang Preiß) in Lang's last film, *Die 1000 Augen des Dr Mabuse/The 1000 Eyes of Dr Mabuse* (1960).

8 See, for example, Kaes (1987: 23) and Sloterdijk (1988: 509–10) for discussions of the dominance of visual culture in urban areas of Weimar Germany.

9 Hervé Dumont asserts that Ulmer's contribution to the direction is fairly negligible, having left the shoot after only ten days due to arguments within the team (1992: 143).

10 Berthold Viertel's *Die Abenteuer eines Zehnmarkschein* (1926) and Wilfried Basse's *Markt am Wittenbergplatz* (1929) are typical examples of the cross-section film (see Kappelhoff 2003).

11 The English intertitle omits the words 'zur Zeit' (meaning 'currently', or 'for the time being') in translation. However, the reference 'currently' hints at the probability that von Waltershausen will not be working as a 'wine trader' for long, drawing attention to areas of instability and transience in his life.

12 Wilder's script is similar in themes and style to the detached, ironic and sober formal aspects of the so-called 'Gebrauchslyrik' ('functional poetry'), which emerged in Germany in the 1920s. Well-known Berlin authors of 'Gebrauchslyrik' are Brecht and, in particular, Erich Kästner, whose poems engage with the discrepancy between traditional ideals about romantic love and the reality of anonymity and casual sexual consumption in the modern city. Kästner's well-known poem 'Sachliche Romanze' ('Matter-of-fact Romance') takes a sober look at the uncertainty of loving relationships in modern times. Kästner's widely published *Dr Erich Käst-*

ners Lyrische Hausapotheke, a collection of 'Gebrauchslyrik' written during the 1920s, perceptively responds to the isolation of individuals and their (unfulfilled) desires in the anonymity of the modern metropolis.

13 Discussing the link between radical industrialisation, New Objectivity and the new class of salaried workers during Weimar's stabilisation period, David Durst argues: 'In "new objectivity", the psychological dimension of intense subjectivity and uneasy angst of German expressionism yield to a more stabilised culture of impersonality and anti-individual sobriety of mass production and consumption. This new sobriety is concentrated especially in the urban centres of Weimar Germany, for it is there that the erasure of residual zones of "Irratio" resistant to the rationalisation of production and the dilation of capitalist commodification in the realm of culture and consumption are most advanced' (2004: xxxi).

14 An advertisement for such a '5 Uhr Tee' dance is visible in the shot of the trains passing through Bahnhof Zoo, prior to von Waltershausen's encounter with Christl Ehlers on the station forecourt.

15 A review by Andor Kraszna-Krausz stands out in drawing attention to the stylistic vacillation between sobriety and sentiment in the film: 'That there's such a thing as desire. Not just my own desire. That everything is much more confusing than we think, but also much simpler. One can hardly make sense of it, one can only see it. Especially on Sundays' (1930:14).

16 The 1973 Suhrkamp edition *Bertolt Brecht: Kuhle Wampe: Protokoll des Films und Materialien*, edited by Wolfgang Gersch and Werner Hecht, has proved an inestimable source in writing this chapter. It contains not only the full script (with reference to the cuts and changes demanded by the censor) but also a comprehensive account of the battle to secure its release and a wide range of reviews after the film's eventual premiere in Moscow and Berlin in May 1932.

17 See Stooss (1977); Korte (1978); and Silberman (1995) for detailed historical accounts of Weimar's extensive proletarian film culture.

18 During Brecht's lifetime, his oeuvre spanning the years 1926–32 was considered mostly as a transition phase from the early plays to the completion of his concept of the epic theatre. In contemporary Brecht scholarship this 'middle' phase is regarded as a time of creative experimentation with a range of theatrical modes rather than merely as a 'precursor' to the epic model (see Payrhuber 1995: 45–6). This exploration of various theatrical forms included opera, the Lehrstück and the epic theatre in its earliest stages. It can, therefore, be regarded as a time of the dramatist's critical engagement with a range of political aesthetic strategies, ranging from the didactic intention of the Lehrstück to the more open-ended methods of later works. Rooted in the dialectics of historical materialist thought, these overtly didactic forms were intended as models for a new (that is, socialist) society which, though envisaged by the left in the early 1930s, ultimately failed to materialise giving way to fascist rule instead. My use of the term 'didactic' in the context of this essay therefore refers to its explicit political function at this stage in Brecht's career, though I will argue in this chapter that the extent of the political function of certain methods were of interest to Brecht and *Kuhle Wampe*'s filmmaking collective.

19 In the film's original version, the mother responds to the father's comment about the loss of state benefit by replying: 'Don't shove the emergency decree under his nose.' However, the

producers cut this reference to the immediate political situation in order to appease the censor (see Gersch & Hecht 1973: 78), who considered the line an attack on the government.

20 Though we see the workers marching it can be assumed that they would not have walked the whole distance from the city to Müggelsee at its outskirts.

BIBLIOGRAPHY

All translations from German sources by Iris Luppa unless stated otherwise.

Adank, Thomas (1977) 'Hanns Eisler und die Musik in Kuhle Wampe', in Neue Gesellschaft für Bildende Kunst (NGBK) and Freunde der Deutschen Kinemathek (eds) *Erobert den Film! Proletariat und Film in der Weimarer Republik*. Berlin: NGBK, 65–7.

Arnheim, Rudolf (1930) 'Tauberton und Studio', *Die Weltbühne*, 7, 246–7.

Bauer, Ludwig (1988) 'Zeichen und kulturelles Wissen: Die Rekonstruktion des Bedeutungspotentials visueller Zeichen am Beispiel von Menschen am Sonntag', in Elfriede Ledig (ed.) *Der Stummfilm: Konstruktion und Rekonstruktion*. Munich: Schaudig, Bauer, Ledig, 33–68.

Bessel, Richard (1993) *Germany After the First World War*. Oxford: Clarendon.

Brecht, Bertolt (1973) *Gesammelte Werke*, Vol. 18. Frankfurt: Suhrkamp.

_____ (1974) 'A Small Contribution to the Theme of Realism', *Screen*, 15, 45–8.

_____ (1992a [1931]) 'The Literarisation of the Theatre (Notes to the *Threepenny Opera*)', in *Brecht on Theatre: The Development of an Aesthetic*, ed. and trans. John Willett. London: Methuen, 43–6.

_____ (1992b [1931]) 'The Film, The Novel and the Epic Theatre', in *Brecht on Theatre: The Development of an Aesthetic*, ed. and trans. John Willett. London: Methuen, 47–51.

_____ (1992c [1957]) 'Theatre for Pleasure or Theatre for Instruction', in *Brecht on Theatre: The Development of an Aesthetic*, ed. and trans. John Willett. London: Methuen, 69–76.

_____ (1992d [1958]) 'The Popular and the Realistic', in *Brecht on Theatre: The Development of an Aesthetic*, ed. and trans. John Willett. London: Methuen, 107–12.

_____ (2000a) 'No Insight through Photography', in *Brecht on Film and Radio*, ed. and trans. Marc Silberman. London: Methuen, 144.

_____ (2000b) 'The Threepenny Lawsuit', in *Brecht on Film and Radio*, ed. and trans. Marc Silberman. London: Methuen, 147–99.

Burch, Noel (1980) 'Fritz Lang: German Period', in Richard Roud (ed.) *Cinema: A Critical Dictionary: Volume One*. London: Secker and Warburg, 583–99.

Coates, Paul (1991) *The Gorgon's Gaze: German Cinema, Expressionism and the Image of Horror*. Cambridge: Cambridge University Press.

Decker, Peter and Konrad Hecker (2002) *Das Proletariat*. Munich: GegenStandpunkt.

Dumont, Hervé (1992) 'Robert Siodmaks avantgardistische Filme', in Uli Jung and Walter Schatzberg (eds) *Filmkultur zur Zeit der Weimarer Republik*. Munich: Saur, 142–52.

Durst, David (2004) *Weimar Modernism*. New York and Oxford: Lexington.

Eisler, Hanns (1973) 'Funktion und Dramaturgie (der Filmmusik)', in Walter Gersch and Werner Hecht (eds) *Bertolt Brecht. Kuhle Wampe. Protokoll des Films und Materialien*. Frankfurt: Suhrkamp, 97–100.

Eisner, Lotte (1969 [1952]) *The Haunted Screen*. London. Thames & Hudson.

'E. L.' (1930) 'Kritik der Kinomusik: Der Illustrierte Studio-Film', *Reichsfilmblatt*, 6, 5 (Archive Stiftung Deutsche Kinemathek, Filmmuseum Berlin).

Elsaesser, Thomas (1997) 'Traps For the Mind and Eye', *Sight and Sound*, 8, 28–30.

_____ (2000) *Weimar Cinema and After: Germany's Historical Imaginary*. London: Routledge.

Gersch, Walter and Werner Hecht (eds) (1973) *Bertolt Brecht. Kuhle Wampe. Protokoll des Films und Materialien*. Frankfurt: Suhrkamp.

Gibbs, John (2002) *Mise-en-scène: Film Style and Interpretation*. London: Wallflower Press.

Grafe, Frieda (1987) 'Für Fritz Lang: Einen Platz, kein Denkmal', in Frieda Grafe, Enno Patalas and Hans Helmut Prinzler (eds) *Fritz Lang: Reihe Film 7*. Munich: Hanser.

Gunning, Tom (2000) *The Films of Fritz Lang: Allegories of Vision and Modernity*. London: British Film Institute.

Hake, Sabine (1987) 'Girls and Crisis: The Other Side of Diversion', *New German Critique*, 40, 147–66.

_____ (1993) *The Cinema's Third Machine: Writing on Film in Germany 1907–1933*. Lincoln and London: University of Nebraska Press.

_____ (1994) 'Urban Spectacle in Walter Ruttmann's *Berlin, Symphony of the Big City* ', in Thomas Kniesche and Stephen Brockmann (eds) *Dancing on the Volcano: Essays on the Culture of the Weimar Republic*. Columbia, Sc: Camden House, 127–42.

Happel, Ralf and Margot Michaelis (1978) 'Wem gehört die Welt? Filme der Arbeiterbewegung in der Weimarer Republik', in Helmut Korte (ed.) *Film und Realität in der Weimarer Republik*. Munich: Hanser, 93–212.

Haustedt, Birgit (1999) *Die Wilden Jahre in Berlin*. Edition Ebersbach.

Hermand, Jost (1994) '*Neue Sachlichkeit:* Ideology, Lifestyle, or Artistic Movement?', in Thomas Kniesche and Stephen Brockmann (eds) *Dancing on the Volcano: Essays on the Culture of the Weimar Republic*. Columbia, Sc: Camden House, 57–67.

Ihering, Herbert (1958) *Von Reinhardt bis Brecht, Volume 1 (1909–1923)*. Berlin: Aufbau-Verlag, 272–75.

_____ (1961 [1930]) '*Menschen am Sonntag*', in Herbert Ihering *Von Reinhardt bis Brecht, Volume 3 (1930–1932)*. Berlin: Aufbau-Verlag, 300–1.

_____ (1973 [1932]) 'Review of *Kuhle Wampe*', in Walter Gersch and Werner Hecht (eds) *Bertolt Brecht. Kuhle Wampe. Protokoll des Films und Materialien*. Frankfurt: Suhrkamp, 143.

Jacques, Norbert (1996 [1921–22]) *Dr. Mabuse, der Spieler*. Hamburg: Rowohlt.

Kaes, Anton (1987) 'Literary Intellectuals and the Cinema: Charting a Controversy (1909–1929)', *New German Critique*, 40, 7–34.

_____ (1994) 'Cinema from Expressionism to Social Realism', in Anton Kaes, Martin Jay and Edward Dimendberg (eds) *The Weimar Republic Source Book*. Berkeley: University of California Press, 617–19.

Kappelhoff, Hermann (2003) 'Eine neue Gegenständlichkeit: Die Bildidee der Neuen Sachlichkeit und der Film', in Thomas Koebner (ed.) *Diesseits der 'Dämonischen Leinwand': Neue Perspektiven auf das späte Weimarer Kino*. Munich: edition text + kritik, 119–38.

Koebner, Thomas (ed.) (2003) *Diesseits der 'Dämonischen Leinwand': Neue Perspektiven auf das späte Weimarer Kino*. Munich: text + kritik.

Korte, Helmut (ed.) (1978) *Film und Realität in der Weimarer Republik*. Munich: Hanser.

Kracauer, Siegfried (1947) *From Caligari to Hitler*. Princeton. Princeton University Press.

_____ (1995) 'Those Who Wait', in *The Mass Ornament: Weimar Essays*, trans. Thomas Y. Levin. Cambridge, Massachusetts: Harvard University Press, 129–40.

Kraszna-Krausz, Andor (1930) 'Startum, Tendenz, Reportage', *Filmtechnik-Filmkunst*, 4, 13–15 (Archive Filmmuseum Berlin).

Kraus, Karl (1974 [1926]) *The Last Days of Mankind: A Tragedy in Five Acts*. New York: Frederick Ungar.

Kreimeier, Klaus (1987) 'Der Schlafwandler: Fritz Lang und seine deutschen Filme', in Uta Berg-Ganschow and Wolfgang Jacobsen (eds) *...Film ...Stadt...Kino...Berlin*. Argon: Berlin, 89–112.

_____ (1992) *Die Ufa Story*. Munich: Hanser.

Kunzmann, Peter, Franz-Peter Burkard and Franz Wiedmann (eds) (1993) *dtv-Atlas zur Philosophie*. Munich: dtv.

Lang, Fritz (2003 [1969]) 'Fritz Lang in Venice', in Barry Keith Grant (ed.) *Fritz Lang: Interviews*. Jackson: University of Mississippi, 91–100.

Leonard, Yvonne (1977) 'Die verdoppelte Illusion', in Neue Gesellschaft für Bildende Kunst (NGBK) and Freunde der Deutschen Kinemathek (eds) *Erobert den Film! Proletariat und Film in der Weimarer Republik*. Berlin: NGBK, 48–64.

Lüdecke, Heinz (1973 [1932]) 'Review of *Kuhle Wampe*', in Walter Gersch and Werner Hecht (eds) *Bertolt Brecht. Kuhle Wampe. Protokoll des Films und Materialien*. Frankfurt: Suhrkamp, 155.

Ludendorff, Erich (1977 [1917]) 'Letter to War Ministry, Berlin', in Neue Gesellschaft für Bildende Kunst (NGBK) and Freunde der Deutschen Kinemathek (eds) *Erobert den Film! Proletariat und Film in der Weimarer Republik*. Berlin: NGBK, 68–9.

McCormick, Richard (2001) *Gender and Sexuality in Weimar Modernity: Film, Literature and 'New Objectivity'*. New York: Palgrave.

Neue Gesellschaft für Bildende Kunst (NGBK) and Freunde der Deutschen Kinemathek (eds) *Erobert den Film! Proletariat und Film in der Weimarer Republik*. Berlin: NGBK.

Paech, Joachim (1988) *Literatur und Film*. Stuttgart: Metzler.

Paucker, H. R. (1991) *Neue Sachlichkeit Literatur im 'Dritten Reich' und im Exil*. Stuttgart: Reclam.

Payrhuber, Franz-Josef (1995) *Literaturwissen Bertolt Brecht*. Stuttgart: Reclam.

Perez, Gilberto (1998) *The Material Ghost: Films and their Medium*. Baltimore. The Johns Hopkins University Press.

Pettifer, James (1974) 'Against the Stream – *Kuhle Wampe*', *Screen*, 15, 49–64.

Pinthus, Kurt (2001 [1922]) 'Dr. Mabuses Welt', trans. Catherine Kerkhoff-Saxon, in Rolf Aurich, Wolfgang Jacobsen and Cornelius Schnauber (eds) *Fritz Lang: Leben und Werk*. Berlin: Deutsche Kinemathek and Jovis, 74–80.

Pye, Douglas (1988) 'Seeing By Glimpses: Fritz Lang's *The Blue Gardenia*', *CineAction!*, 12/3, 74–82.

_____ (1992) 'Film Noir and Suppressive Narrative: *Beyond a Reasonable Doubt*', in Ian Cameron (ed.) *The Movie Book of Film Noir*. London: Studio Vista, 98–109.

_____ (2000a) 'Movies and Point of View', *Movie*, 36, 2–34.

_____ (2000b) 'Demonstration and Disguise: Observations on Lang's Style' (unpublished article).

Salt, Barry (1979) 'From Caligari to who?', *Sight and Sound*, 48, 2, Spring,119–23.

Schacht, Roland (2001 [1922]) '*Dr. Mabuse, der Spieler*', in Klaus Hoeppner (ed.) *Fritz Lang: FilmHeft 6*. Berlin: Deutsche Kinemathek, 24.

Schmied, Wieland (1979) 'Neue Sachlichkeit and the German Realism of the Twenties', in Wieland Schmied (ed.) *Neue Sachlichkeit and the German Realism of the Twenties*. London: Arts Council of Great Britain, 7–33.

Scholdt, Georg (1996) 'Mabuse, ein Deutscher Mythos', in Norbert Jacques *Dr. Mabuse, der Spieler*. Hamburg: Rowohlt, 359–82.

Schönemann, Heide (1992) *Fritz Lang: Filmbilder-Vorbilder*. Berlin: Filmmuseum Potsdam and Edition Hentrich.

Silberman, Mark (1995) *German Cinema: Texts in Context*. Detroit: Wayne State University Press.

Sloterdijk, Peter (1988) *Critique of Cynical Reason*. London: Verso.

Smith, Murray (1995) *Engaging Characters: Fiction, Emotion, and the Cinema*. Oxford: Clarendon.

Stooss, Toni (1977) 'Erobert den Film! Oder "Prometheus" gegen "Ufa" & Co' in Neue Gesellschaft für Bildende Kunst (NGBK) and Freunde der Deutschen Kinemathek (eds) *Erobert den Film! Proletariat und Film in der Weimarer Republik*. Berlin: NGBK, 4–48.

Timms, Edward (1986) *Karl Kraus Apocalyptic Satirist*. New Haven and London: Yale University Press.

Wilson, George M. (1986) *Narration in Light*. Baltimore: The Johns Hopkins University Press.

3.3 MEN'S CINEMA
Stella Bruzzi

ACKNOWLEDGEMENTS

I would like to begin by thanking Doug Pye for waiting so patiently for my manuscript and for then editing what I finally sent him with such precision and engagement. His comments were always constructive and have made this study much better than it was otherwise shaping up to be. I am also immensely grateful to Alastair Phillips and Charlotte Brunsdon for making me believe I could actually finish this. Above all I would like to thank my family for letting me carve out the time to write: to Mick for doing all the ballet, judo and riding lessons and to Frank and Phyllis for falling in love with *Master and Commander*, *Gladiator* and *Troy*. The subject of men's cinema has been with me in my teaching for many years, and my biggest debt is to all the groups of students that have, over the last twelve or so years, taken my courses on masculinity. *Men's Cinema* is dedicated above all to the first of these, the class of 1997, who were inspirational and to the last, the class of 2008, who resisted so firmly but with such good humour all my attempts to make them see that *The Deer Hunter* is a great film.

Introduction: Towards a Masculine Aesthetic

Mission: Impossible 2 (2000) effectively has two beginnings, the first kick-starts the plot and centres on the villains; the second establishes the heroic credentials of its hero, Ethan Hunt (Tom Cruise), the man who will fight and eventually defeat these villains. The first beginning ends in violence: a hijacked plane crashing into a mountain as Sean Ambrose (Dougray Scott) and the other bad guys parachute to safety. The plane's explosion on impact cuts sharply to two speeded-up, slaloming aerial shots around dry red canyons, swerving like a hungry bird trying to locate its prey. The pace slows right down as the dwarfed figure of Hunt becomes discernible, climbing a sheer rock face; the camera moves in to a medium shot of him before cutting to a wider angle, the camera circling Hunt: a speck against the hard, vast, roughly-hewn rock formations. The circular move continues but from a higher angle; there is minimal distracting sound – although this is the title sequence too – except Cruise's breath as he exerts himself and the playful beginning of 'Iko-Iko' on the soundtrack (Fig. 0.1). Hunt crouches in a nook for a rest, again filmed from three different angles and distances, the camera (mounted on both rocks and helicopters) perpetually in motion. There follows an

Fig. 0.1

edit to a close-up of Hunt's chalky hand gripping the rock, swiftly replaced by an almost vertical high-angle shot looking down at the daredevil climber attempting this implausibly terrifying vertiginous climb (2,000 feet up, with no safety net apparently). A few more contrasting shots are juxtaposed, followed by a close-up of Hunt's face, looking at something below. A reverse zoom into a tiny ridge indicates what had caught his attention, then three more contrasting images (the first two in slow motion) capture Hunt jumping the 15 feet onto that ridge. All looks well until Hunt loses his footing and slips, the near death fall comprising six different short shots, cumulatively adding to our tension and disorientation. Things briefly come to rest on a close-up of Hunt's hand gripping a small ledge, but this gives way quickly to two high circular shots of Hunt hanging from the rock using one hand. As the camera moves towards him he smiles and swings round into an iron cross shape, facing outwards (Fig. 0.2). With an edit to a frontal close-up of Cruise as Hunt, his bright, muscular arms contrasted with his black vest and unkempt dark hair, there is a zoom into his face and his eyes slowly open, fixing the camera – and us – with a stare that is both steely and ecstatic. *Mission: Impossible 2* displays an interesting relationship to desire and the erotic: although action can take the hero to sex (as demonstrated in the subsequent scene as Hunt and Nyah Nordoff-Hall (Thandie Newton), a deft thief, hide in a hotel after she has stolen a Bulgari

Fig. 0.2

necklace) it frequently supplants it. The end of this sequence is marked by a change of pace with a series of majestic, swooping helicopter shots as Cruise reaches a plateau at the rock's summit; there is momentary tranquillity until mundanity and plot again interrupt in the form of a helicopter, delivering agent Hunt his new mission.

The title sequence of *Mission: Impossible 2* establishes the film's very particular tone, as irony sits alongside but does not subvert the staggering spectacle of the action sequences.[1] The spectator is placed here, as in many other examples of 'men's cinema', in the position of quasi-identification with not only the hero but with the film's visual style. The film's own positioning of itself as masculine is not merely down to how it represents masculinity but also because of the feelings it generates in its audience. The excitement and camaraderie the film tries to make us feel as we are watching the action sequences occur, it seems to me, within mainstream cinema in relation to men and masculinity, if not exclusively then predominantly. These adrenalin-driven emotions are, I will argue, the result of more than a conventionalised identification with the muscular male hero, the figure of idealised masculinity on the screen; they are responses – less intellectual, more spontaneous, physical, visceral even – shaped by the conjunction of stylistic elements, not just a response to representation and narrative. Frequently spectacular, 'men's cinema' uses mise-en-scène alongside character and narrative to convey masculinity, not merely to represent it. Such evocation of masculinity or transmutation of its sensibility onto a film's aesthetics is the reason for it having become imperative to go beyond the critical preoccupation with issues of representation and the body and for feeling the necessity to posit a non-genderised model of response that supplants older models of identification. Taking the discussion away from issues of representation and identification is thereby fundamental.

Mulvey, Neale and problems with representation

This is a study of how, within Hollywood, masculinity is interpreted, understood and conveyed via aesthetics. The title of this Introduction, 'Towards a Masculine Aesthetic', is adapted from Silvia Bovenschen's essay 'Is There a Feminine Aesthetic?', which was written in 1976 and which attempted a definition of the style, not merely the ideology, of 'women's cinema'. Three decades have elapsed and much criticism has been written but it still seems that, for all the writing about masculinity and cinema, a comparable, extended study of 'men's cinema', of masculinity and aesthetics, has not been attempted. Instead, masculinity in cinema is still being understood in ways almost exclusively indebted to feminist film criticism and in particular to Laura Mulvey's essay 'Visual Pleasure and Narrative Cinema' (1975). Just as this work has become the automatic – in many instances *only* – starting point for subsequent feminist analyses of cinema, so Steve Neale's 1983 essay 'Masculinity as Spectacle', which takes as its starting point 'Visual Pleasure', has, almost as frequently and unquestioningly, been taken as the theoretical basis for discussions of masculinity and cinema. In a study of spectatorship written as recently as 2007, Michele Aaron frames her brief discussion of male spectacle (an interesting slippage that in the end sidelines issues of male spectatorship in favour of yet another discussion of male representation) through references to 'Visual Pleasure', Richard Dyer's 1982 essay 'Don't Look Now' about the male pin-up and 'Masculinity as Spectacle'. I will discuss here why these early articles are still considered important, whilst also suggesting ways in which the arguments they formulate can be moved on.

Mulvey polemically issued the manifesto-like declaration, 'It is said that analysing pleasure, or beauty, destroys it. That is the intention of this article',[2] whilst Neale concluded 'Masculinity as Spectacle' (like so much writing on gender in the 1980s) with binary oppositions: 'Where women are investigated, men are tested. Masculinity, as an ideal, at least, is implicitly known. Femininity is, by contrast, a mystery' (1983: 19). Such declarations resound both with accepted notions of difference and confrontation between male and female, masculine and feminine and with an awareness that the *status quo* is and should be under attack.

I have not only become troubled by how Mulvey's radical and incomplete template (which Neale explicitly follows) has become reduced to its famous sound-bites ('Woman as object/man as bearer of the look') but also by how her polemic, her feminist rallying cry, has been taken as fact rather than argument. As a result of these reductions, subsequent readings of Mulvey's original essay have been mobilised to form and perpetuate comparably limited interpretations of masculinity as well as femininity and film, centring almost exclusively, as Neale did and Mulvey was assumed to do, on issues of the look and the body.

Neale, having identified the need to analyse heterosexual masculinity in a similar way to femininity (not yet identified more particularly as *heterosexual* femininity), states his intention in 'Masculinity and Spectacle' to use 'Visual Pleasure and Narrative Cinema' as 'a central, structuring reference point' for examining in particular 'identification, looking and spectacle as she [Mulvey] has discussed them' (1983: 10). Neale's specific attention to these aspects centres specifically on two sorts of looking and concomitant patterns of identification: 'narcissistic' and 'voyeuristic'. An internal struggle seems to run through Neale's article – perhaps between what he would like to discuss and what he feels he ought to discuss – that revolves around how, using Mulvey, men can be identified to be the new women, displaying similar tendencies towards masochism, vulnerability, objectification and eroticisation. However, Neale intimates the existence of a potentially just as interesting theorisation of masculinity in cinema that centres not on representation but on film style and aesthetics when, for example, he refers to the westerns of Sergio Leone, whose heroes 'are rendered almost godlike, hardly qualified at all. Hence, perhaps, the extent to which they are built around ritualised scenes which in many ways are devoid of genuine suspense' (1983: 12). The argument returns to issues other than representation when again Neale talks about Leone's shoot-outs in which, he suggests:

the exchange of aggressive looks marking most western gun-duels is taken to the point of fetishistic parody through the use of extreme and repetitive close-ups. At which point the look begins to oscillate between voyeurism and fetishism as the narrative starts to freeze and spectacle take over. (1983: 17)

Mulvey's psychodynamic paradigm is then reiterated and reinforced over the remaining two pages or so of the article, at the expense of further discussion of style as a generator of meaning. Neale suggests a division – predicated upon Mulvey's active/passive binary model – between male bodies on display in 'masculine' genres such as westerns and action films and the more feminised representations of men in 'feminine' genres such as melodrama, and inevitably proposes a reductive difference between men's and women's cinema based on an essentialist conception of gender. In the more 'masculine' films, Neale argues:

> we are offered the spectacle of male bodies, but bodies unmarked as objects of erotic display. There is no trace of an acknowledgement or recognition of those bodies as displayed solely for the gaze of the spectator. (1983: 18)

Whereas in the more 'feminine' films the male body can explicitly become 'the object of the erotic look' through being feminised (1983:18). 'Feminised' and 'feminisation' as terms are put in inverted commas or italicised, as if we are meant to simply take as read this hugely problematic conflation of gender identities.

The centrality of the body to discussions of masculinity in cinema continues through subsequent film criticism: 'The Body' is the first subheading of Pat Kirkham and Janet Thumim's introduction to their anthology *You Tarzan: Masculinity, Movies and Men* (1993); Steven Cohan's *Masked Men: Masculinity and the Movies in the Fifties* (1997) contains two chapters explicitly focused on the body ('The Body in the Blockbuster', 'The Age of the Chest') as well as several further allusions to its predominance; Yvonne Tasker's *Spectacular Bodies: Gender, Genre and the Action Cinema* (1993), as its title suggests, equates strong masculinity with muscularity; Peter Lehman's edited collection of essays, *Masculinity* (2001), is subtitled *'Bodies, Movies, Culture'*. It is also notable that all these titles place a bare-chested image of a man – usually an actor – on the front cover: Johnny Weissmuller, Kirk Douglas, William Holden, Jean-Claude van Damme and so on. Whether the masculine body is 'triumphant' or 'in crisis', it is through images of muscularity that masculinity is defined (see Tasker 1993: 109). The recent anthology of essays *The Trouble with Men: Masculinities in European and Hollywood Cinema* (2004) sets out the genealogy I have outlined above once more as if it is fact. Its introduction, after stating 'The study of men in film has assumed increasing importance since the 1990s', declares that:

> The study of *the representation of men in films* has been widespread in Film Studies; after all, it is hardly possible to write about a number of film genres – the western, the war film, the gangster film, romantic comedy, the biblical epic, film noir all spring immediately to mind – without touching on masculinities. *However, what concerns us in this volume –*

the systematic exploration of masculinities anchored in the gender paradigm, and which we shall call 'Masculinity in Film Studies' for short – *developed as an afterthought of the feminist-inspired spectatorship paradigm of the period 1975–1985.* (Powrie, Davies & Babington 2004: 1; emphasis added)

Here the automatic conclusion is that the sum total of 'masculinity in Film Studies' is 'the representation of men in films'. Powrie *et al.* make the additional assumption that such critical reductivism is due to the over-reliance of 'masculinity in Film Studies' on 'the feminist-inspired spectatorship paradigm of the period 1975–1985'. It is true that this is, as I have indicated above, the received view of the way in which masculinity has been approached by Film Studies, but it is not the only way, as I hope this study will demonstrate.

Discussions of gender and cinema, and more specifically masculinity and cinema, could have developed along different lines had alternative pieces of early film criticism become the automatic reference points of later criticism. After having discussed the work of Claire Johnston, for instance, Alison Butler, with reference to Christine Gledhill, suggests the potential usefulness and value of an approach to women's cinema 'which prioritises discursive structures over looking relations' (2002: 13), meaning being potentially generated not merely through form and narrative but less systematically via 'a variety of articulations, which may be aesthetic, semantic, ideological and social' (ibid.). The definition of 'women's cinema' was always a different project from any potentially comparable definition of 'men's cinema', as the former necessarily had an active political as well as ideological root, and aesthetics were inevitably allied to this political struggle. However, the manner in which Johnston or E. Ann Kaplan, for instance, sought to define women's cinema in the 1970s and 1980s or how Bovenschen and Mulvey negotiated whether or not there could be a purpose to formulating what might constitute 'a feminine aesthetic', went beyond the debates focused on by the main body of feminist film criticism. As Bovenschen notes in 'Is There a Feminine Aesthetic?':

The exclusion of women from vast areas of production and the public sphere has directed women's imagination along other lines … Is there a feminine aesthetic? Certainly there is, if one is talking about *aesthetic awareness* and *modes of sensory perception*. Certainly not, if one is talking about an unusual variant of artistic production or about a painstakingly constructed theory of art. (1976: 49; emphasis in original)

Several notable feminists argued that women have been compelled to communicate using 'man-made language'[3] and that part of the feminist struggle was to find alternative means and modes of articulating female subjectivity and of describing feminine experience. In the words of British feminist Sheila Rowbotham, 'As soon as we learn words we find ourselves outside them … Language is part of the political and ideological power of the rulers' (1973: 32–3). From a very different perspective, the writings of French literary theorist Hélène Cixous to an extent have formulated and advocated alternative and 'feminine' modes of expression, clustered around the idea of 'l'écriture feminine'. Although Cixous is specifically not saying that 'l'écriture feminine' (loosely translatable as 'feminine writing') is tied to biological difference, she is referring to the idea that an opposition to patriarchy is the foundation for an alternative form of expression, which she allies to the feminine. Within Film Studies, the articulation of a similar opposition has taken various forms and, like Cixous, a writer such as Claire Johnston, in her essay 'Women's Cinema as Counter-Cinema' (1974), advocated the importance to women of working within the mainstream, within the realm of entertainment as well as finding alternative forms through which they could conceptualise their political struggle.

At the outset of 'Male Sexuality in the Media' Richard Dyer posits the possible reason for the absence of critical writing on masculinity as a concept and a style:

> One would think that writing about images of male sexuality would be as easy as anything. We live in a world saturated with images, drenched in sexuality. But this is one of the reasons why it is in fact difficult to write about. Male sexuality is a bit like air – you breathe it in all the time, but you aren't aware of it much. Until quite recently, what was talked about was the mysterious topic of female sexuality, or else, the subject of deviant male practices. Ordinary male sexuality was simple sexuality, and everyone knew what it was. (1985: 28)

The 'masculine' has been the universal, the known, not the 'other' that merits and necessitates critical definition and scrutiny. This study takes as its starting point the need to examine what 'everyone knows', namely the most mainstream, omnipresent and 'ordinary' (as Dyer puts it) forms of cinema, and identifies within this universal what can positively be defined as 'men's cinema' as opposed to what is merely taken for granted. Although masculinity and cinema has, since Dyer wrote this, become a persistent and common subject of film criticism, there is, as indicated by Powrie *et al.* above, still relatively little criticism that engages with what men's cinema looks and feels like.

This discussion of masculinity and mise-en-scène is divided loosely into two halves, both of them more explorative than definitive. It is the second half (chapter two) that articulates in greater detail what I have started out by saying about masculinity being expressed through style as well as through representation and narrative. I examine a series of tropes and motifs that appear in conjunction with masculinity in a variety of films and develop the first stages of a definition of men's cinema as a style and not just an intellectual category. The purpose of chapter one is to ground this discussion by illustrating some of the ways in which masculinity has been expressed via mise-en-scène. The underpinning intention behind the wide-ranging discussions in this first section is to explore some of the ways in which mise-en-scène has always – in some films much more than others – been used to articulate issues of masculinity.

Governing my thinking for this study has always been an interest in 'The Sexual Aberrations' (1905), the first essay of Freud's *Three Essays on Sexuality*, in which Freud outlines – among other things – what constitutes 'normal' sexuality and, by extension (and for the purposes of this argument), 'normal' masculinity. I want to discuss this essay not because I want to then impose a Freudian 'reading' on the films to be examined here, but because Freud's articulation of what constitutes the 'normal' sexual aim and what constitutes a 'perversion' offers an invaluable insight into why definitions of masculinity might have proved so problematic. Firstly, I feel it is necessary to stress that I think 'The Sexual Aberrations' ought to be read as a polemic, in which Freud himself can be seen to be grappling with and deliberately exaggerating the fundamental issues and problems of human sexuality. So what, to Freud, in this seminal essay is 'normal' sex? At the outset of 'The Sexual Aberrations' he establishes the '*sexual object*' as 'the person from whom sexual attraction proceeds' (1991: 45–6)[4] and the '*sexual aim*' as 'the act towards which the instincts tend' (1991: 46); he then, throughout the essay, offers various carefully nuanced definitions of the 'normal sexual aim' and the perversions' relationship to this. The 'normal' sexual aim for Freud in this essay is 'the union of the genitals in the act known as copulation' (1991: 61); the 'normal sexual aim' is thus defined in an excessively and even parodically narrow way – and in such a way that the essay itself seems to be straining to believe. Count, for example, the number of times Freud uses the word 'normal': he doth protest too much and does not himself define 'normal' sexual activity as narrowly as he initially purports to.

Against this definition of the 'normal sexual aim' are the various perversions Freud identifies, starting with the most significant – 'inversion' – before progressing to 'bisexuality', 'fetishism', 'touching and looking' and 'sadism and masochism'. In each case he argues that these become 'perversions' if they take the place of and supplant the act of (heterosexual) copulation, that is, if they pervert the course of 'normal' sex. Although the major part of 'The Sexual Aberrations' is dedicated (in keeping with its title) to these perversions, Freud identifies quite readily the basic problem with the central 'normal' vs. 'perversion' binary, namely that 'even in the most normal sexual process we may detect rudiments which, if they had developed, would have led to the deviations described as "perversions"' (1991: 61–2). As he later elaborates under 'The Perversions in General':

No healthy person, it appears, can fail to make some addition that might be called perverse to the normal sexual aim; and the universality of this finding is in itself enough to show how inappropriate it is to use the word perversion as a term of reproach. (1991: 74)

Freud's argument is, intentionally I am sure, contradictory, in that he itemises in such detail each 'perversion' and identifies why and how it might be pathological, only to say that by and large 'perversions' are part of the 'normal sexual aim' and so not perversions as he has defined them at all.

If one is then to treat 'The Sexual Aberrations' as a polemical and inherently contradictory piece, then the 'normal sexual aim' becomes the ultimate perversion because it is so impossible to attain in its pure state and is predicated upon the insistent, incessant (and ultimately hypocritical) disavowal of sexual acts the majority of us, according to Freud, practice. Likewise masculinity (the *active* partner, in Freud's estimation, of that 'normal' act) is repeatedly defined by what it is not – and through the repression of various perversions, homosexuality in particular. But in thinking about masculinity and cinema, so many examples exist in which the struggle between 'normal' and 'perverse' forces is clearly being enacted via aesthetics, acting, editing, let alone narrative, that masculinity, like the sexual 'normality' it embodies, does not simply exist in opposition to or separate from the repressed aspects of male sexuality, but because of them. There is an argument to be made for masculinity as cinema's ultimate perversion, because it is perpetually defined in relation to the perversions around which it is constructed, but which the ultimate representative of that masculinity (the 'man') so actively represses. With 'The Sexual Aberrations' in the back of my mind, it is now to the unbearable strain of being a man that I now turn.

This is a different 'strain' to that found in Neale, for example, in which 'strain' was seen on the level of representation as the strenuous activity of the male body to become a mechanism by which it fends off potentially weakening objectification, feminisation and eroticisation. More in keeping with Freud's polemical formulation in 'The Sexual Aberrations' is the argument that forms the basis for Dyer's essay on the male pin-up, Dyer suggesting here that the implied activity of the pin-up's body stems more directly from a desire to maintain a distance from both homosexuality and a barely disavowed acknowledgement that heterosexual masculinity is hard to maintain.

1. Masculinity and Visual Style

Under discussion in this first chapter are various examples of mise-en-scène and film style being used to express something about masculinity and a film's male characters that otherwise would remain unacknowledged. There is a significant amount of mise-en-scène analysis that centres on women, particularly within melodrama, and visual style was, from early film criticism of the 1970s, perceived to be, in this genre at least, a conveyor of meaning. As Thomas Elsaesser identified in his pioneering essay 'Tales of Sound and Fury' (1972): 'The domestic melodrama in colour and widescreen, as it appeared in the 1940s and 1950s, is perhaps the most elaborate, complex mode of cinematic signification that the American cinema has produced' (1987: 52). The relationships between masculinity and mise-en-scène in the examples I am about to discuss are not driven exclusively by repression (as Geoffrey Nowell-Smith, for instance, in 'Minnelli and Melodrama' (1987) argues) and, as I argue in relation to film noir, the psychological motivation, when it pertains to masculinity, functions as an outward expression of the heroes' internalised disillusionment or delusion. Conversely, the male anxieties that emerge through the visual style of the 1950s melodramas I then look at are only in part motivated by repression; this might be the case for Kyle Hadley (Robert Stack) in *Written on the Wind* (1956) but in both *There's Always Tomorrow* (1956) and *Rebel Without a Cause* (1955) – discussed here – the relationship between tortured mise-en-scène and the male protagonists' psyches is more convoluted as both Clifford (Fred MacMurray), the unhappy father in *There's Always Tomorrow*, and Jim (James Dean), the unhappy son in *Rebel Without a Cause*, know that they are so even if they persist, to an extent, in disavowing this knowledge. Similarly, the discussion of *The Deer Hunter* (1978) examines in detail the repression – in this instance by the film and not just the characters – of its homosexual subtext, which finds its sub- or pre-conscious expression in the editing. Then, when the discussion moves to the distinctive mise-en-scène elements of *Raging Bull* (1980), repression of all anxieties becomes impossible. This chapter concludes with an analysis of *The Right Stuff* (1983) and phallic imagery; again the somewhat permeable, flexible division between repression and more conscious instincts is acted out in the film's central opposition between Chuck Yeager (Sam Shepard) and the Mercury 7.

Out of the Past and The Lady From Shanghai

In 'How Hollywood Deals with the Deviant Male', Deborah Thomas examines how the strain of masculinity is played out in noir as anxiety clarified by the films' mise-en-scène. She examines in detail the shared sense 'of the essential male-centredness of film noir and of its pervasive mood of anxiety', which she argues:

> ... pervades the entire fabric of such films, and does not merely accrue to its duplicitous women, appearing to linger on despite the resolutions of the narrative and the frequent

restoration of its hero to his 'rightful' place. (1992: 59)

Thomas couches the masculine anxieties in noirs principally in terms of motifs and narrative and uses slightly different psychoanalytic terms to the ones I have outlined above, remarking, for example, that 'much of Hollywood cinema has grappled more or less explicitly with a kind of male schizophrenia which both puts an enormous pressure on men to be "normal" and yet represents such normality in contradictory terms' (ibid.). Nevertheless, the acting out of male anxiety in noir on the level of mise-en-scène is a fundamental idea that I would like to explore further.

Anxiety is frequently attributed to noir's expressionist mise-en-scène but also, on an extended level, permeates much of the criticism surrounding noir – that, for example, there remains so little consensus about how noir can be defined and whether or not it is in fact a genre. One of the broadest but most helpful definitions of noir comes from Paul Schrader, who argues:

> It is not defined, as are the westerns and gangster genres, by conventions of setting and conflict, but rather by the more subtle qualities of tone and mood. (1990: 81)

The contours of noir's style are too well known to rehearse again (the indebtedness to German Expressionism of the films' chiaroscuro lighting, disorientating camera angles, wide-angle lenses, disconcerting close-ups) so what I want to do instead is to examine two sequences in detail that, coming when they do in their respective films, serve to indicate how the underpinning anxiety of noir's mise-en-scène works in relation to masculinity. Frequently it seems as if noir's extreme visual style works on a film's spectator in conjunction with – or perhaps it would be more accurate to say at odds with – the hero's perspective and relative ignorance of the situation evolving around him. We thereby feel an anxiety the hero is oblivious to until in terms of the narrative it is too late. Although the conventional noir mise-en-scène is expressive and rich in style, it is also oblique and elusive when it comes to proffering meaning, in direct contrast to the films' frequently complicated plots that are seldom neatly resolved.

Dictating the tone of the group of films traditionally grouped as Hollywood films noirs is the (vain) attempt to control chaos. Richard Dyer has identified the basic structure of noir as 'a labyrinth with the hero as the thread running through it' (1993: 53) and there are various ways in which I would like to extend this. There are in most noirs three interlinked levels to the male protagonist's embroilment in the labyrinthine plot. Firstly, what occurs in several noirs of the 1940s and 1950s (*Double Indemnity* (1944), *The Postman Always Rings Twice* (1946), *Out of the Past* (1947)) is that, as the hero gets sucked into it, the plot becomes less comprehensible or solvable, thereby functioning in contradistinction, as Dyer notes (see 1993: 53–4), to the classic thriller conventions of Agatha Christie or Arthur Conan Doyle, in which each twist and turn takes the hero and reader closer to solving the mystery, not further away. Secondly, it seems that in many cases the more complex the labyrinthine plot becomes, the less possible it becomes for the hero to exert any control over it, although this is not evident to the hero himself at the time. Finally and paradoxically, the more control over and independence from the plot the hero thinks he has, the less independent or in control he in fact is and the more embroiled in the plot he is becoming. This last stage of the hero's imprisonment is, for the viewer, particularly satisfying and compelling because it is often enacted on the level of mise-en-scène, and so is not tied exclusively to character but open to more instinctual and emotive patterns of response.

Out of the Past illustrates the duality at the centre of the male experience in noir, and the paradox is contained within its structure and by the undermining of Jeff's (Robert Mitchum) voice-over (often indicative of control and conviction) by the uncertainties and chaos indicated by the mise-en-scène. Jacques Tourneur imposes a superficially coherent narrative structure (for example, its cyclic quality) onto events that are not satisfactorily resolved (for example, the film ends on a lie). Symptomatic of Jeff's status within this paradoxical structure is how he is situated within the mise-en-scène. At the heart of the film is an extended sequence in San Francisco, with Jeff going in search of Kathie (Jane Greer) and Leonard Eels (Ken Niles). Despite early on remarking to his cab driver that he realises he is being framed, 'but all I can see is the frame', it is in this section that Jeff feels he is closest to unravelling the deceits of Whit Sterling (Kirk Douglas) and Kathie. How Tourneur uses this motif of 'framing' is crucial to the sequence's tone and to how it conveys that Jeff is more trapped than ever in a labyrinthine plot he does not understand (Figs 1.1–1.3). Between his first conversation with the cabbie to finding the dead body of Leonard Eels, Jeff enters and exits numerous dimly-lit buildings and doors – going through, as it were, frame upon frame, a suggestion of entrapment and ignorance emphasised by the bareness of many of the doorways and buildings he traverses, which at times resemble stark German Expressionist sets. There is a purposefulness to Jeff's chasing but ultimately he gets nowhere, futility that is underlined by the number of doors, apartment buildings and clubs he goes in and out of. When, after finding Eels' body, he encounters Kathie (who tells Jeff she was forced to have Eels killed) he senses he is getting closer to

Fig. 1.1

Fig. 1.2

Fig. 1.3

the truth, but again the mise-en-scène contradicts this, as the lovers are so deeply in shadow as to be almost indecipherable.

A variant on this relationship between the noir protagonist's voice-over and mise-en-scène is the end of Orson Welles' *The Lady from Shanghai* (1947). As Michael (Welles) is coming to, having been rendered unconscious, in the 'Crazy House', his voice-over starts with conviction and certainty: 'I was right, she was the killer, she killed Grisby and now she was going to kill me.' But he talks about his sanity against the expressionist backdrops of wild, intersecting lines, tilted and distorted images and stage sets reminiscent of *Das Cabinet des Dr Caligari* (*The Cabinet of Dr Caligari*, 1920). It is as he is working out that he has been the fall guy that the frequently excessive mise-en-scène of *The Lady from Shanghai* becomes particularly unstable and fragmented, with Michael careering down a slide, being propelled across spinning stages and ending up in a hall of distorting mirrors. Of the parallels between Expressionism and noir Frank Krutnik has commented that 'the distorted mise-en-scène serves as a correlative of the hero's psychological destabilisation' (1991: 5). As Elsa (the 'she' of the initial voice-over, played by Rita Hayworth) enters the hall of mirrors, images multiply and the screen comes to resemble a chaotic kaleidoscope, compounded by the entry of Elsa's husband, Arthur Bannister (Everett Sloane) who, on his crutches, moves across the various mirrors like a tired clockwork toy. The final shoot-out between Elsa and Bannister is almost comic in its chaotic imagery: glass shatters as each shoots randomly at any of the images of the other, not knowing which one is 'real' and which are reflections. The hall of mirrors becomes the ultimate metaphor for the duplicity of noir, the lack of certainty, stable identities and sound knowledge. Only as Michael walks out into the palpable sanity of the blank outside world does the craziness end, but even here there is ambiguity as Michael's last voice-over starts: 'Well, everybody is somebody's fool.'

Sigmund Freud and Josef Breuer's notion of 'conversion hysteria' – the manifestation on the body (via some psychosomatic debilitation) of a repressed psychological trauma – is very much applicable to such moments in noirs, as the films' visual style is used to express or explain things that the heroes do not understand or do not want to recognise about themselves. The conjunction between visual excess and the male protagonists in noir is specifically that the men's traumas (internalised and repressed by them until it is too late) are explicated on the level of mise-en-scène, although a satisfactory point of self-realisation is seldom reached. Nowell-Smith identifies hysteria as 'the energy attached to an idea that has been repressed [and] returns converted into a bodily symptom', then going on to comment: 'The "return of the repressed" takes place, not in the conscious discourse, but displaced onto the body of the patient' (1987: 73). By extension, there is always material that cannot be expressed in the discourse of actions and characters, and so a 'conversion takes place onto the body of the text' (ibid.). It is through visual style rather than plot or dialogue that noirs convey what the male protagonists refuse to acknowledge, namely that they are done for. Even Michael in *The Lady from Shanghai*, who walks away from the final shoot-out unscathed, indicates through his morose voice-over that the effect of Elsa will never leave him.

There's Always Tomorrow and Rebel Without a Cause

As alluded to above, there is a tradition within melodrama criticism of interpreting meaning via mise-en-scène analysis. The tensions and conflicts that come out in the excessively stylised mise-en-scène of many of these melodramas are indirectly compensating for the characters' repressed or disavowed emotions and desires. My intention here is to discuss a series of scenes in male-centred 1950s melodramas in order to illustrate some of the different ways in which mise-en-scène is deployed to relay or act out male anxieties that otherwise remain unarticulated in dialogue and narrative. What is compelling, however, in so many cases (and exemplified by the scenes discussed below) is that the male anxieties expressed via the films' visual style are much closer to the surface and to consciousness than they are in the noir examples. Particularly apparent in the melodramas is not merely that the elaborate visual style *compensates for* the male characters' repressive instincts and lack of introspection or self knowledge; it is more as if the male characters – whose bodily gestures act in conjunction with the films' visual excesses – *are aware of but are consciously disavowing* the tensions and anxieties conclusively expressed through the films' heightened mise-en-scène.

There's Always Tomorrow is one of the most melancholy of Douglas Sirk's melodramas and, in terms of its portrayal of male unhappiness and desperation, one of the most depressing. Elsewhere I have discussed *There's Always Tomorrow* as one of a cluster of mid-1950s Hollywood films, principally melodramas (the others, all from 1956, being *The Wrong Man*, *Bigger than Life* and *The Man in the Gray Flannel Suit*) in which the breadwinner, the supposedly hegemonic male of 1950s America, is shown not to be content and secure as might be expected but as miserable, desperate and insecure.[5] The pervasive and enduring malaise of these films is far from alleviated by their tacked on and deeply implausible 'happy endings'; the hopelessness by this point is woven into the films' fabric and has been signalled in the first instance on the level of mise-en-scène.

The second sequence of *There's Always Tomorrow* is in this respect exemplary, resonating with Clifford's redundancy and unhappiness and setting the tone for the rest of the film. Clifford arrives home from the office, having bought flowers and two tickets for the theatre in anticipation of being able to celebrate his wife Marion's (Joan Bennett) birthday with her *a deux*. As he opens the front door to the family home he enters a deep focus shot dominated by Vinnie (William Reynolds), his teenage son, who is on the telephone arranging a date (Fig. 1.4). Coming home proves to be an alienating, not a welcoming event. As Clifford hovers around him, Vinnie tells his father to 'ssshhh' and Clifford obliges. In an analysis of the scene focusing on performance, Andrew Klevan comments of this moment: 'This begins a pattern

Fig. 1.4

Fig. 1.5

Fig. 1.6

in the sequence of Clifford left behind, left stranded in his house' (2005: 54); the ensuing action that revolves around Clifford is busy and he is literally left behind, as Klevan goes on to observe, when all the other characters eventually leave him at home alone. Frankie (Judy Nugent), the youngest of two daughters, rushes past him on the stairs, barely acknowledging him, and he continues up to the landing, where he presents Marion with the bouquet of flowers. As he does so he leans forward to kiss her, an advance from which she visibly recoils, thankful it seems that one of her children has called out to her so she can go and tend to them instead (Figs 1.5–1.6). This brief exchange is shot from a low angle further down the staircase and through the spindles, heightening again the sense of Clifford's marginalisation and now adding the notion of him being trapped, within the family and within the home. He then tries to improve the situation by telling Marion how special she is and how this, her birthday, is the one day of the year which should be dedicated to her. Marion tells him regretfully that she cannot go to the theatre as it is Frankie's first ballet performance and she had promised to go to it. Here, Clifford and Marion are centre frame, but his speech is interrupted both by Frankie, fussing about getting ready, and then by their other daughter Ellen (Gigi Perreau), on her way out to discuss 'emotional problems' with her friend Gloria. Clifford (all of whose actions so far have been reactive and insignificant) once more follows the action, this time back downstairs, now pleading with Marion, 'Let's go away some place … alone'. Marion is only half listening but promises to go away with her husband the following weekend. Here the framing and the inelegantly high camera angle reflect Clifford's growing redundancy as he hovers on the outskirts of the frame as if about to fall out of it. He tries to interest both Vinnie and Ellen in his wasted theatre tickets and finally asks the cook if she wants them, but even she cannot take them as she is going to look after her grandchild. Everyone except Clifford tumbles out of the door and he is left to have dinner alone.

This sequence so far has been marked by frenetic choreography – children and wife running up and down the stairs, going in and out of different rooms and, most importantly, rushing past Cliff, blocking, framing and iconography being used in tandem to construct a domestic world that barely remembers he is there. If ever there was an example of a man rendered insignificant by the female domain of the home it was this – but then the doorbell rings and at the door is Norma Vale (Barbara Stanwyck), who years earlier had left Los Angeles because she was in love with Clifford. At this point he finally becomes both central to the narrative and central to the frame. He had gone to the door wearing an apron and carrying the coffee pot he has just taken off the stove because it was bubbling over. The coffee escaping from the percolator is an apt concluding simile for his state, now matched and counterbalanced by Norma's arrival – the return, just as Clifford has reached a nadir of despair, of a repressed love. Boundaries are important here and just as the coffee had broken free of its pot, so Norma has intruded upon and disrupted the sterile stability of Clifford's family home.

The marginalisation of the breadwinner father remains the emotional epicentre of *There's Always Tomorrow* and later Clifford reaches a point of being able to articulate his discontent to Marion when telling her:

> I'm tired of the children taking over, I'm tired of being pushed in the corner, I'm tired of being taken for granted … I'm becoming like one of my own toys: Clifford Groves the walkie-talkie robot; wind me up in the morning and I walk and talk and I go to work all day. Wind me up again and I come home at night, eat dinner and go to bed … I'm sick and tired of the sameness, day in day out.

Thus, the eloquence of the film's mise-en-scène intensifies and elaborates what we can also see and hear, our empathetic pain generated by a straightforward identification with Clifford's unhappiness as well as via the visual excesses. Sirk layers on the pain and permits a certain interaction between the spectator's perception of an incident (via excess and symbolism) and the character's not entirely successfully repressed realisation of their state.

A more grandiose but equally pregnant 1950s example of male anxiety being 'siphoned off' (as Nowell-Smith terms it) onto and articulated through the fraught melodramatic mise-en-scène is the opening scene of Nicholas Ray's *Rebel Without a Cause*. Jim Stark, Judy (Natalie Wood) and Plato (Sal Mineo) are the adolescents who have separately ended up being detained at the local police station (Jim having been brought to the station – as the title sequence shows – for underage drinking). I am here going to look specifically at the exchange between Jim, his parents and his grandmother, which in terms of its heightened visual style establishes the tense mood of the rest of the film. Jim is in the station's public area waiting to be interviewed, while the resident counsellor/psychologist talks to first Judy then Plato. Offscreen comes the sound of Jim's mother (Ann Doran) calling his name. Jim is seated on a leather chair set on a raised platform; as he hears his parents' and grandmother's arrival, he slowly stands up, an action marked – as are subsequent parent/son confrontations – by an intrusive and mannered mise-en-scène (Fig. 1.7). For the arrival of his parents, Jim is firstly positioned to the extreme left of the Cinemascope frame; the camera is also set at a low angle, which serves to destabilise the scene, an effect accentuated by the

Fig. 1.7

height at which Jim is standing – his feet almost level with the bottom of the frame. On the extreme left of frame, he takes up very little of Ray's stretched screen space, underscoring through literal marginalisation his as yet unverbalised personal insecurities. As he moves to stand up (slowly, tentatively, drunkenly – all traits further emphasised by the destabilising framing), Jim never gets to the point of being upright, and in remaining slightly bent appears to be – again literally – constrained by and trapped within the frame. His parents and grandmother (Virginia Brissac) then come into shot, low in the frame due to the angle of the camera, and Jim is left hanging over them, precariously as opposed to threateningly positioned. The juxtaposition of Cinemascope and tight framing has a literalness about it, creating the physical sense of Jim not fitting the frame, rather like Lewis Carroll's Alice being squeezed into an undersized house.

Fig. 1.8

Jim then falls back into the leather chair and finally comes down to his family's level, at which point he does stand straight. After the psychologist has talked with Plato, he brings Jim and his family into his office (Fig. 1.8). The contrast between this office and the public space outside it is marked; the use of Cinemascope again contributes to a feeling of entrapment, as the office is cramped and the five characters are squeezed into it. It is this more visually mundane sequence that explains or rather gives a context to the excesses of its predecessor, as Jim and his parents start to squabble. Immediately, this local argument about Jim's drunkenness becomes a wider metaphorical one about parent/son relations, as Jim's father, Frank (Jim Backus), asks of his son (*a propos* of nothing much) why he keeps 'slamming the door in my face', before progressing to: 'We give you love and affection, don't we? Then what is it?' It is after this escalation of the petty argument that Jim cries out, 'You're tearing me apart!', a grossly exaggerated response to the classic and bad-tempered familial exchange but one that is entirely in keeping with the film's highly wrought visual style.

The tensions of the sequence in the police station are accentuated throughout by Ray's pointed use of Cinemascope, the depth of field and the breadth of the image (anomalously majestic for such a prosaic setting) being used in two ways: to lose Jim within the frame by prioritising or drawing attention to subsidiary actions and to show him trapped by and within it. Thus the opening scene with Jim sets up the relationship between the melodramatic emotional dynamics in *Rebel Without a Cause* and the mannerist use of the camera throughout, for example in the scene when Jim returns home after the 'chicken run', in which the prelude for another key confrontation between son and parents is the camera moving from upside down through ninety degrees, mimicking Jim getting up from the sofa. In addition to establishing the audience's affinity with Jim, the film's visual expressiveness again provides a means of exploring and conveying Jim's internalised angst on a primal, physical level, the audience having been invited to empathise with him by being moved not only vicariously by his narrative situation but also more directly by the emotiveness of the mise-en-scène. It is not only that Jim's repressed anxiety finds its most fulsome expression in the mise-en-scène nor that the extravagances of the melodrama's mise-en-scène relates exclusively to the characters (Elsaesser's (1987) comment, for instance, that the men in these films are trying to live up to an exalted vision of man), but that our empathetic anxiety is awakened by the paralleling of what is going on in the film at a literal, narrative level with what is being implied via its visual style: hence the tilted camera, for example, becoming in more than one scene an externalised extension of Jim's feelings of entrapment and confinement.

Melodrama, repression and excess in *The Deer Hunter*

Rebel Without a Cause and other male melodramas of the 1950s centre on the notion of 'being', or of 'becoming', a man, and the expressive visual style of these films evokes and gives an aesthetic context to the specific traumas of the transition to manhood or of not matching up to an imaginary masculine ideal. Clifford in *There's Always Tomorrow* and Jim in *Rebel Without a Cause* are further linked by how their internalised anxieties find expression in the highly wrought mise-en-scène, namely that they find themselves acting out these anxieties as if they are not so much *repressed* as *suppressed* or *disavowed*. There are many other ways besides different levels of repression in which the crises of masculinity are enacted, confronted and voiced on the level of mise-en-scène. Before moving the discussion on to a consideration of the active, subjective evocation of masculine identity through visual style, I would like to return to one last repression, perhaps the most fundamental to the construction of masculinity: the repression of homosexuality.

Freud's idea that heterosexual masculinity is predicated upon the (successful) repression of homosexuality is exemplified by a film such as Michael Cimino's *The Deer Hunter*, a film ostensibly 'about' the Vietnam War (as its narrative revolves around the wartime experiences of its three central characters) but which signals, primarily through its editing, the presence of a deeply repressed and unresolved homosexual narrative. Unlike the almost acknowledged repressions that drove the male characters of the noirs and melodramas previously discussed, the characters of Michael (Robert de Niro) and Nick (Christopher Walken) in *The Deer Hunter* remain deeply repressed on all levels, but, arguably, here such repression also characterises the film itself. What several critics, myself included, have offered are therefore 'against the grain' readings of *The Deer Hunter*.

The fear of homosexuality drives many cultural representations of masculinity; positive masculine identification is so hysterically tied up with an obsession with *not being homosexual* that – rather like the ultimate conundrum offered by 'The Sexual Aberrations' (Freud 1905) being that perversity is the ultimate normality – homosexuality, through needing to be systematically repressed, becomes the *sine qua non* of masculinity. In so many narratives the man's fear is the fear of an externalised 'other' that is actually, as it turns out, the embodiment of his own perceived internal inadequacies, most significantly homosexuality.[6] Discussions of repressed homosexuality in *The Deer Hunter* have centred on the homoerotic undertones sounded by the feminisation of Nick; as Christine Gledhill has argued in her discussion of the bar scene on the eve of Steven's (John Savage) wedding, in which Nick dances and sings along to 'I Can't Take My Eyes Off You', Walken's 'androgynous' performance 'momentarily escapes the constricting male stereotypes of leader or lead' (1995: 80). Walken, who trained as a dancer (and much later in his career shimmied his way effortlessly through Spike Jonze's video for Fat Boy Slim's 'Weapon of Choice' and danced memorably with his wife in *Catch Me If You Can* (2002)), offers an intriguing disruption to the declared heterosexuality of Steven's stag night. Robin Wood also discusses Walken's persona as mediating 'the cultural definitions of masculinity and femininity' (2003: 260) and his performance as projecting 'those properly human qualities which our culture ... chooses to label feminine' (2003: 261). Wood argues that:

> The narrative of *The Deer Hunter* is posited on, largely motivated by, the love of two men for each other, but this, far from being a problem, is assumed to be unequivocally positive and beautiful; therefore, the film is compelled to permit the spectator to pretend that its sexual implications do not exist. At the same time, it leaves remarkably clear, if not always coherent and consistent, traces, so that those who wish to see may do so. (2003: 260)

The crux of Wood's interpretation is the eroticised permeability of the heterosexual war film text by the homosexual melodrama, as it invites the spectator not merely to read the film against the grain by unearthing a submerged subversive subtext, but also to see that subversive subtext come out at a textual level. Wood identifies key points on a narrative level when this occurs, while I would like to discuss in detail a couple of scenes in which the tense interrelationship with homosexuality is drawn out through editing.

The first is the exchange of looks between Michael and Nick during the dancing at Steve and Angela's (Rutanya Alda) wedding. This wedding in Clairton, Pennsylvania, is not unproblematically joyous as it is coloured by its 'ominous proximity to Vietnam' (Wood 2003: 252), as Michael, Nick and Steven are leaving for the war the next day, an eventuality signalled by a banner wishing them well and black and white high school photos of the three of them adorning the walls. At this Russian Orthodox wedding, Nick and Linda (Meryl Streep) form part of a dancing group alongside Steven and others while Michael is drinking at the bar. His first look over towards the dance floor is ostensibly aimed at Linda, as in the reverse shot she is central. Shortly after, however, there is another shot of the dancing group, and this time Nick is clearly centre frame, after which there is a brief shot of an older couple eating, before a cut back to Michael, walking away from the men at the bar and towards a doorway, where he stands looking again and more intently at the revellers. On this occasion the reverse shot indicates that Michael's look definitely alights on Nick. When we return to Michael he is still looking in the general direction of the dancing but now turned slightly to his left, looking as it turns out, towards the large photo of a younger Nick hanging on the wall (Figs 1.9–1.12). When Michael then reverts to watching the dancers again, there is an exchange of looks between Nick and Michael, although it is Linda who gets self-conscious as she wrongly senses she is the one being looked at, an attraction tentatively confirmed a little later as Michael makes a drunken pass at her at the bar.

Fig. 1.9

This rapid sequence of shot/reverse-shots can only really imply one thing: that, as Wood suggests, *The Deer Hunter* revolves around a love story between two men, Michael and Nick, lent a bit of legitimacy through the implication of Linda as the third corner of their erotic triangle – the woman through whom the men indirectly express and consummate their illicit love for each other. The most erotically charged and poignant look is Michael's at the old photo of Nick, an enigmatic and dreamy image of Walken in a home-knit sweater gazing out into the middle distance, a sort of matinee idol shot weighed down by innocence and nostalgia: the innocence of youth (prior to the 'experience' of an adulthood represented first by Steven's marriage and then by Vietnam) and the nostalgia for a pre-adult stage when loving your friend as Michael does Nick was not so problematic. It is important, therefore, that there is never a comparable exchange of glances between Michael and Nick to the one between Michael and Linda; homosexual possibilities are here buried deep within the sensuous dreaminess of homosocialism, a concept that will be elaborated below.

Fig. 1.10

Fig. 1.11

Fig. 1.12

The doomed and repressed homosexual desire resurfaces again most keenly around the time of Nick's disappearance in Saigon, as he is spirited away by a mysterious Frenchman, Julien (Pierre Segui). Nick has just left hospital, where we had seen him traumatised, hardly able to recall his parents' names. Sitting on a veranda wall, he opens his wallet and slides a passport shot of Linda out of one of the compartments, an action he repeats when, having been discharged, he tries unsuccessfully to put a call through to her. Then, in Saigon, Nick mistakes another man for Michael, a misrecognition that triggers a frenetic and self-destructive series of events, beginning with his abortive visit to a prostitute from whom he flees, only to find himself irresistibly drawn towards the sound of a revolver being fired. In a dim alley he meets Julien, who offers him a glass of champagne and warns, 'When a man says no to champagne, he says no to life.' The gunshot had come from a game of Russian roulette and the Frenchman tries to get Nick interested in going to see it, but Nick protests: 'You've got the wrong guy.' However, in an indirect echo of the wedding dance sequence, Nick does go and while he is watching the roulette, he finds himself the focus of both the Frenchman's gaze and Michael's, who coincidentally happens to be there. After the players have fired the gun, Nick snatches it and puts it to his head, pulling the trigger before running off (the chamber is empty); Michael runs after him, but Nick gets into the Frenchman's car; he turns round and presumably sees Michael (the object of his quest only a little while earlier), but rather than leave the Frenchman for Michael, he instead turns away from his friend with an expression close to annoyance before hurling a wad of money into the air, an act that effectively separates him from Michael as a swarm of Saigonese get down off their scooters to grab what notes they can, blocking the road. Michael is left looking on, helpless.

Fig. 1.13

Fig. 1.14

The next scene is Michael's return to Clairton. On getting to his hotel room, Michael squats against the wall (in a pose reminiscent of Nick's on the hospital veranda) and takes out Nick's wallet (which he must have salvaged in Saigon), repeating Nick's gesture of slipping out the photo of Linda, an action followed by a shot of Michael and then another shot of the photo, exactly as it had been in the hospital with Nick (Figs 1.13–1.14). Heterosexuality in *The Deer Hunter* is problematic. As the epicentre of the film's heterosexuality, Steven and Angela are troubled: after their shotgun wedding Steven leaves immediately for Vietnam only to return having lost both his legs, an injury that, in the context, could be seen to indicate castration. Then there is Linda's surprise and inconclusive engagement to Nick. As a riposte to the homoerotically charged but deeply repressed wedding sequence, the urgency of the Saigon sequence seems important in that it signals this as the moment when Nick turns his back on his old life and embraces a new one less obliquely framed as homosexual. The abandon with which Nick flings the money into the air in Saigon as if unshackling himself from Michael (and by extension Linda) suggests this, as does the fact that the Frenchman appears to spot something in Nick that marks him out as different. Ostensibly this special quality is the death wish that prompts Nick to become a Russian roulette player; that it is homosexuality is implied through the Frenchman's gesture of plying Nick with champagne and whisking him off in his fancy car, much as a client might a prostitute. Also, there is Michael's later mirroring of Nick's action with the photo of Linda and also that he found and saved his friend's wallet. Upon his return to Clairton Michael starts a sexual relationship with Linda, but their shared melancholy suggests that both are sleeping with the other as a substitute for Nick.

That the relationship between Michael and Nick can be called a 'love affair' is underlined in the film's penultimate sequence when Michael goes back to Saigon to find Nick, just as the city is about to fall. As Victor Perkins pointed out to me, there are unmistakeable similarities with the myth of Orpheus's descent into the underworld to save Euridice. Making the parallel with Orpheus also helps explain not only the intensity of the roulette contest Michael engineers against Nick in which Nick dies, but also the fact that, after so much time being lucky and not dying, his luck turns at precisely the moment at which his lover comes back for him. Just as Orpheus cannot help himself and turns round to see that Euridice is following him despite having been told that if he does so he will lose her forever, so Nick's recognition of Michael (and the association of 'one shot' to his deer hunting past) precipitates the luck running out. The love affair is compelled to remain unconsummated and repressed.

The formative role played by the repression of homosexuality in the formation of masculinity is outlined by Eve Kosofsky Sedgwick as she puts forward her definition of 'homosocialism' in the opening chapter of *Between Men: English Literature and Male Homosocial Desire* (1985), a critique of masculinity that is extremely useful for an analysis of *The Deer Hunter*. Sedgwick posits that heterosexual masculinity can only be satisfactorily constructed if its opposite, homosexuality, is denied and actively repressed. Sedgwick argues, however, that men, having successfully repressed homosexuality, will still need to find a means of interacting erotically with other men via what she terms 'male homosocial desire', which she defines thus:

'Male homosocial desire': the phrase in the title of this study is intended to mark both discriminations and paradoxes. 'Homosocial desire', to begin with, is a kind of oxymoron. 'Homosocial' is a word occasionally used in history and the social sciences, where it describes social bonds between persons of the same sex; it is a neologism, obviously formed by analogy with 'homosexual', and just as obviously meant to be distinguished from 'homosexual'. In fact, it applies to such activities as 'male bonding', which may, as in our society, be characterised by intense homophobia, fear and hatred of homosexuality. (1985: 1)

Having identified her terrain as that which centres on desire, Sedgwick then develops her idea of the 'continuum' that links the polarities of both male and female sexual, erotic experience when she argues that, while in men the opposition between the 'homosocial' and the 'homosexual' is dichotomous and discontinuous, for women there is a fluid continuum from one potential polarity to another, that 'however conflicting the feelings … women in our society who love women, women who teach, study, nurture, suckle, write about, march for, vote for, give jobs to, or otherwise promote the interests of other women, are pursuing congruent and closely related activities' (1985: 2–3). For Sedgwick there is a simplicity and relaxedness about the various sexual and non-sexual women's relations and how they inform and interact with each other that is lacking in the comparable relations between men. Sedgwick's argument about men is more convincing than her argument about women on this point of the continuum, and it becomes increasingly clear that it is men and the complexities of desire that surround and define them, that really intrigue her. The proposal that all female experience is part of a solid continuum is utopian and, as a theoretical idea, relatively unformed. Writing in the mid-1980s (the 'hard-bodied' Reagan era covered by Susan Jeffords)[7], Sedgwick argues convincingly that 'it has apparently been impossible to imagine a form of patriarchy that was not homophobic', that 'homophobia directed against both males and females is not arbitrary or gratuitous, but tightly knit into the texture of family, gender, age, class and race relations. Our society could not cease to be homophobic and have its economic and political structures remain unchanged' (1985: 3–4). In order to believe in itself, Sedgwick suggests, heterosexual masculinity must repress and vilify homosexuality; desire between men is siphoned off into intense 'bonding' activity whose direct link to sexual desire has been broken but which nevertheless still possesses a suppressed erotic component.

In the subsequent chapter Sedgwick outlines and applies René Girard's idea that an 'erotic triangle' exists between a woman and two men in which 'the bond that links the two rivals is as intense and potent as the bond that links either of the rivals to the beloved; that the bonds of "rivalry" and "love", differently as they are experienced, are equally powerful and in many senses equivalent' (1985: 21). A woman desired by two men thereby becomes the figure through whom two men, unable to express their desire for each other openly, can find an outlet for this desire. This could have been written with the triangular relationship between Michael, Nick and Linda in mind. What is strikingly relevant about Sedgwick's notion of homosocialism to my definition of men's cinema is that it enforces both the repression of homosexuality by masculinity while still permitting homosexuality to have a role in defining masculinity. There are few texts that illustrate this quite as clearly as *The Deer Hunter*, a film emblazoned with its disavowal, proclaiming itself to be a film *about* Vietnam, while really being about a set of personal relationships wrecked by Vietnam, most notably the shattered friendship between Michael and Nick.

The body and the text: *Raging Bull*

In many of Martin Scorsese's films there exists a strong correlation between style, meaning and masculinity. There is, for instance, a uniformity about the moment when the male protagonist first spies the woman with whom he is about to fall in love. Whether (to cite three Robert de Niro examples) it is Travis Bickle noticing Betsy (Cybill Shepherd) for the first time in *Taxi Driver* (1976) or Jake La Motta seeing the underage Vickie (Cathy Moriarty) by the pool in *Raging Bull* or Ace spotting Ginger (Sharon Stone) playing the tables in *Casino* (1995), this event is always marked first by its specified relation to the male protagonist's lusting gaze and second by the mobilisation of a series of stylistic tropes that serve to fetishise, eroticise and objectify the (mute) woman, such as slow motion, close-up or a zoom or track into her body. In *Raging Bull*, Jake is still married to his first wife when he asks his brother Joey (Joe Pesci) who Vickie is. The point at which he falls in love with her is marked not just by action and dialogue but by how it is filmed: the slightly slow-motion shot of Vickie's legs moving to and fro in the water, the sensuous ripples caressing her young flesh as Jake imagines he would like to.

Raging Bull is a nostalgic film and the languidness of these shots of Vickie hark back to classical examples of male infatuation, such as the moment when Jeff's voice-over in Out of the Past says dreamily, 'And then I saw her...', as he first sees Kathie coming into a bar in Acapulco. In Raging Bull, however, the domains of masculine and feminine are not so definitively demarcated, for either side of the short sequence of shots of Vickie at the poolside there is the fleeting use of close-up and sensuous slow motion in specific conjunction with images of Sal (Frank Vincent) and other Mafiosi friends, a far less conventional eroticisation of the masculine form that Scorsese uses a number of times in this film and elsewhere – for example the opening sequence of Goodfellas (1990). Whereas in Goodfellas it is categorically Henry Hill's (Christopher Serrone, later Ray Liotta) attraction to Paulie Cicero (Paul Sorvino) and the other Mafia guys who own the taxi rank across the street that is being indicated by the specific conjunction of his introductory voice-over and the fetishistic slow-motion close-ups of their gaudy accessories and flashy shoes as they emerge from their cars, this affinity between male protagonist and desire for the Mafia is, in Raging Bull, far more tentatively defined and these slow-motion interludes are more there for the spectators' enjoyment than directly suggestive of Jake's attraction or jealousy.

Masculinity is problematised and rendered complex via mise-en-scène early in Raging Bull, thereby complementing another recurrent feature of Scorsese's treatment of masculinity, which is the male protagonist being shown at the beginning to be confident and in control, only for the remainder of the film to be taken up with his demise. The transition from one state to the other is particularly marked in Raging Bull as a couple of minutes into the film, just after the elegiac beauty of the title sequence (of which more in a moment), there is an abrasive cut to the older, fatter, uglier Jake preparing, in 1964, the dreary anecdotes and gags for 'An Evening with Jake la Motta' (Figs 1.15–1.16). On the one hand, Raging Bull is exemplary of the supremacy-to-defeat narrative structure, as it is propelled by the struggles between victory and defeat, between personal happiness and jealousy and so on. On the other, it plays out these struggles not just on the level of narrative but also on the level of mise-en-scène.

Fig. 1.15

The ease and beauty of the film's title sequence has been remarked upon frequently. With its breathtaking elegance, it lures us in; in soft, grainy black and white[8] and to the accompaniment of the intermezzo from Mascagni's Cavalleria Rusticana, Jake shadow-boxes around a ring dressed in his trademark leopard-print robe. The images – captured largely through the ropes along one side of the ring – are slightly slowed down, making this

Fig. 1.16

otherwise ugly pugilist (La Motta was no Ali) seem almost dainty as he dances around the ring and swings at the air, an air filled with smoke that shrouds the ambiguous figure of Jake in mystique, even majesty. The music, the fluidity of the movements (both Jake's and the camera's) and the soft monochrome film stock all suggest these titles form an elegy rather than an opening, but for what? Pam Cook, in still the most emotive and moving article on *Raging Bull*, argued that the film's tragedy centres on masculinity and loss: that 'masculinity is put into crisis so that we can mourn its loss' (1982: 40). Certainly, the juxtaposition of beauty and loss is enacted starkly at the outset, as the lithe, fit and idealised Jake of the titles is swiftly replaced by the prosthetically deformed Jake of 1964, in his too-tight shirt and dinner jacket, rehearsing under his crude and unsubtle dressing room lights. The flat ugliness of this latter image also contrasts significantly with the depth and beauty of the title sequence.

Later, amid her discussion of *Raging Bull* and cinephilia, Cook remarks:

Then there is the film's visual pleasure: the excitement of the mise-en-scène which alternates between long, reflective shots which allow us to contemplate the scene in safety, at a distance, and explosions of rapid montage which assault our eyes and ears, bringing us right into the ring with the fighters. Sometimes we almost literally get a punch in the eye. I don't like boxing; but the illusion of 'being there', the risk involved, is a real turn-on. The film moves and excites by making the past immediately present, by making us present in history. For women, perhaps, this illusion of presence is doubly exciting, since we are generally represented as outside history. But the price of that pleasure is an identification with masculinity on its terms rather than our own. (1982: 42)

Cook is worth quoting at length here, as it is important for my commentary on the film to get from the diverse pleasures of *Raging Bull*'s mise-en-scène to issues of excitement and identification. I am less concerned – no doubt in part because I am writing 25 years after Cook – with matters of gender and difference and more interested in questions of how a film conveys masculine subjectivity (Jake's and that assumed by the mise-en-scène) and how such subjectivity flourishes, so prompting the instinctual and non-cerebral audience identification Cook touches on. Up until this point my primary focus has been films in which the mise-en-scène is linked expressively to masculinity and its representations. With *Raging Bull* – and inspired in this instance by Cook's response to it – the argument is moving on towards identifying certain repeated stylistic tropes that have become identified within Hollywood with masculinity, and which elicit from their films' audiences emotive and instinctual responses. The implications of the relationship between image and audience that I am proposing here opens up the possibility that the expressiveness of a film's mise-en-scène can be mobilised to urge or compel those watching and enjoying to become part of this expressiveness, to physically and emotionally respond, in these instances, to a film's conceptualisation of masculinity. 'Conceptualisation' is used here as a term to indicate the drawing together of representation and mise-en-scène, to indicate that the latter can be used to explain or convey the essence or character of the former. Unlike Cook, who differentiates not only between Scorsese's 'long, reflective shots' and the 'explosions of rapid montage' but also between their effects on the audience (that the former allows us to stand back from a scene, whereas the latter 'brings us right into the ring'), I tend to see the vast array of visual tropes and editing styles as all part of *Raging Bull*'s overriding preoccupation with the essence of masculinity and how to evoke it – its inconsistencies, its fragmentation, its complexity.

Fig. 1.17

One of the key shots in the film is the 90-second Steadicam shot of Jake La Motta walking from his dressing room to the ring to fight Marcel Cerdan (Louis Raftis) in Detroit, 1949, for the middleweight title (which La Motta wins) (Figs 1.17–1.20). The shot charts Jake's final preparations in the dressing room, his journey through the corridors and tunnels that lead to the arena and his eventual emergence into the crowd awaiting the start of the title fight. In his discussion of this shot Todd Berliner gives a useful potted history of the Steadicam, a system that enables the camera operator to obtain smooth tracking shots using a harnessed-on hand-held camera and without the need for tracks, dollies or cranes (see 2005: 50–1). In 1980, the Steadicam was a recent invention, first used commercially by Haskell Wexler in *Bound for Glory* (1976). Scorsese and his cameraman, Michael Chapman, also used the small, lightweight Arriflex 35 BL camera. Berliner makes the comparison with the generic follow-the-star-onto-stage shot of so many music and performance documentaries (*Dont Look Back* (1967) and *The Last*

Fig. 1.18

Fig. 1.19

Fig. 1.20

Waltz (1978) are two of Berliner's examples) that is parodied so effectively in Rob Reiner's *This is Spinal Tap* (1984), as the band get lost trying to find the stage. It is also reminiscent of Albert Maysles' long hand-held tracking shot in Robert Drew's documentary *Primary* (1960), following John Kennedy as he makes his way through swelling crowds into a hall where he is due to make a speech. That shot at that time was, in technical terms, a show-off, macho, 'look at what I can do with the new lightweight cameras' moment that befitted its subject matter: the rise and imminent victory of John Kennedy, the fresh, dynamic new face of American politics, about to clear out Eisenhower's 1950s Republicans by defeating the incumbent vice president, Richard Nixon. The Steadicam shot in *Raging Bull* makes, initially at least, a similar impact: encapsulating and allowing us to revel in Jake's big moment of success. The straightforwardness, however, of this relationship to the mise-en-scène is short-lived as the shot's implied linearity is rendered more complex by how the sequence goes on to end and by how it is contrasted with the subsequent scene, as will be developed in a moment.

What makes the Steadicam tracking shot in *Raging Bull* both compelling and satisfying as a viewing experience is the synchronisation of gesture, sound, meaning and camera movement. Although Berliner remarks that, at the point when the 'backward tracking shot becomes, with hardly a pause, a forward tracking shot' we, the audience, lose our 'sense of privilege' and become merely one of the fans (2005: 51), the shifts in direction do not fundamentally interrupt fluidity and tone. It seems more important that this shot's smooth grandiloquence exists beyond the immediate confines of narrative and character and is used instead to connote or translate the intermingling of triumph and masculinity. Contrary to Berliner, I actually feel that the moment at which the camera peels away from La Motta and starts to soar and circle the action as he continues through the roaring crowds to the ring is the moment of maximum adrenalin and heightened identification. Our point of identification is not so much La Motta as the rush of power he is shown to be experiencing. That is, until it stops. Unlike the music, which keeps going, the soaring camera move is unexpectedly cut short before it has reached any natural end, replaced by the relative mundanity of the referee in the centre of the ring introducing Jake. This technique of interrupting a shot or camera move with a sharp edit occurs elsewhere as well and signals the deflation of whatever idealisation of masculinity precedes it. Cook likens the structure of *Raging Bull* to tragedy, and these brusque truncations could be viewed as interruptions to our cathartic enjoyment of tragedy, all part of the film's preoccupation not with masculine success but with masculine disintegration. In keeping with this, when La Motta finally wins the middleweight championship at the end of the bout with Cerdan, his crowning moment is resolutely undermined by an edit even more cruel than the transition from title sequence to 'An Evening with Jake La Motta'. Jake's moment of triumph is conspicuously disjointed and shortlived. The referee comes over to La Motta to declare him the winner, Cerdan being unable to continue. The sound becomes muted and dreamlike (we can hear the referee's words but they are definitely subsidiary) as Jake raises his arms, goes over to Cerdan's corner, then is held aloft, images that are juxtaposed with shots of a sea of press cameras, flashbulbs popping with arhythmic speed. Jake is then lowered to the floor and, with his gloved fists in the air once more, he looks down (framed in a medium shot) to the World Champion's belt being put around his waist, distant chants resonating in the background. There is a cut to a tighter shot that has Jake to the right of frame, his arms around the men beside him and tears in his eyes. This has been slowed down slightly, and the slow motion is held over into the next shot, a repeat image of the belt being put on Jake, this time from a low angle. The muffled fizz of the flashbulbs firing continues over a final image, a close-up of the belt around Jake's middle, the last bulb sounding in synch with the edit to the next scene and the subtitle 'Pelham Parkway, New York, 1950', a scene that opens with a ballooning La

Motta in opened shirt and shorts bashing his television set in a vain attempt to obtain a picture, while scoffing a sandwich.

Raging Bull's masochism has often been remarked upon, largely in relation to the pummelling endured by Jake's body during the boxing bouts; the brutal battering he suffers and the masochism he displays when being subjected to this repeatedly signals the loss of any stable notion of the masculine subjectivity so mourned by Cook. Equally resonant is a certain masochistic tendency inherent within the film's style – for example, interrupting a flowing camera move, the disjointed editing or denying the spectator a straightforward cathartic response to the boxing bouts. *Raging Bull* is frenetic and disjointed; pockets of fluidity reside amidst a pervasive visual style that is fragmentary and wholly antithetical to the ponderous predictability of the more traditional boxing movies such as *Rocky* (1976) that Scorsese consciously did not want to emulate. Shots, particularly bombastic ones, are not permitted to remain unqualified; the big aesthetic moments in *Raging Bull* are integrated, not show-stopping *tours de forces* like big musical numbers. Berliner starts his article by saying provocatively: 'Visually, *Raging Bull* is almost an artistic fiasco. The film's visual style seems often on the point of falling to pieces' (2005: 41). He refers to its 'ludicrous' images and illogical shot sequences – all true, in terms of the repeated, virtually ritualistic defiance of the 180-degree rule, for instance – although this 'visual absurdity' masks an intellectual and emotional cohesiveness that Berliner somewhat elides.

One place in which this intellectual coherence comes out is in the parallel between body and film, so that what is happening on a narrative level, principally to Jake's body (the violence, the pain, the masochism) is also being transmitted and felt on the body of the film, the surface of the text. This is what renders *Raging Bull* moving and, if anything, effects some form of catharsis. One fight that Berliner and others have focused on is the last of the film and the third bout with Sugar Ray Robinson (Johnny Barnes), when Sugar Ray wins back the middleweight title. Berliner picks out the slow-motion shot of Robinson winding up for a punch, his body surrounded by smoke or steam, as one of the many 'implausible images' that 'permeate the film, especially its fight sequences' (ibid.), further commenting that Robinson's stance is 'ridiculously awkward … like a third-grader pretending to be a fighter' (ibid.) (Fig. 1.21). The degree of critical distance Berliner is exercising here, though, ignores or marginalises the sequence's affective power, for the illogicality of the shots is redolently expressive of both our mixed, equivocal responses as spectators and Jake's own internalised contradictions. Towards the end (Round 13) of this terrible fight La Motta takes a barrage of punches from Robinson of which the wheeling, expressionistic punch described above is just one. La Motta is on the ropes, tempting Robinson to have another go at him ('Come on Ray'). Silence descends briefly and Robinson, centre-frame, surges towards both La Motta and, through the point-of-view angle, the camera, then there follows a reverse shot of Jake

Fig. 1.21

and another of Ray, the splicing together of 'implausible images' mirroring the battery La Motta is receiving. During these gruesome close-ups, the destruction of Jake's body is emphasised not only via the close-ups themselves of blood and other liquids spurting from him, but by the tempestuous collisions on the level of mise-en-scène and sound: the mismatched angles, the amplified noises, the slow motion, the dark, unpopulated backdrop to Ray's killer punch.

In this final fight there are the consecutive close-ups of Jake's bloodied and bloated face, taking Sugar Ray's punches; the images defy sense and are from conflicting high angles. In a Soviet, notably Kuleshovian way, the sequence is made sense of by the spectator; its internal dynamics defy spatial, temporal and generic logic entirely. I would argue that the supposed illogicality and fragmentariness of *Raging Bull*'s mise-en-scène can be viewed as part of the film's pervasive masochism, as the disjointedness of its visual construction interrupts and interferes with our potentially more straightforward responses to its emotional core. Thus, Jake's pleasure at finally becoming world champion is fleeting, just as the beauty of the title sequence cuts rudely to the overweight, disfigured Jake rehearsing his clunky nightclub gags. We are offered cathartic potential only for this to be interrupted or denied. At the end of La Motta's losing fight with Robinson, Chapman's camera makes elegant, swooping, circular moves around the ring, similar to the ones we have seen before, but this time, the pan circles the ring, the ropes and Sugar Ray, only to come to rest on a close-up of one of the ropes, from which blood drips in graceful slow motion as Sugar Ray is pronounced world champion. Although in many ways 'tragic', *Raging Bull* is so overwhelmingly draining because, unlike most tragedies, what its images make us feel is so frequently at odds with what we want to feel. Here, I would posit, the slow, dejected, wary pan across the ring makes us mourn La Motta's painful demise, but without extending us the satisfaction of identifying with it or him.

The Deer Hunter and *Raging Bull* are films which centre on male protagonists who lack self-awareness or a tendency towards introversion, but which are, nevertheless, manifestly preoccupied with looking beyond an individual's surface or façade. In part as a result of this oppositional pull between what the protagonists know or want to explore about themselves and what is conveyed about them to the audience, the male protagonists in both films suffer extreme trauma and/or death, their suffering – though in markedly different ways – conveyed via an unusually suggestive mise-en-scène that goes some way towards unravelling the traumas' origins, which otherwise would remain incompletely explained. Male identity traumas are thus rendered accessible via visual style. There are examples of films in which, as in melodramas, hidden facets of identities and characters are explained through style and in which the transference of knowledge to the audience is not merely intellectual but also emotive and physical. Mise-en-scène in these films is not used to decipher a mystery (as it is, for example, in several films noirs) but to convey some of the essence of masculinity, producing an affinity and understanding between audience and male protagonists that goes beyond straightforward identification with a figure on the screen.

The Right Stuff, symbols and the phallus

The penis and its relationship to the phallus will always be somewhere close to the heart of any representation of masculinity, although not always as overtly as it is here. In 'Male Sexuality in the Media' (1985) Richard Dyer argued strongly and wittily for a demystification of the relationship between the penis and the phallus, having previously written in 'Don't Look Now: The Instabilities of the Male Pin-up' that 'the penis isn't a patch on the phallus' (1982: 116). As Dyer then observed in 'Male Sexuality in the Media':

> One of the striking characteristics about penis symbols is the discrepancy between the symbols and what penises are actually like. Male genitals are fragile, squashy, delicate things; even when erect, the penis is spongy, seldom straight and rounded at the tip, while the testicles are imperfect spheres, always vulnerable, never still ... far more commonly [than the use of flowers as phallic symbols in Genet's *Un Chant d'Amour*] the soft, vulnerable charm of male genitals is evoked as hard, tough and dangerous. It is not flowers that most commonly symbolise male genitals but swords, knives, fists, guns. (1985: 30)

In contrast to the majority of critics writing on masculinity and film, Dyer dwelt not on the phallic potential of the male body but on the reductiveness of such an attachment, which wrongly equates masculinity with the penis (1985: 31). The affiliation between the penis and hard phallic imagery, Dyer suggested, was not only unerotic but also separated men from the source of their erotic pleasure by promoting the notion that the penis had 'a life of its own' and was an object over which the man had 'no control' (ibid.). Denial of the erotic potential of the male form is, of course, the underlying theoretical rationale for several of the other critiques of masculinity on film referenced in my Introduction.

The conclusion of Dyer's essay examines certain significant parallels between 'basic storytelling grammar' and male sexuality, suggesting that:

> The argument can be taken further to suggest that virtually all narratives, regardless of what medium they are in, reproduce the way male sexuality is organised ... There is a suggestive similarity in the way both male sexuality and narrative are commonly described. Male sexuality is said to be goal-orientated; seduction and foreplay are merely the means by which one gets to the 'real thing', an orgasm, the great single climax ... It is no accident that the word climax applies to orgasm and narrative. In both, the climax is at once what sex and story aim at; the climax is also the signal that the sex and the story are over ... The male drives himself, or his penis drives him; it is he who 'reaches' the climax. (1985: 40–1)

Dyer's analysis of male sexuality, unlike Steve Neale's arguments about masculinity and spectacle, assumed and was built upon a relationship between style and meaning; Neale offered an intellectual response, while Dyer allowed for a spectatorial response to male

Fig. 1.22

Fig. 1.23

narratives that was also physical, emotive, psychological. He also took issue with traditional phallic symbolism, whereas Neale (through his emphasis on sadism, battles, fights, duels and struggles) still evidently believed in the symbolic ideal of masculinity.

The Right Stuff offers the clearest Hollywood critique I have come across of masculinity and symbolism (represented as the struggle for supremacy between the magnificent men and their flying machines) while, like Dyer, remaining positively attached to masculinity itself. What I want to explore in particular here is the relationship in The Right Stuff between the debates (within the film) surrounding masculinity and phallic symbolism and the evocatively rich mise-en-scène. The film contains various moments of 'pure spectacle' (as Neale might put it), although in this case they are not invariably linked to the exploits of the male body. The effect of these stylistic excesses is particularly marked in the 70mm, six-track stereo version of this three-hour film. The Right Stuff opens with a monochrome sequence composed of archive footage of an X-1 being released from a B-29, mixed with point-of-view shots from inside the X-1 as a pilot tries and fails to break the sound barrier. The plane judders as the pilot's dial goes further and further up the Machmeter, reaching 9.9, at which point there is an explosion, not caused by, as Tom Charity succinctly remarks, 'the supersonic boom, but the test plane crashing to the ground' (1997: 34). At the point of the plane's impact with the ground, the film explodes into colour and the image ratio jumps from 1:1.33 to 1:2.33 Cinemascope (Figs 1.22–1.23). As Charity continues:

> The audacity of this cut (reminiscent of the first cut in Welles' *Touch of Evil*) heightens the impact of the explosion and marks the end of the preamble. This dramatic crash is the movie's take-off point. The sudden shift to colour and widescreen heightens our appreciation of these aesthetic pleasures. It's a bold announcement of the scale of this picture. (Ibid.)

As *The Deer Hunter* and *Raging Bull* have suggested, the construction of an idea of masculinity through the synchronisation of diverse elements of narrative and mise-en-scène is a recurrent feature of much 'men's cinema'. The effect of this widening of the screen at the beginning of *The Right Stuff* to the accompaniment of the triumphant, soaring soundtrack (the music subsequently used for Chuck Yeager's repeated, successful test flights) is dramatic and intense – especially in the stretched 70mm version. It is also specifically related to masculinity in that it is the first of many moments in the film when we as spectators can experience and understand the pilots' adrenalin rush, triumphs and fears; conventional, character-driven forms of identification are supplanted at the start of *The Right Stuff* by a more abstract identificatory pattern rooted in an instinctive and emotional, even primal, audience response to its non-narrative textual elements. This is a form of identification with mise-en-scène that I will come to argue is an essential trope of 'men's cinema' and transcends the more conventional character and gender recognition through which most forms of identification are understood.

The use of non-narrative elements such as colour, ratio and music in this instance is expressive, serving to instil, through transference of emotional response to us, the audience, the emotions that drive the interpersonal and internalised struggles the film's story narrativises. The construction of masculine identity in *The Right Stuff* centres on the ultimately intangible and unrealistic notion of 'the right stuff', a symbolic construction (frequently comically conceived) that links the battle to be the 'best pilot' of them all with increasingly abstract notions of authentic and heroic masculinity. The majority of the film is dedicated to the Mercury space programme of the 1950s and early 1960s, before the Apollo programme took over, from the first successful single-manned flights of Alan Shepherd and Gus Grissom to the orbital flights of John Glenn and Gordon Cooper. *The Right Stuff* starts, however, with Chuck Yeager, who never became an astronaut but rather remained a test pilot (he failed to conform to the government profile for the job – he did not go to college, for example). Unlike the astronauts' flying, Yeager's is instinctual and strenuous; history – and the middle portion of *The Right Stuff* – might marginalise Yeager and give preference to the space programme, but this programme of testing diminishes the Mercury 7 rather than builds them up. 'The right stuff' and authentic masculinity is, ironically, exemplified most concretely in Kaufman's adaptation by Yeager – the one omitted from the Mercury programme – rather than by the endlessly tried and tested astronauts.

The film's equivocal attitude to the phallus is repeatedly and comically illustrated by the series of tests the would-be astronauts have to endure during the Mercury programme selection process: they have to ejaculate into a small metal penis-shaped container, they are walked down the corridor with a catheter up them, they are wired to machines in a claustrophobic capsule and they have to see for how long they can keep a ping-pong ball afloat by blowing into water-filled tubes. The tests that ostensibly prove their suitability as astronauts are demeaning and belittling, more adept at accentuating their mortality and frailty than their heroism. The Mercury pilots were beaten into space not only by Yuri Gagarin but by a chimp, and when the NASA scientists are testing the various incarnations of the rocket that will finally launch an American man into space, the earlier models' performances are distinctly Monty Python-esque.

There is, in fact, a *Monty Python* sketch this rocket-testing sequence recalls: 'Erotic Films' (part of Episode 5, Series 1 – *Man's Crisis for Identity in the Latter Half of the Twentieth Century*) in which a couple in their underwear (played by Terry Jones and Carol Cleveland) kiss heartily before falling back onto a double bed. A montage of film clips start up that includes: a tower being erected, water crashing against rocks, fireworks, a rocket launch, a train entering a tunnel, an udder being milked, a plane crash-landing on water, a tree being felled, the tower from the start of the sequence being demolished. These images supplant the sexual act and most (the image of Richard Nixon grinning being the exception) make comic reference to it. At the end of the montage sequence the woman is sitting up in bed having a cigarette complaining about being made to watch films, whilst Jones – crouched next to a portable projector – assures her there is 'just one more, dear'. In Philip Kaufman's 1983 adaptation of Tom Wolfe's *The Right Stuff*, about the 7 Mercury astronauts who took part in the first American space programme, there is a comparable sequence, as NASA, in the wake of the first successful Sputnik flight, test a series of their own rockets, only for these to explode on the launch pad, shoot up a few feet then shrink back into the earth, leave the ground only to fizzle back to earth like a timid party popper and refuse to launch at all. Throughout *The Right Stuff* rockets and being able to tame them are at the heart of how masculinity becomes defined; these are not just failed rockets.

In direct contrast to the way in which the astronauts and rockets are filmed Yeager – although nearly defeated – is never humiliated. Unlike the early space missions, which are filmed from inside the cramped capsules, the astronauts' discomfort mirrored by the oppressiveness of the close-ups, Yeager's flights are captured largely from outside, his plane shooting through perfect clouds hanging in infinite blue skies, intermingled with a few shots of Yeager inside the cockpit straining to keep his plane under control. The liberation and exhilaration of the image and the scenes' fast editing opens up the potential for identification with Yeager, not a straightforwardly narcissistic identification as envisaged by Neale, for instance, but a more nebulous response both to him and to his at-one-ness with the skies, with the movement and music and with the dimensions of the image. The importance of the scale of the image to the film's articulation of masculinity is made clear in its last, prolonged sequence, in which Yeager testing the air force's new jet (ironically as the pilot test programme is to be scrapped) is intercut with a night of lavish Texan entertainment laid on for the Mercury astronauts by Texan Vice President Lyndon Johnson, head of the space programme (just as *their* programme is about to be superseded by the Apollo programme).

The difference between Yeager and the Mercury pilots is enforced on various levels and exemplified by their overall situation: as the astronauts eat pork and beans off disposable plates while watching a fancy fan dance, Yeager is hurtling – on his own – through the skies (Figs 1.24–1.27). Going Icarus-like into the upper atmosphere, Yeager loses consciousness and then control of his aircraft, just managing to eject himself in time. As his fellow pilots drive to the crash site, one – having spied a glint of silver amidst the black smoke – turns to the other and asks: 'Sir, over there – is that a man?' As Yeager emerges, defiant and angry, striding towards them, his face badly burnt, the other replies with the wry smile of shared pride in his buddy's macho exploits, 'Yeah, you're darn right it is!' This last image of Yeager in *The Right Stuff* is – for all the supposed supremacy of the astronauts and the space programme – the film's triumphant conclusion and 'among the most transcendent images in contemporary cinema' (Charity 1997: 84). The transcendence is ultimately a masculine one and up there in the pantheon of transcendent male images with Butch Cassidy and Sundance jumping into the river or the man with no name as he rides into *A Fistful of Dollars* (1964).

Fig. 1.24

Why is Yeager's masculinity never in question? It is partly because, unlike the astronauts strapped up to endless machines or stuck immobile in their capsule, Yeager never relinquishes independence or control. His masculinity escapes problematisation also because of the manner in which Kaufman's mise-en-scène reinforces his mastery. In the final sequence there exists a contrast between the crowded interiors of the Texan celebrations and the expansive exteriors of Yeager's last flight. Crucially, both the astronauts and Yeager are rendered insignificant by their respective environments, but whereas the astronauts are swamped by and lost amidst the throngs around them, Yeager, after the crash, is still not confined or constrained. While the astronauts find themselves undermined, Yeager's reputation as the one with 'the right stuff' is consolidated: the 'best pilot'[9] and the best man, a status complemented and enhanced by Kaufman's use of mise-en-scène. While the film's use of phallic symbolism (often crude, usually ironic, sometimes adolescent) undercuts the astronauts' ostensible claims to masculine supremacy, the stretched image, the soaring music, the vast, flat desert landscape and the open skies, conjure up a nostalgic attachment to an older, more stable and traditional image of masculinity exemplified by Yeager.

Fig. 1.25

Fig. 1.26

Fig. 1.27

Yeager and the other test pilots in the late 1940s characterised Mach 1, or at least what resided on the other side of the sound barrier, as 'the demon in the sky'. Just as the demon remains both imaginary and unattainable, so the pursuit of idealised masculinity, the film (even in the case of Yeager) seems to be saying, is futile. What *The Right Stuff* and so many other films ultimately celebrate is the pursuit of masculinity as opposed to the possession of it; the abstractness and elusiveness of idealised masculinity is what Kaufman captures through his use of mise-en-scène: the vast expanse of luminous blue skies, for example, that Yeager dissects with his plane. The infinity of skies and space serves as an appropriate metaphor for masculinity's unobtainability as its boundaries can never be reached. *The Right Stuff* makes us both yearn for – and through that yearning almost believe in – the intangible essence of masculinity; it also, however, treats the striving for masculine perfection ironically, and to this not even Yeager is quite immune: shot through with romanticism and nostalgia, Kaufman's rendition of him – for all its old-fashioned heroism – is nevertheless imperfect, for Yeager ultimately *was* left behind, superseded by the pilots selected for the space programmes. This contradictory relationship with what masculinity might mean or be can, using other terminology, be characterised as the enforced distinction between consciousness and more repressive instincts: what you would like to be, what you are and what you would like to forget you could ever be.

This attachment to such an unrealisable ideal of 'the right stuff' serves perhaps to make sense of Jacques Lacan's conceptualisation in 'The Signification of the Phallus' (1958) of the phallus as a symbolic construct, a signifier empty of meaning until given significance by a process of interaction with other signs. It is clear throughout Lacan's writing generally that to see or name a symbol is to divest it of potency, so the phallus is really only powerful if absent – for if seen, rather as Dyer identifies, the discrepancy between the hard, frightening, potent symbol and the penis (which the phallus is mistakenly assumed to represent) becomes abundantly clear. The classic Freudian notion of the power of the phallus being constituted through a fear of loss (castration) confirms this fear of being found out; masculinity is thus predicated upon a false attribution of phallic power to the male, the assumption that the body finds its correlative in the symbol being misplaced. So the phallus can be important only, as Lacan suggests, when it remains veiled, just as the 'right stuff' retains its own symbolic power through being perpetually out of reach.

2. Men's Cinema

The underpinning aim of this chapter is to propose a tentative definition of 'men's cinema' as the cinematic expression of masculinity via mise-en-scène. The analysis will focus on some of the most notable constituent parts of this mise-en-scène. Consistencies and repetitions are always intriguing and of interest here is how such familiar and repeatedly used tropes – when used in conjunction with masculinity – make the spectator feel, often engendering solidarity and camaraderie with the image, or a more abstract sense of solidity, self-belief, power, heroism, triumphalism or machismo, reflected in that image. Whereas chapter one was concerned with the expressive use of mise-en-scène in relation to masculinity (often, significantly, centring on trauma), chapter two is about the evolution of what I very tentatively call a rhetoric designed to convey what it is to be a man. This chapter's arguments are introduced by means of a discussion of Ron Howard's *Backdraft* (1991) although I subsequently adopt a broadly chronological approach as I argue the development of men's cinema is not entirely ahistorical.

Backdraft: a film about firefighters, a film about men

Backdraft, despite its limitations as a film, is an archetypal example of men's cinema. Whereas for the most part I have identified and discussed sequences that are interesting in terms of their use of mise-en-scène in relation to masculinity, my intention with *Backdraft* is to discuss a series of moments that offer a collective demonstration of how a whole film can work as an example of men's cinema. Ron Howard's movie about a family of firefighters is strongly masculinist, 'masculinism' being, as defined memorably by Robin Wood, the 'assumption of the rightness – the *naturalness* – of male *dominance* ... the *cult* of masculinity' (2003: xvii–xviii). 'Masculinism' is woven into *Backdraft*'s very fabric, its characters, narratives and its mise-en-scène; although characters are flawed the fundamental belief in 'the cult of masculinity' remains intact, as it does in so many of Howard's films (even the ostensibly more sensitive, 'feminine' ones such as *A Beautiful Mind* (2001)).

Backdraft's pre-title sequence, set twenty years before the main story, contains the favoured ingredients of men's cinema: the recurrent Hollywood plot line of a son's equivocal veneration of the lost/dead father, the macho job and the synchronisation of character, action, music and visual style in the formation of an idealised, unapologetically traditional masculinity. At the film's core is the unresolved sibling rivalry between two brothers, Stephen and Brian McCaffrey (Kurt Russell and William Baldwin), both firefighters and the sons of a heroic fireman whose death Brian witnesses in the pretitle sequence of 1971. Brian had been taken by his father (also played by Kurt Russell) on a seemingly routine firefighting mission; marking the engine's exit from the station Hans Zimmer's music starts (quiet but expectant), gradually building in momentum, pace and depth, indicators that the men are about to be asked to prove themselves.[10] Brian's father tells him to give the rope that sounds the horn 'a good yank' as the engine is about to negotiate a busy interchange. Shots of the interior of the engine are intercut with shots onto and of the street, the most memorable being the image of bystanders looking up admiringly as the engine speeds by. There is then a fast track into the engine as it speeds round a corner, gleaming red with the music soaring. The engine comes to a halt near a burning building and Brian's father looks up at the fire and with heady anticipation declares, 'there it is', a statement accompanied by a wobbly point-of-view shot of the fire (echoing Brian's perspective). As the music rises to its tumescent climax, it becomes clear that in *Backdraft's* terms the moment at which men are tested is the moment of male triumph; Howard's (and other directors') penchant for synchronicity between the various cinematic elements is perpetually indicative of this notion that masculinity is predicated upon ambivalence, upon testing and triumph and potential loss. The soundtrack builds up again (the brass section, appropriately enough considering the luminous brass detailing of the pristine Chicago engines, is given special prominence) as the firefighters go in to the blaze; Brian waves up at his dad who is in the process of saving a baby girl, but then the music abruptly changes to a minor, melancholy, foreboding key (with strings prominent this time): the fire

is unexpectedly fierce and as an explosion sounds and the flames rage, Brian despairingly calls up 'dad' as his father's helmet tumbles to the ground. This establishing sequence concludes with a mute, slow-motion image of McCaffrey's distraught colleague, John Adcox (Scott Glenn), comforting Brian who picks up his father's helmet as a vertical crane shot pulls out slowly from this tableau of trauma

Fig. 2.1

(Fig. 2.1). This image – or one similar to it – becomes a *Life* magazine cover and immortalises the moment when Brian takes up the talisman that, in death, becomes the signifier for his father.

Like an operatic overture, this opening flashback contains tasters of what is to follow, setting out the unity of iconography, character, narrative and stylistic tropes that will thereafter predominate. The use of slow motion to draw attention to heroic masculine exploits, for instance, returns very soon after the titles as firemen walk into a doorway, silhouetted against the smoke and flames belching from within the building and then again as Stephen McCaffrey emerges from the same door once the blaze is under control. The narrative of *Backdraft* has various points of focus, both literal and metaphorical: firefighting, an arson investigation, the sibling rivalry between Brian and Stephen, the testing and defining of masculinity and the symbolism of fire itself. Its predictable mise-en-scène becomes the vehicle for the interweaving of these various strands and, through looking in more detail at certain sequences that clearly demonstrate how this functions, I will examine the cumulative effect of such tropes and mannerisms.

Backdraft is replete with with several extended sequences that are in themselves mini narratives about 'being a man'. One such is an extended composite montage of 'being a fireman' (Figs 2.2–2.6), synchronously edited to the truly awful *The Show Goes On*, by Bruce Hornsby and the Range (and so once again conforming to the structural formulae of the three-minute narrative pop song). The music starts over the end of the previous sequence, thus suggesting that what follows is of particular importance. The series of images that then comprise the montage sequence are a mixture of the dramatic (Adcox trying in vain to revive a woman just pulled out from a blaze; firefighters silhouetted against the flames; a fireman saving a smiling boy; a fireman on a high crane fighting a blaze; a man being cut out of a wrecked car), the recreational and cooling off (a game of basketball replete with high fives; slow-motion shots of tired, hot fireman hosing down their faces), the routine (Brian kicking a street fire hydrant in frustration as he tries and fails to attach a hose to it; two episodes of training) and the comic (the unit trying to rescue several escaped chickens; Brian being woken by the unit's dog). That the representative identity being constructed here is cohesive and integrated is signalled by the synchronisation with the music – that when the unit is playing basketball, for example, the lyrics are 'he's the one keeping the score'. Even more banal is the editing together of Bruce Hornsby singing 'the show must go on' to the car crash. The one non-synchronous element is the sibling relationship between Stephen and Brian, which inevitably concludes the montage as the music peters out when they crash onto the roof of a building during a competitive training exercise of racing up a fire escape carrying a hose. *Backdraft* provides an intensely – but not unsatisfyingly – formulaic example of the mechanics of men's cinema. In this sequence the formula is to bring together, couched in the sort of music-led montage that has become a genre movie staple within contemporary Hollywood, a series of stereotypical images of masculinity and to achieve this via marked shifts in tone – from traumatic to heroic to light and bathetic. A significant feature of

Fig. 2.2

Fig. 2.3

Fig. 2.4

Fig. 2.5

Fig. 2.6

a sequence such as this and *Backdraft* as a whole is how hard it is not to be swept along by its momentum; our enjoyment of such a sequence is predicated to an extent upon finding it difficult to view it with much critical distance.

An essential component of the satisfaction *Backdraft* offers its audience is precisely this accessibility and predictability: that it signals clearly not only where it is at but also where it is going. Even if elements of its plot keep us guessing, where it ends up in terms of emotional and psychological closure or narrative and iconographic stability is where earlier the film had telegraphed it would end up. The role of mise-en-scène in cementing the ending's tone and in constructing a strong sense of closure is fundamental. Against yet another backdrop of soaring orange flames various plot strands are resolved and Brian and Stephen McCaffrey finally reach a state of rapprochement – but only once Adcox, their flawed surrogate father, has plunged to his death and Stephen lies dying.

So what is *Backdraft* ultimately about? The background of the final fire's cascading ramparts – the uncontrollable, writhing hose spewing forth its unstemmable liquid and the violent flames that suck morally equivocal men to their deaths – resembles the iconography of hell. Fire in *Backdraft* is an ambivalent symbol; although firemen refer to the

Fig. 2.7

need to tame it and not to let it sense their fear (thus implying that fire might share certain traits with femininity) they most commonly evoke its affinity to masculinity. Just as Tim had said of Stephen that he 'took that fire by the balls', so Adcox welcomes the two rookies to 'the world of old man fire' and the arson investigator Donald Rimgale (Robert de Niro) tells Brian that 'the only way to beat it is to think like it … the only way to kill it is to love it a little'. Stephen in particular has, until the very end, the sort of equivocal, homosocial response to fire that suggests fire – rather like the 'right stuff' – is a subliminal, ultimately unknowable masculine force (Fig. 2.7).

What is most clearly resolved via the convoluted imagery of these final scenes is the brothers' relationship. Stephen implausibly survives the fall that kills Adcox by landing on a platform jutting out into the cavernous warehouse's flaming abyss and although Brian does tend to him, he then leaves his brother in favour of finally finding the hero inside by helping to stem the fire instead. Brian – who until this point has been sensitive and a little toughness short of a real man – looks up at the marauding blaze with a mixture of attraction and awe, belatedly understanding the ambivalent rapport with fire that, he has been told, good firemen possess. He grabs the convulsive hose, brings it under control and aims it at the blanket of flames. Something resembling Russian marching music starts up, the camera cranes upwards and, in slow motion, Brian demonstrates that he is, after all, a man, as Stephen looks on and exclaims exultantly: 'Look at him, that's my brother, goddammit.' Stephen then dies in the ambulance holding Brian's hand, but as he (perhaps because he) loses a brother Brian finally reaches a state of manhood.

In chapter one I proposed and embellished a notion of masculinity predicated upon the instinct to repress unhappiness and a fear of perversity (especially homosexuality), and while this repressive instinct is still present in the films under discussion here, it has a different relationship to visual style. In *Backdraft* the strain of masculinity – its ambivalence, the fear of contradictions and equivocations – comes out in the hysterical, protesting mise-en-scène, the flamboyant bombast of which is used to mask male doubts and potential fissures. Whereas repression in films such as *There's Always Tomorrow* or *The Deer Hunter* has the effect of drawing the audience's attention to what is being repressed and its importance to the definition of masculinity, in the films being examined in this chapter the attraction is not towards the act of repression itself as the impulse to disavow potential frailty and ambivalence is, like the emphatic mise-en-scène, far stronger. The insistent and uniform visual style of a film such as *Backdraft* becomes a hysterical over-statement of a belief in the integrity, straightforwardness and straightness of masculinity, but just as Freud's adamant reaffirmation of 'normal' sex ends up flagging up just how 'abnormal' this prescriptive normality is, *Backdraft*'s powerful attachment to strong (hetero) masculinity – as expressed via the simple stridency of its mise-en-scène – shows itself also to be protesting too much.

After the most well attended funeral since Annie's in *Imitation of Life* (1959), a fire station bell rings and a fast-cut series of images of men getting into a fire engine establishes that they are responding to an emergency call. Brian does not look as if he is going to join them but then at the last minute slides down the pole and jumps into the engine as it moves off, just as he had done on his first day. As Adcox had done with him on that day as well, so Brian takes a probationer under his wing. As the music rises to a crescendo, a zoom into Brian shows him going from contemplative and uncertain to serenely knowing. The image then cuts to an aerial shot of a long straight road stretching all the way to the centre of Chicago with, at the end of it where smoke is sidling into the sky, a fire that needs quelling. The music is unambiguously triumphant again; the omniscient camera tells us the road Brian is on is the straight and sure road towards manliness.

One of the things that characterises men's cinema is that the tropes it deploys are at the very least positive in their evocation of men and masculinity, even though the presentation of masculinity is also frequently marked by irony. In a heavily ironic film such as Quentin Tarantino's *Reservoir Dogs* (1992), for example, there is nevertheless a residual sense, however fleeting, of masculinity as powerful. This albeit ambivalent attachment to masculinity's potential even for transitory invincibility or omnipotence is an indirect backlash, no doubt, against men having been, as a result of feminism, over-scrutinised and beleaguered. Like its antecedents discussed in chapter one, men's cinema therefore comes out of a traumatic moment of criticism and self-doubt but – on the surface at least – for all those anxieties and doubts, the films remain emphatically conservative. It becomes important to read men's cinema against the grain to identify the continuing schism, frailty and ambivalence at the heart of masculinity, namely its root in the repression of alternatives to traditional masculine identities, such as homosexuality. Men's cinema, whilst embodying these contradictions and ambiguities, is uplifting, exhilarating and frequently spectacular, and we as the audience, finding ourselves swept along with this, also find ourselves embodying those same contradictions and ambiguities. What I am now intent on telling is the – less straight and sure, perhaps – road to *Backdraft*, starting with an analysis of elements of Sergio Leone's *C'era una volta il West/Once Upon a Time in the West* (1968), in many ways the Ur-text of men's cinema.

Once Upon a Time in the West

Historically, perhaps, the most significant example of 'men's cinema' is Sergio Leone's *Once Upon a Time in the West* which, alongside his other 'spaghetti westerns', the *Fistful of Dollars* cycle, remains one of the most iconic moments in the history of masculinity and film. *Backdraft* is an example of a film that takes its masculine ideals without irony (straight, perhaps!), whereas Leone's play on convention and self-conscious handling of genre, performance and style speaks of a different relationship to masculine ideals. It affirms them, but it also doubts them. *Once Upon a Time in the West* believes, above all, in the performative basis of masculinity, its grounding in symbolic power. During the course of an undergraduate module on melodrama I was teaching some years ago, I asked a seminar group of predominantly men what made them cry. They had seemed singularly resistant a term before to the charms and effects of the melodramas (even the male-centred ones) of Max Ophuls, Vincente Minnelli and Douglas Sirk and so I wanted to discover what, if anything, might provoke them to tears. Probably I was envisaging an ironic answer reminiscent of the scene in *Sleepless in Seattle* (1993) when Tom Hanks and a friend pretend to be moved to tears as they recount the ending of *The Dirty Dozen*. Instead, the answer I got was unexpected as one of the many male cinephiles in the group offered, with little hesitation, 'the crane shot at the beginning of *Once Upon a Time in the West* as Claudia Cardinale arrives at the station'. The student was moved, it transpired, by the arching movement of the crane itself, the surety of its magisterial swoop and the sheer scope of the image. In fact, there are two spectacular crane shots around the time of Cardinale's arrival in Flagstone, one that precedes her emergence from the train and one that marks her exit from the station building. The student was referring to the second.

In the first, a train is pulling into the station. As the train is still drawing to a stop and coming ever closer to the lens, the previously static camera starts to crane up and left in a gentle arc around and above the train, thus continuing the movement of the train itself. It comes to rest and then a series of cuts take one to Cardinale dismounting from her carriage, expectant as she returns to her family after several years (she does not yet know that they have all just been killed). She is put out by there being no one at the station to greet her and goes in search of a ride. The second crane shot starts through the window of the station building, then rises slightly faster than the first over its roof, to the accompaniment of one of the film's musical themes: its lusher, orchestral strand. The music grows and then hits its peak just as the strong, assertive crane shot reaches its own; Cardinale is, by now, insignificant and small, almost lost amidst the dust and the crowds (Figs 2.8–2.11).

What was it about this second shot that might move one to tears? One thing that is unusual about such a response is that it is not rooted in conventional character identification as this is the first time we are introduced to Cardinale, although we have witnessed the massacre of her family, so we feel some indirect sympathy with her. The film is thereby playing with certain key disparities in audience and character knowledge, making use of the strength and visual elegance of the crane shot to assert an alternative form of knowledge and power, one that enables us to engage with the opening of the film on the level of sensibility.

Fig. 2.8

Fig. 2.9

As the film progresses Leone establishes the connection between strong aesthetic elegance and masculinity in a number of key scenes. One reason for this might well be (here and in his earlier westerns as well) that expressiveness has to come from somewhere and the men in *Once Upon a Time in the West* express very little verbally. I tend to think that the shedding of tears at movies comes from an awareness of lack as well as from an engagement with emotions, gestures or moods that are visible and present. The impact of grand visual gestures such as Leone's in *Once Upon a Time in the West* function hysterically in that they have the effect of accentuating what is being masked or absent (what I would term 'normal', functioning masculinity) as well as what is there (omniscience and sensibility)

Fig. 2.10

Fig. 2.11

via the very expressiveness that remains incompatible with the distance between style and character the scene generates.

There is in this crane shot a particular collusion and a particular beauty, which centres on or is evocative of the film's emotional attachment to masculinity. In this regard, there are two sections of *Once Upon a Time in the West* I will examine here: its opening and the final shoot-out between Frank (Henry Fonda) and Harmonica (Charles Bronson). The opening twelve minutes or so of the film are mesmerisingly (for many irritatingly) slow and in them nothing much either happens or is said, testifying to the fact that speed and action are not necessarily the only means by which cinema evokes masculinity. As three of Frank's henchmen arrive at the station, menace the station master and then wait for a train that brings Harmonica into town, there is no music and very little sound, beyond the squeak of a hinge and the buzz of a fly. The men do not respond logically to the small things that do happen in these languid minutes of screen time: the one being irritated by the fly does not simply bat him away with his hat, just as the one being plagued by water dripping through the ceiling does not move away but rather shields his head by putting on his hat, later drinking the water that collects in its brim. This extreme self-consciousness is augmented through the exaggeratedly composed mise-en-scène: the slow pans, for example, or the close-ups of faces positioned to the side of the widescreen frame and juxtaposed – through Leone's persistent use of deep focus – against the vast expanse of the big country behind them. Finally, there is the sound of a train approaching the station and Harmonica alights. The studied slowness, quiet and surety of the past few minutes are eventually scarred by the swift and noisy exchange of bullets that erupts between the four men and which Harmonica wins, having shot dead all three of his rivals. The convulsive puncturing of the prolonged silence is, of course, in part parodic; we have spent twenty minutes or so studying a group of men who are doing excessively little and who turn out to be narratively unimportant.

This opening comprises many of the film's notable visual tropes: the jolting alternation of pace, the use of extreme close-up in the foreground of a deep focus shot and leisurely camera moves. It is only later, though, after Frank's arrival in the subsequent scene, that these can start to be understood as part of the film's residual fascination, not just with stylisation but with the stylistic reinforcement of masculinity through mise-en-scène, as well as through narrative and character. After another unhurried introduction, this time to the doomed McBain family, Ennio Morricone's score finally starts up and, out of the scrubby bushes, emerges a posse of men in their dustcoats. Filmed from a low angle Frank and his men walk in the direction of the camera; the image then cuts to a long shot from behind them, then a close-up, at which point a ninety-degree pan circles around Frank and comes to rest, still in extreme close-up, on his face. Probably still captivated by the contrast between the sparkling blueness of Fonda's eyes and his darkened, grubby skin, we are summarily jolted out of this state as shots ring out when Frank shoots the youngest McBain child.

The image of a group of men walking – invariably slowly or in slow motion, frequently not quite in focus and almost always in widescreen – towards a low-angle lens has become, since *Once Upon a Time in the West*, an iconic trope of men's cinema. Leone's rendition of the shot conveys so much: power, menace, group identity and camaraderie; its pace – coupled with the enveloping swoop of the pan that circles Frank and comes to rest on his face – in this instance draws us into a complex form of identification not with the men so much as with the feelings provoked by the synchronisation of the men's actions with the camera's angle and movement. What characterises this and several other examples of men walking (such as the title sequence of *Reservoir Dogs*, discussed later) is the synchronicity between action and visual evocation of masculinity through the gesture of a group of men walking slowly, purposefully, menacingly through space. What makes this narrative moment in *Once Upon a Time in the West* so rich is that we find ourselves torn: we are irresistibly drawn to the momentum and power of Frank and his men invading the domestic screen/scene (and as such find ourselves with the 'bad men' as our natural point of identification) while simultaneously sharing the McBain family's fear of Frank and thus forming an attachment with them. The feelings evoked in us by the strong, menacing gesture of Frank and his henchmen walking are, though, different from the mixed emotional responses to the men walking to their deaths at the end of Sam Peckinpah's *The Wild Bunch* (1969), for example, although I would posit that the pessimism embodied by the latter – as in *Reservoir Dogs* – is so richly affecting precisely because it recalls and embodies the majestic potency of the men walking motif in its more triumphant form. It also embodies – and pastiches – the irony of Leone's posturing, the weighty but vapid elegance of the final shoot-out, for instance.

Not much happens in *Once Upon a Time in the West* (so little, in fact, that the triple 'story' credit for Dario Argento, Bernardo Bertolucci and Sergio Leone plus separate 'screenplay' credits for Leone and Sergio Donati are a touch absurd). The culmination of its visually exquisite drawn-out action is the duel between Frank and Harmonica, a long (eight-minute) sequence. The denouement begins as Fonda and Bronson enter what is almost literally an arena, eyeing each other up from opposite sides of a circle as the familiar electric guitar and harmonica refrain starts up. They then walk in the same direction, keeping pace with each other and still at a distance. Henry Fonda's walk is extremely distinctive; his legs are long and he takes few strides, rather like a racehorse ambling elegantly around the paddock. The languid but purposeful pace of *Once Upon a Time in the West* mirrors or maybe was inspired by the way Fonda moves. The film repeatedly uses an inverse waltz rhythm (the opening, the murder of the McBain son, this final shoot-out), starting sequences lethargically slowly only to then conclude them extremely rapidly through sudden gunfire. The two distinct aspects of such sequences – the slow and the quick – reflect our ambivalent reactions to Fonda as Frank. There is a notable collision in the casting of Fonda as the coldly and extremely violent Frank with his previously dominant star persona as the dependable, upright male (of *Twelve Angry Men* (1957), for example). Although Leone had wanted him to wear brown contact lenses, Fonda, at his own insistence, retained his familiar, beautiful blue eyes. The elegant Fonda finds himself compatible with the elegant, languid side of Leone's visual style, while the unexpectedly violent side of Fonda such a star persona camouflages finds expression in his character's sadism and concomitantly the brutal violence with which Leone concludes so many of Frank's scenes.

Back to the sequence of shots (Figs 2.12–2.15): having observed the two men eyeing each other, as it were, the camera then begins to slowly crane up and then away from them. Todd Berliner remarked of the moment when the camera in *Raging Bull* cranes away from La Motta as he walks towards the ring for his successful title fight that, at this juncture, we (the audience) lose the 'sense of privilege' we had enjoyed previously and become merely one of his fans (2005: 51). It is not inevitably the case, however, that literal distance creates metaphoric distance; a move away by the camera is not inevitably indicative of a retreat from or a renunciation of identification with the figure who had hitherto been followed. Instead it frequently feels that, particularly once a strong camera move (such as an upwards crane shot) has been established, that spectatorial affinity could lie with the movement and the power embodied by the gliding, omniscient

Fig. 2.12

Fig. 2.13

Fig. 2.14

Fig. 2.15

camera, as opposed to the figure on the screen. There remains, though, a residual affinity between male characters and camera movement here as the circular pans encircle and envelop the action, creating another ring around and beyond the arena. It is the circling camera that cements this idea of compatibility between masculinity and mise-en-scène, whilst also – via its sweeping gesture – making us notice that there are other points of identification beyond the men on the screen. When the crane move stops the high-angle shot is replaced by a different high long shot of the two men, and the imposition of some distance between us and the duelling men is made clear, just as it was at the end of William Wyler's *The Big Country* (1958), in which the tough men about to slug it out became as inconsequential as a couple of insects scrubbing about in the grubby sand.

The image then cuts to a closer ground-level shot of Frank's legs, clad in black trousers tucked into brown boots. He then discards his jacket, which falls to the ground between him and the camera. As Frank starts to walk forward, the camera switches again to a high angle, to the side of Frank, then cutting to a close-up as the orchestral leitmotif resumes, once more echoing the cool, confident stride pattern as he continues walking. Then follows an exchange of shots and reverse shots that presage the battle to come: a circling point-of-view shot of Harmonica as Frank circles him followed by a close-up of Harmonica's face, still from the point of view of Frank circling round him, followed by several images of Frank, who finally stands still. The two men have been circling each other, as it were, since Harmonica was revealed by the train pulling out from Flagstone station, and the build up to their culminating duel is elegantly predictable on the one hand but wittily unpredictable on the other. We have been fooled, to an extent, by Tonino delli Colli's majestic cinematography, which has ostensibly confirmed that the balance of power resides with Frank, when it has, in fact, shifted to Harmonica, the one who, from the outset, is centred, who stands still but who observes the movements of others around him. There are echoes of both formal dancing and chess here: Harmonica leads while Frank follows and he now executes his first decisive and aggressive move, which is to walk towards his adversary, thus breaking the fluid yet cagey circularity. There is then an exchange of close-ups (yet another prelude to the shoot-out still to come) and a final zoom into Harmonica's face, at which point a flashback starts.

This is an exaggeratedly significant interruption and one that explains what past events Harmonica wants to avenge. The flashback begins with a shot we have seen twice before of a younger Frank walking towards the camera. The image started off blurred and indistinct and has gradually got clearer, until our suspicion that Harmonica is recalling a previous meeting with Frank is confirmed as Frank walks (in sharp focus now) towards the lens, takes a harmonica from his pocket and offers it in the direction of the camera. It is the flashback that is interrupted now as we revert to a close-up of Harmonica's eyes and a further zoom into them, before cutting back to Frank and a further reverse shot of Harmonica, but this time as a boy in the flashback, having the harmonica rammed into his mouth. There then follows another of the film's majestic crane shots – to the strains of the soaring harmonica refrain – as the camera pulls up from Harmonica to reveal he is standing under a man with a noose round his neck, hanging from a brick arch, stranded in the expanse of dust. The younger Frank smiles and they swap yet another sequence of close-ups, concluding with the boy falling to the ground, his teeth loosening their grip on the harmonica.

For one last time, Leone lets speed and noise break the spell of a slow build up as the youthful Harmonica's face falling into the dust is swiftly followed by the sound of gunshots ringing out and a reciprocal ground-level image of Frank (in the present), mimicking the boy's similar slump in an earlier flashback. Frank has time to ask of Harmonica, 'Who are you?', at which point Harmonica shoves a harmonica in his mouth and Frank, in another parallel gesture, crashes to the ground and dies. The inevitability of this series of images is significant in terms of audience response, as was any formal predictability elsewhere in *Once Upon a Time in the West* sequences built up via movement and synchronicity, not just between actors and camera, but also, as discussed earlier, between fluidity of editing and camera movement and music. After two and a half hours, Leone has tutored us in how to read *Once Upon a Time in the West* and has guided our emotional, psychological and also physiological responses to the composition of images and sound on the screen. In many ways this is a cold film and I do not want to suggest that we feel great empathy or sympathy for any character in the end. Rather like Jill McBain (Cardinale) who, following the massacre of her family, scouts around for the most likely man to look after her, our character attachments are often inconsistent, even illogical. It is this which has led me to suggest that it is the film's visual style (for instance, its repetitive tropes) or its use of Morricone's score, that draw us in and provide our channels of emotional release, supplanting more straightforward character identification. Leone's construction of masculinity is emotive yet ambivalent, and it seems to me that it is such ambivalence that leads to our identification with *Once Upon a Time in the West* – as with other examples of 'men's cinema' – not being necessarily gender specific. It appears to be that the expansiveness granted by the importance of mise-en-scène in men's cinema and the concomitant marginalisation of a more traditional identification with character, may also be liberating for the audience. The universality of this appeal, coupled with the compatibility between mise-en-scène and masculinity discussed above – makes the viewing of the film both moving and paradoxical.

Dirty Harry

Although stylistic excess is a more prominent feature of men's cinema than minimalism, there does exist a secondary tradition (exemplified by the spare, economical style of directors such as Don Siegel, Walter Hill and – outside Hollywood – Jean-Pierre Melville) that I will acknowledge here via a discussion of Siegel's *Dirty Harry* (1971). *Dirty Harry* is slick and functional and, when contrasted with Leone's flamboyance, complements Clint Eastwood's own minimalist acting style (as cop Harry Callahan) in much the same way as Leone's style complemented Fonda's. Synchronicity between style and protagonist is doubly significant in men's cinema, maybe, because in many films male characters are less than verbally expansive, so gesture and visual expressiveness are key. A lack of verbosity characterised many of Eastwood's earlier roles, which conformed to the cliché of the 'strong, silent type' and Eastwood himself offers an important link with Leone, as cinematically he rose to prominence as the 'man with no name' in the *Fistful of Dollars* cycle from 1964–1966. Like his character in *A Fistful of Dollars*, Eastwood's Callahan is a loner who enters *Dirty Harry* alone, prefers to work alone, stalks the serial killer Scorpio (Andy Robinson) alone and, now that his wife is dead, lives alone. There are other parallels, such as Eastwood's own languorous and unflustered walk, that echoes both his persona in his earlier Leone films and Henry Fonda's in *Once Upon a Time in the West* and is used in *Dirty Harry*, as it was in the Leone, to signal the sense of the male protagonist's surety and control.

Dirty Harry opens (pre-titles) with a pan down the names inscribed on the memorial to the San Francisco Police Department members who have been killed in the line of duty, cutting abruptly to an extreme close-up, low-angle image up the barrel of a silencer and gun, which we soon learn is being trained by 'Scorpio' on a woman swimming in her roof-top pool. Scorpio then aims at the woman (we see this via a reverse shot down his gun's viewfinder), followed by another shot up the barrel of his silencer followed by a muffled shot ringing out as the woman writhes and dies. However, when Harry subsequently arrives at the crime scene (coinciding with the start of the credits) the visual style becomes, rather like its object, much straighter. Harry is shown frequently in static medium shot, and even when the camera does move (photography is by Bruce Surtees, a favourite Seigel/Eastwood cameraman at the time) it does so sparingly and in tandem with Eastwood. Towards the end of the titles, for example, Eastwood is up on the roof from which the woman was shot, walking around its perimeter and towards the spot where he finds an empty gun cartridge and then Scorpio's note. The camera here tracks him from a slight distance, but – like the editing – it remains functional and clean, never operatic as Leone's was. Siegel's crispness complements Harry Callahan's straightness, the clean traditional look – his suits, ties, tank tops, tweeds and leather elbow pads – he is over-attached to, as when he refuses to let the doctor tending a leg wound cut his trousers, preferring to take them down (although this will prove more painful) because they cost $29.95.

Eastwood as Callahan stands tall and adopts, as I have already mentioned, the aloofness and easy, confident gait of his earlier cowboy persona; he also unfailingly talks tough ('Make my day…'). The unshowy mise-en-scène, and particularly Surtees' economical camerawork, works in tandem with this persona as Callahan's authority is signalled not by the audience being drawn to him but by being kept at a distance, like Jean-Pierre Melville's treatment of the similarly cold Jef Costello (Alain Delon) in *Le Samouraï* (1967). A little way into *Dirty Harry* there is a failed bank robbery, a sequence that shows Harry at a crisis moment, behaving in much the same cool way as he had done in the title sequence. Around him chaos ensues as the getaway car overturns, men slump down wounded and onlookers scream, but both Callahan and the mise-en-scène remain unflustered and unmoved, the camera tracking him as he saunters over to the scene of the robbery, still chewing on his hot dog, a .44 Magnum in his hand. There is none of the sensuality you find in Leone's work, nor is there any of the breathless cutting now virtually mandatory in high action chase sequences; instead, the functional mise-en-scène reaffirms, through its stillness, Harry Callahan's hardness as he retains the calmness and authority that all those around him have seemingly renounced.

Whereas the effect of *Once Upon a Time in the West* is to affect the audience via the emotive and symbolic use of aesthetics and certain visual and stylised tropes, the effect of *Dirty Harry*, conversely, is to convey Callahan's masculine supremacy through analytical distance, the effect almost Brechtian (although the techniques definitely not). Detachment is part of mainstream cinema's lexicon of masculinity, but it has increasingly been marginalised in favour of a form of men's cinema centred on affect and identification. Not all 'men's cinema', therefore, is pregnant with evocative, emotive or showy mise-en-scène (see, for instance, the classical Hollywood western).

Reservoir Dogs and men walking

Quentin Tarantino's *Reservoir Dogs* centres on a group of men, while women are almost entirely marginalised. Although the macho swagger of Tarantino's first feature and its notable lack of female characters proclaim its masculinity, the film also possesses a more fragile, less macho side that emerges, for instance, in the emotional bond that develops between Mr White (Harvey Keitel) and Mr Orange (Tim Roth). The film's pervasive sensuality and ambivalent eroticism are rooted in its fluent and adrenalin-inducing visual style; *Reservoir Dogs* articulates the narrative's inherent attitudes to masculinity through its use of mise-en-scène. By way of trying to define (or at least convey) the excitement the film's visual style produces in its audience, I will focus on the post-title sequence of the 'reservoir dogs' walking in a group out of the diner where they have been having breakfast.

The film opens with the male characters in a diner for breakfast (about to embark on a heist), engaged in one of Tarantino's now-familiar stream of consciousness riffs that culminates in an argument with Mr Pink (Steve Buscemi) about the pros and cons of tipping. For the most part – especially on first viewing – what is being said is not as important as how it is being said. With the first frame, we enter the fast-talking banter mid-sentence; the camera – also mid-thought as it were – tracks slowly around a table at which are seated the men, most of whom are dressed in black suits and white shirts except Joe (Lawrence Tierney) and his son (Chris Penn) in his garish shell suit and adorned in bling. The tracking shot cuts from medium- to close-up, but the strong, methodical, insistent circular movement continues virtually uninterrupted until the camera stops as Mr White snatches a notebook off Joe. After this brief hiatus, the circular camera movement resumes, stopping once again as Joe gets up to pay and the tipping argument starts. Joe, these moves suggest, is the boss.

After Joe persuades the reluctant Mr Pink to chip in with his dollar for the tip, a radio playing 'K-Billy's Super Sounds of the Seventies' intrudes. The image cuts to outside the diner, as the 'dogs' emerge in slow motion from right of frame in monochrome costumes, smoking and putting on their sunglasses. The framing and angle changes as the

Fig. 2.16

men switch to walking towards the camera (at head height) in close-up as the titles go through each actor in turn, their names appearing under them (Figs 2.16–2.17). Their effortless cool (Susan Fraiman, for example, begins her book *Cool Men and the Second Sex* by referring to being 'confronted by coolness' (2003: 1) as she started to write about Tarantino) is echoed by the definite but at the same time playful bass intro of 'Little Green Bag'. Tarantino's soundtrack music – as meticulously selected as Scorsese's – is as cool as the men it accompanies. Tarantino has referred to Jean-Pierre Melville's suited gangsters as wearing suits of armour,[11] and here during the title sequence of *Reservoir Dogs* there is a comparably strong sense of Tarantino's gangsters going into battle; instead of armour they have suits, instead of weapons they carry shades, and the slow motion accentuates the nonchalant swagger in their step (Figs 2.18–2.19).

Fig. 2.17

Fig. 2.18

Once the main actors have been introduced, the framing changes to a low level long shot from behind; the jaunty chorus of 'Little Green Bag' plays as the men walk away from the camera and the film's title rolls upwards into frame, proclaiming that these men 'are … *Reservoir Dogs*', a collective identity that is enigmatic and impenetrable. There is then a cut to black for the remainder of the credits, towards the end of which one begins to pick out the gasps and groans of Mr Orange who has been

Fig. 2.19

shot and is bleeding profusely all over the pristine pale leather backseat of a car as he is being comforted by the driver, Mr White, also attempting to reassure him that he is not going to die. The 'dogs' have thus remained unblemished, virile and active symbols of functioning, superlative masculinity until precisely the end of the title sequence and the ease, grace and confidence they ooze at the outset is resolutely undermined by the remainder of the film, beginning with the messy and bloody puncturing of Mr Orange's suit of armour.

The allure of *Reservoir Dogs* was, at the time of its release, complex. Tarantino remarked: 'I've always said that the mark of any good action movie is that when you get through seeing it, you want to dress like the character' (in Dargis 1994: 17). It is intriguing that Tarantino equates the existence of desire- and narcissism-drenched identification with the action film, and I am arguing here for a correspondingly layered form of identification in relation to masculinity and mise-en-scène; not that the films necessarily make audiences want to look like the characters, but that one key motivational force is to want to offer the sense of what it is like to be them. This is clearly not a straightforward form of identification and it is certainly not one that presumes the idealisation of the image on the screen as the film also dwells upon the men's shortcomings and failures. The ambivalence and complexity of our affinity to the men, however, is tied to Tarantino's use of mise-en-scène, for on the level of image only the 'reservoir dogs' – in their swaggering majesty – come across as unified, strong, butch. The residual fear that masculinity might be insubstantial, fragile or the ultimate illusion is compensated for and masked by the manner in which the men are styled. The aim, I think, of Tarantino's opening to *Reservoir Dogs* is to sweep us along with the momentum of the slow-motion walk, the culty soundtrack, the men's cool costumes and shades and to make us then interpret the subsequently far less perfect representation of masculinity with this supremely confident opening always in mind. The cameraman on the film, Andrej Sekula, commented that the 'dogs' swagger out of the diner at the beginning '*Wild Bunch* style' and with 'a sort of unnatural slowness' (in Dawson 1995: 62). *Reservoir Dogs* – the product of Hollywood's best-known film nerd – is knowing, ironic and reflexive. It defines itself in relation to past cinema as well as having become, virtually instantaneously, a trend-setting, definitive film in its own right. The dogs' cool is transferable and tangible.

If the specific qualities of *Reservoir Dogs*' style are then linked to Tarantino's reflexivity, then how the motifs and tropes of men's cinema are established becomes much clearer. The cameraman of *Reservoir Dogs* recalls *The Wild Bunch*; he could equally have recalled *Once Upon a Time in the West* or numerous Hollywood films since that have used the group of men walking in slow motion to embody strident masculinity and the (ultimately flimsy, futile) 'let's go to work' ethos at the heart of *Reservoir Dogs*. The opening titles make us feel one way about the men, while the remainder of the film makes us question their stridency and our belief at that moment in the performance of strident masculinity. As in Freud and Lacan's writings about masculinity, *Reservoir Dogs* retains in tandem a residual belief in the integrity of idealised, heterosexual masculinity while confronting it as illusory. The swaggering title sequence thereby becomes an attempt to paper over the cracks of the frailties that emerge soon after, the most persistent of which is the homosocial bond that forms between Mr White and Mr Orange.

A significant factor in the effectiveness of the potency of the 'men walking together' motif is that it is recognisable and familiar: *Reservoir Dogs* works at framing and conveying masculinity not just because of what it does, but because of the fact that it self-consciously recalls *The Wild Bunch*, *Once Upon a Time in the West* or *The Right Stuff* and such films' use of the group of men walking purposefully in slow motion to fight or work. The iconic status of a group of men walking in this way is played on in *The Right Stuff* as the astronauts, having stood up to the NASA scientists by insisting that their capsule design should include a window,[12] stride 'in slow motion ... manfully abreast towards the camera through the long NASA corridor, with shafts of light rippling on their shiny silver space suits' (Charity 1997: 66). About this scene Philip Kaufman commented on the peculiar Americanness of such iconography:

> They have that swagger almost like they're a gang from *The Wanderers*, about to get into a battle with a neighbouring gang, in this case the Russians – that sort of American swagger ... For me, that's freedom without viciousness, that kind of bonding and team spirit which, within proper bounds, I really like. (In Charity 1997: 66)

Kaufman here picks out the particular conjunction of conservatism and confidence that marks many examples of men walking; the self-belief epitomised by this collective gesture usually has a reactionary ideological root, which for many of those swept up – as Kaufman is – by its 'spirit', is inherently problematic. This ambivalence is demonstrably shared by many of the more recent (and post-feminist) examples of men walking: the men swagger, but this is pride before a fall. There is something undeniably powerful in such images of bonding and supportiveness, but in many instances what is ultimately exposed is the instability of a form of male bonding overly reliant on gesture and performance.

Goodfellas and *The American President*: the single male figure walking

As an adjunct to this analysis of men walking in tandem, I will now examine another recurrent trope of men's cinema that is similarly expressive of male confidence and power: the lone man walking. This is just as iconic as the male group walking; in many westerns, for example, the hero walks or rides into and out of town alone. The solitary male figure generally exemplifies a different type of masculinity – untouchable and lonelier, but also more self-sufficient than his buddied counterpart. What I am going to look at here are two very different sequences that nevertheless share the trait of a man in a position of power walking, accompanied by a woman. In both, there is a sense of bravura and showing off, of performing for the benefit of those watching; in *Goodfellas* (1990) technical ostentatiousness complements Henry Hill's (Ray Liotta) walk into the Copaca-bana looking to impress Karen (Lorraine Bracco) on their first date, and in *The American President* (1995) similar elements are brought together for President Andrew Shepherd's (Michael Douglas) walk to the Oval Office on a Monday morning, the mise-en-scène complementing the sense of this action's routineness. Both sequences show men walk-ing to a defined, significant destination, but whereas the sequence from *Goodfellas* is a single-take Steadicam shot, that from *The American President* is made up of a series of individual shots edited together to form a comparably seamless impression. Both clearly required meticulous logistical planning, which is emphasised rather than concealed.

The Steadicam shot in *Goodfellas* – a technical *tour de force* – shows young Irish gangster Henry Hill escorting Karen into a club. Michael Balhaus, *Goodfellas*' cinematog-rapher, evidently influenced the film's camera style as much as Scorsese did as director.[13] Henry Hill has just picked up Karen from home; the Steadicam shot starts after they have got out of the car, with a medium close-up of Henry handing a parking valet his keys and is synchronised with The Crystals' 1963 single 'Then He Kissed Me', which begins just on the edit into Henry's hand and draws to a close just as Henry and Karen take their seats in the Copacabana. The timing of this single shot to the Crystals' song is significant not just because of what the song is about (a girl's old-fashioned, quaintly naïve account of being kissed and proposed to) but because it renders the shot self-contained, dreamy, slightly detached from the rest of the film – as from Karen's perspective (as she is willingly swept off her feet by Henry Hill) it undoubtedly is. The classic perfection of the three-minute pop song is emulated by the comparable perfection of the long single-take, doubly significant perhaps because *Goodfellas* is not full of such 'look at me' sequences. The Steadicam fol-lows behind Henry and Karen until the very end and, unless remarked upon, their move-ment is continuous.

After handing over his car keys Henry, with one arm protectively around Karen's back, crosses the street. On the other side Henry takes Karen into the Copacabana the back way ('better than waiting in line'), the long queue of those also trying to get in parting for them as they head down some stairs. At the bottom of the stairs Henry opens a door and greets and pays the doorman; they then turn right down a corridor, Henry shaking hands with a couple of men and joshing with a couple canoodling in the corner ('Every time I come here! Every time!'). Henry is at ease here, known, part of the fraternity, a 'made man'; the relaxed, elegant fluidity of the camera moves conveys firstly Henry's mastery of the situation, that he belongs, and secondly the allure of this world to Karen, a nicely brought up middle-class Jewish girl for whom the Crystals' song is far more appropriate than a mafia-run club.

Henry then leads Karen weaving through the brightness and the bustle of the noisy kitchen and tips another doorman as they finally enter the dingy pink of the club itself. The shot remains unbroken but Henry and Karen temporarily stop walking as a member of the waiting staff talks to Henry about where he will put his table (which turns out to be right at the front); the camera then begins to move again, but this time it follows the table that has hastily materialised, being carried aloft by another waiter, negotiating the tightly packed tables already in place, its billowing white tablecloth standing out against the seedy gloom around it. A lamp is found, placed on the little round table and plugged in, at which point Henry and Karen come back into view and sit down, but only after Henry has leant over to greet the people seated behind them. Karen removes her white gloves and raises the issue of Henry having liberally disseminated $20 tips.

Karen's gloves resonate with her demure innocence and conventionality, totally at odds with Henry's ostentatious immorality. Just as Karen has removed the gloves and placed them in front of her (their pristine whiteness sitting easily on the unsullied whiteness of the tablecloth), a hovering waiter presents Henry with a bottle of wine, from 'Mr Tony over there'. The camera then pans over to Mr Tony's nearby table, Tony acknowledging Henry's gratitude. As the camera pans back to Henry and Karen 'Then He Kissed Me' winds down, and as it fades out Karen asks of Henry, 'What do you do?' to which he offers the stock reply that he is 'in construction'. Karen remarks that his hands are too soft for someone in that line of work and Henry counters that he is a union delegate. The camera then pans over to the stage, where 'the king of the one-liners, Henny Youngman' has just arrived, a middle-aged, sexist comedian who opens his set with a weary dig at his wife ('I'm glad to be here – take my wife, please!'). This is the end of the single take, although the sexist gags spill over into the next scene.

This whole sequence, for all its uninterrupted majesty, is about conflict, or rather how conflicts can find themselves subsumed, glossed over, the most obvious of which is Karen's internalised struggle between wanting Henry and knowing that he is no good. Karen's disavowal is important to the effect of the Steadicam shot – that she understands what is going on and realises that Henry is a gangster, but nevertheless is willing to suppress this knowledge because she is in awe of Henry's flamboyant lifestyle and power. The fluidity of the Steadicam's movement itself – the manner in which it sidles and shimmies with effortless ease through the corridors, kitchen and tables – connotes what it feels like to be sucked in willingly to all this and to enjoy both the lifestyle and the act of submission. Although executed differently, this act of succumbing to the allure of the mafia has featured before in *Goodfellas*: the sensuous slow-motion close-ups of Paulie Cicero's (Paul Sorvino) friends' shoes, clothes and accessories as they emerge from their cars at the beginning of the film, representing the schoolboy Henry's fascination with and desire to be part of the gangsters' world, or the classic fetishising pan up the adult Henry's body, from his tassled loafers to his face, as he leans against the bonnet of a car waiting for a consignment to arrive at the airport. Just as the youthful Henry found himself irresistibly drawn to the world of Paulie Cicero, so he is unstoppable in his seduction of Karen.

Karen's role in this, however, is not merely to be duped; just as she realises Henry does not 'work in construction', so the steamroller quality of the extended Steadicam shot enacts an elaborate negotiation between parading the violence, the criminality, at the same time as it brushes past them and pretends they are not there. This long take is also fundamentally erotic, for Karen is not only being sucked into the milieu of the mob but is falling in love with Henry, and although her refinement (the little black dress, the white gloves) might imply she is looking for the straightforward chastity evoked by the Crystals' song, her glances over at Henry as they walk into the club and the eagerness with which she disavows all knowledge of what he does for a living imply she would rather be the mobster's moll. The use of such a fluent and energetic Steadicam serves to underline how a 'nice' girl like Karen could fall for a criminal like Henry by involving and implicating those watching: it is not just Karen who is being swept into the bowels of the Copacabana, but us, via the insistent camera. As with Scorsese's use of an expressive camera style in *Raging Bull*, the ostensible synchronisation of camera and character is only partial; following on from the sequence's inherent ambivalence (that Henry is attractive but also a criminal) is confirmation that our point of view is not synchronous with Karen's. When Henry and Karen stop momentarily as a waiter fetches their table seems extremely important, because it is at this moment – the resumption of the movement of the camera and the characters' movement in front of it notwithstanding – that the critical distance between Karen's limited perspective and our greater omniscience is underscored. The gangsters' world is attractive and smooth, like Balhaus's shot, but the short cessation of movement in the middle of the courting couple's journey to the best table in the house (magicked out of thin air, as it were) serves as a reminder that the shot has been intricately constructed, all the movement going in and out of it meticulously choreographed. With this distance comes the inevitable recognition that the club's and Henry's charms and glamour are merely superficial.

In the opening sequence of Rob Reiner's romantic comedy *The American President*, the fictional titular president, Andrew Shepherd, is walking to the Oval Office at the beginning of the working week. *The American President* was scripted by Aaron Sorkin and the film's opening sequence, though smooth and energetic, has principally become noteworthy retrospectively, having later become a staple moment of Sorkin's later creation *The West Wing* (1999–2006) (and frequently parodied in British comedy series such as *Dead Ringers* (2002–), *The Armstrong and Miller Show* (2007) and *The Graham Norton Show* (2007), in which Martin Sheen, who plays fictional president Josiah 'Jed' Bartlet, performed a mock power walk through the studio).[14] *The West Wing*'s renditions of the power walk prioritised Steadicam, which made them appear slick and robust; what remains interesting about the incarnation in *The American President* of an ostensibly similar cinematic moment is that here a comparable effect is created using more traditional editing and camera techniques alongside Steadicam sections.

The title sequence of *The American President* comprises a montage of the portraits of past American presidents displayed in the White House, edited languidly together using cross-fades and captured by a camera that, though constantly moving, is leisurely and slightly staid as opposed to breathless. The tone of these titles (accompanied by a lush orchestral score) is sonorous and serious and the sequence concludes with a static wide shot of the White House exterior. A sharp edit marks the transition to the start of Shepherd's walk, a brisk contrast with the stroll through the icons of American presidential history that had preceded it (a history he now embodies). A security man whispers into a hidden microphone, announcing that the president (codename 'Liberty') is

Fig. 2.20

Fig. 2.21

Fig. 2.22

Fig. 2.23

on the move (Figs 2.20–2.21). Shepherd emerges with his personal assistant, Jane (Samantha Mathis), who is running through the day's schedule as they walk, briskly and purposefully, through the corridors of power, the sequence thereby collapsing literal meaning and metaphoric meaning, as subsequently occurs in *The West Wing*. Shepherd strides dynamically towards the camera while Jane struggles a bit to keep up; they get closer to the camera and turn, the camera panning round with them. The meetings Jane runs through include one with American Fisheries, at which the president will be presented with a prize fish. Shepherd quips to Jane to remind him 'to schedule more events when someone gives me a really big fish'. The joke is lost on Jane who is busy writing this instruction down. The use of humour here is significant, for although it temporarily detracts attention from the powerfulness of the power walk, Shepherd's pace, look and tone do not alter as he jokes: there is no faltering, no let up; nothing will make the president digress from his mission.

The dialogue continues uninterrupted as Shepherd and Jane enter a lift and exit it, at which point Lewis Rothschild (Shepherd's press secretary, played by Michael J. Fox) joins the president and Jane to express his concern at the omission from a speech the president had made the night before of plans to tighten gun control (Figs 2.22–2.23). Leaving out a piece of liberal policy from a speech about 'the great society' is an important indicator of Shepherd's political tendencies (as well as his caution), but however significant such a detail is, it again does nothing to interrupt or stall him: Shepherd had started walking the moment the lift doors had opened, this time away from the camera and flanked by Lewis to his right and Jane to his left (now framed from the front and side). He then makes his way along a corridor and through another door, at which point there is an edit to a frontal shot, a switch in angle that coincides with both the group's passage through a door and a changeover of security personnel (Figs 2.24–2.26).

Key to the effect of the sequence is that there is no break in momentum, either in Shepherd's tank-like progress towards the Oval Office or in the pace of his conversation, his tone of voice or the direction of his gaze, which remains focused on the middle distance in front of him (signalling both his presidential destination and more generally his determination). The one thing that does change, as the visuals remain constant, is the topic of conversation. On passing through this second set of doors into the loggia running alongside the garden, for example, the conversation turns to Shepherd's high approval ratings, although there is a subsidiary exchange as the gardener addresses the president, Jane tells him *sotto voce* that his name is Charlie and Shepherd extends a return greeting. Again, there is no faltering, no easing of either the walking or the conversational pace as this aside is seamlessly interwoven into the rest of the conversation, the actors' delivery complementing the President's physical movement through the White House. The walk's feeling of purposefulness and momentum is built up using a combination of Steadicam and fixed-mounted shots, individual sequences being built up using a wider shot – usually showing the characters walking towards the camera, a side close-up as the characters walk in front of the camera on their way past it and then a pan or Steadicam track

Fig. 2.24

Fig. 2.25

Fig. 2.26

round to follow them as they continue away from it. Unlike the single take in *Goodfellas*, several camera angles are intercut in *The American President*, but the seamless editing (seamless because the cuts almost invariably come as the direction alters or a door is entered or a character comes in or out of frame) create a similar effect.

Through a third set of doors, the presidential entourage enters the inner sanctum of the Oval Office and the network of offices that surround it. This sequence has got progressively busier, and here, while Shepherd and Lewis continue their discussion of the 'great society' speech, aides bustle around them, a busyness signalled by switches in framing and camera angles: from behind to frontal as Shepherd and Lewis enter the domain of the Oval Office, to close-up as they turn the corner. The rise in adrenalin induced by merely following this sequence is interrupted again by an amusing exchange between Shepherd and Lewis as the President asks his press secretary to cut by half his morning caffeine intake, only to be informed that he does not drink coffee, to which he advises Lewis to hit himself 'over the head with a baseball bat'. Despite the respite offered once again by humour the only shift comes in the tone of the script; there is still no change in vocal register from Michael Douglas. After wishing one of his office workers 'happy birthday', the President swoops past his chief secretary, Mrs Chapil (Anne Haney), who is holding out the mug of coffee that he takes without pausing, as he finally walks into the Oval Office. The conversation between Shepherd and his aides about the rise in his approval ratings continues across another edit, as they enter the room, adopting the by now conventionalised sequence of shots, starting with a closer shot as the actors walk past the camera at the point of Mrs Chapil handing Shepherd his coffee that is then replaced by a shot from behind as they approach the Oval Office door, which in turn cuts to a frontal shot of them entering the door, the camera being mounted just behind the very familiar presidential desk. Finally, as Shepherd comes to rest so does the camera, and throughout the next scene – a Monday morning debrief between the President and his close staff – the editing and framing is a quieter and more conventional mix of mid-close-up shot/reverse-shots.

As it is the opening of the film, the rhythm of this sequence is particularly significant. The effect is to plunge the audience straight into Shepherd's high-pressure world and consequently, while compelling us to marvel at his capacity to manage a situation that could easily (on both a technical and narrative level) unravel, to suck us into his life and the pace at which he lives it. The extended take in *Goodfellas* is more overtly erotic than this opening to *The American President*, but both are symbolic and resonant of male sexuality. Richard Dyer noted, as signalled earlier, the 'goal-orientated' basis of male sexuality, that the male orgasm is sex's grand finale. Whilst Dyer, like *Goodfellas* and *The American President*, does not necessarily believe that male sexuality is this direct, he, like the films, posits the possibility that this is how men see themselves and their sexuality. To then link this to my earlier analysis of Freud's 'The Sexual Aberrations' as a polemic that took an intentionally narrow view of 'normal' sex as heterosexual, pen-etrative copulation in order to more widely examine human sexuality in the light of the *im*possibility of successfully pursuing such 'normality', the stridency and linear trajectory of the 'man walking' sequences in *Goodfellas* or *The American President* mimic Dyer's likewise polemical conceptualisation of the male sex act while simultaneously rendering it rigidly, perversely simplistic. Both Henry Hill and Andrew Shepherd have a strained attachment to not being interrupted or sent off course, an attachment that is hysterical in its intensity.

Although the two sequences are different in tone and offer different attitudes to-wards this masculine fixation with keeping up a powerful appearance, the two examples are useful to discuss in tandem because they approach from alternative perspectives the notion of using smoothness – in the form of a continuous shot or a seamless sequence of shots – to elide ambiguities, much as Tarantino had done in *Reservoir Dogs*. The pace of these two walking sequences creates a quite specific relationship between meaning and mise-en-scène. There is a clear sense in both the *Goodfellas* sequence and that from *The American President* that ambivalences and uncertainties are literally being brushed aside – and symbolically repressed – by the momentum of the men walking. In turn, the spectator's ability to maintain a detachment from the men walking and not to be swept along with the momentum as well is limited. Both sequences are also, as I have indicated, allied to sexuality, for although the one in *The American President* is certainly less fluid, less beautiful, less erotically charged than Henry Hill's entry into the Copacabana, it nevertheless still connotes the equally potent allure of power and control. In this, ultimately, both sequences are compelling – or rather trying to compel – their respective audiences to fall in love with masculinity.

Top Gun and the synchronisation of music and editing

This notion of falling in love with masculinity as opposed to merely the embodiment of a masculine ideal by an actor/character stems from a similar theoretical position to that adopted by Jackie Stacey in relation to psychoanalysis-based feminist film criticism of the 1980s. In 'Desperately Seeking Difference' Stacey argued that:

> The rigid distinction between *either* desire *or* identification ... fails to address the construction of desires which involve a specific interplay of both processes. (1987: 61)

Although Stacey is proposing an ambivalent, eroticised form of identification with, specifically, an onscreen figure, what I am particularly interested in developing here is the comparably ambivalent form of identification with and desire for masculinity proffered by certain tropes and motifs within mise-en-scène. It is not the case, for instance, that the purpose of the slow motion of the 'reservoir dogs' leaving for the heist or the strident pace of Andrew Shepherd's working walk through to the Oval Office is simply to persuade the spectator to identify with or desire the films' protagonists; the effect is more diffuse than this and revolves around the conceptualisation of mise-en-scène as a means of making the spectator desire or identify with an abstract notion – in these instances masculinity – as opposed to a figure. Within this more general framework it seems to me that Hollywood's representation of masculinity has been complemented and enhanced by this development of a series of tropes and motifs through which that masculinity is expressed.

The discussion now moves to the action film, a genre that, especially with the demise and reconfiguration of the western, has become Hollywood's main arena for exhibiting masculine physicality. Again, however, I am less interested in talking about the representation of masculinity than in how that masculinity is conceived through or embodied and enhanced by mise-en-scène. Yvonne Tasker's *Spectacular Bodies* centred on issues of representation when discussing masculinity in the action film, but the genre has also leant itself – through its fascination with spectacle – to the analysis of visual style. One critic to have concentrated on the visual style of contemporary Hollywood action cinema is José Arroyo who, when writing about Brian de Palma's *Mission: Impossible*, remarked upon how such 'high concept cinema ... strives to offer a theme park of attractions: music, colour, story, performance, delight and the sense of improbably fast action' (2000: 22). Arroyo then asserts that the aim of the collision between all these elements is to 'seduce the audience into surrendering to the ride' (ibid.). In a similar vein, Richard Dyer, writing about Jan de Bont's *Speed* (1994), makes the point that 'To go to an action movie is to sink back in the seat and say, "show me a good time"', despite the pervasive cultural and political anxiety generated by passivity, especially in relation to masculinity (2000: 20). He continues:

The worst thing imaginable is to go to the cinema to lie back and enjoy it. Which suggests another terror, lurking beneath the fear of being like, and being treated like, a woman. For what kind of man is it who lies back and enjoys it? A queer, of course. (2000: 21)

For Dyer, the 'delicious paradox' of action movies is that the films promote an 'active engagement with the world' whilst also promoting a passive sense of enjoyment as they 'come to you, take you over, do you' (ibid.). The conclusion to Dyer's argument for action cinema as sex[15] is the assertion that 'for the male viewer action movies have a lot in common with being fellated', a position that compromises masculinity because:

it's the other person … who's doing the work, really being active. So it is with action movies. In imagination, men can be Arnie or Keanu; in the seat, it's Arnie or Keanu pleasuring them. Now that's what I call speed. (Ibid.)

What is refreshing about Dyer's analysis of the pleasures of action cinema in this essay is its attention to the physical act of watching the films. However, in contradistinction to Dyer I will here argue (in relation to the use of mise-en-scène in the action film as a mechanism for generating pleasurable viewing) for a nebulous association of imagination, identification and pleasure more in keeping with Stacey's idea of erotic identification and less attached to the idea that watching action movies is physically a passive experience. As I see it, the emotion generated by an identification not only with the character but also with the spectacle and movement within the mise-en-scène – because of the physical responses of excitement generated through this – does not have to feel passive; the eroticism does not simply stem from things being done to us as Dyer posits but from the transference of that power from what is happening on the screen to us via a dynamic use of mise-en-scène.

What I am interested in doing now is to identify, as I did above with the motif of men walking, some of the persistent key tropes of action cinema and to discuss them as illustrative of this active spectatorial response. When writing about *Mission: Impossible*, Arroyo commented:

Applying the Frankfurt School's critique of mass culture to this type of filmmaking would not be hard: *Mission: Impossible* is not very original; the structure of the whole doesn't depend on details; it respects conventional norms of what constitutes intelligibility on contemporary filmmaking. It could be seen as an example of pseudo-individuation, that which seems different but is in fact the same, whose object is to affirm capitalist culture. (2000: 23)

Arroyo might be right about the action cinema's sameness and its unconscious ideological allegiance to capitalism; the genre's homogeneity, however, is, I would argue, also dependent on an understanding of the films' detail or at least on an analysis of their intricate construction, hence my desire in this study to focus closely on specific elements of their mise-en-scène.

The discussion of Tony Scott's *Top Gun* to follow centres on a specific issue in relation to the analysis of detail, namely the film's most significant subtext: its homosocialism and suppression of homosexuality. The relationship of action cinema to homosexuality is noted, explicitly in Dyer's essay on *Speed* and implicitly in Arroyo's on *Mission:
Impossible*. Part of the action genre's predictability and its affirmation of capitalist culture
is – equally predictably – its repression of homosexuality. However – and with this I wish
to recall once again Freud's polemic in 'The Sexual Aberrations' – certain action films
(such as *Top Gun*) are specifically constructed, it would seem, around situations that
are inherently and defiantly homosocial and explicitly afford images of masculinity that
invite the erotic gaze (male or female) towards the masculine body that Steve Neale, for
instance, found so troubling. Action cinema is about display and about the male body
on display while engaging in extreme acts. The mise-en-scène of a film such as *Top
Gun* is directly in synchronisation with and supportive of the genre's zealous attachment to straightness, but in this case it proves impossible to entirely repress the latent
homosexuality and with it the fear of perversity that would expose the fraudulence of
the film's dominant performance of masculinity, its hysterical protestations of machismo
that point, almost directly, towards what they are denying the existence of (namely, homosexuality). *Top Gun* remains both a great action movie and one of the campest films
of this supposedly straight canon. Available on the Internet are queered versions of *Top
Gun*; but *Top Gun* does not require queering, groaning as it does under the strain of its
own futile internalised battles against its queer core.

Tony Scott in *Top Gun* repeatedly uses the synchronisation of music, rhythm and
energy as a means of constructing the archetype of the young action hero, exemplified
by a series of sequences that intermingle recreation and intensive fighter pilot training, starting with the sweaty game of volleyball in which Pete 'Maverick' Mitchell (Tom
Cruise) and his co-pilot 'Goose' (Anthony Edwards) take on 'Iceman' (Val Kilmer) and his
co-pilot 'Slider' (Rick Rossovich). In terms of the theme of masculine rivalry on which
Top Gun pivots, Maverick and Iceman are the only two real contenders for the 'Top Gun'
slot – the best pilot of a cohort – a competition that underpins all the film's competitive
exchanges.

In a Top Gun classroom, Maverick walks past Slider who, model aeroplane in hand,
mutters: 'Crash and burn, ha Maverick?' (Slider is here hurling back at Maverick a
phrase he has used more than once, thus mimicking Maverick's own posturing machismo); Maverick stops, leans over Slider and snarls back: 'Slider, you stink', at which
Slider looks embarrassed. The introductory beats to a song start up – quietly at first
– as Slider sniffs under his arms to check. This penchant for overlaying onto the end of
one sequence the main driving music track for the next is a central component of Tony
Scott's editing style (*Top Gun*, like *Backdraft*, is basically edited as if it is an extended
pop promo) and is used in *Top Gun* several times: an anticipatory tactic that emphasises
synchronicity, raising the audience's expectations and getting them pumped up before
even the main characters realise they are about to get pumped up. This continual hyp-
ing up is a symptom of *Top Gun*'s pervasive hysteria, its need to constantly reaffirm in

the most exaggerated ways the presence and importance of masculinity, a masculinity that is never permitted just to be normal or even just to be, except in the couple of quiet (heterosexual) romantic scenes between Maverick and Charlie (Kelly McGillis). The concluding frames, as the song starts up, of Maverick getting back at Slider function as a prelude to the next big performance of larger-than-life masculinity, an up-beat action sequence in which machismo is defined through the classic generic conjunction of brash music and fast editing. The choice of music track in such a sequence is equally characteristic: a thumping, insistent, bland 1980s' dance/pop number, its own generic blandness complementing perhaps the generic unoriginality Arroyo detected – and enjoyed – in *Mission: Impossible*. We, the audience for *Top Gun*, are by now familiar with the film's routine packaging of masculinity and this familiarity informs and shapes our enjoyment. A contradictory result of *Top Gun*'s visual and aural elements appearing to be so straightforward and oversimplifying is that they telegraph the potential complexities and contradictions they mask, and so the very predictability of the film's mise-en-scène establishes a framework within which a critique of its portrayal of masculinity can take place.

Straight after the chastened Slider sniffs his armpits there is a sequence of short close-ups and medium close-ups establishing that a game of volleyball is being played, commencing with a close-up of a pilot's sweaty back (who turns out to be Iceman) and

Fig. 2.27

the pilot then spinning a ball on the forefinger of a partially bandaged hand (Fig. 2.27). The iconography is key here: sweaty bodies adorned with that most masculine of accessories, the soldier's metal identity tag, alongside the aviator sunglasses *Top Gun* made so fashionable and desirable and contrasted with Iceman's bandage. From this not too badly injured hand the image cuts to Maverick, who checks his watch, shouts, 'Let's go!' to Goose and claps a motivational, manly sort of a clap. Iceman serves, Maverick receives and Goose hits back to Maverick; the words to the song started in synch with Maverick's first strike of the ball, and thus the complementarity of music to editing effortlessly sucks the audience into synchronicity with Maverick especially, making him the motivational force of the sequence.

Then, following this establishing male-centred montage of close-ups, the camera pulls out to a high-angle shot of the sandy court, a move of strength, certainty and ostentation. The game itself is not as important, this move indicates, as the rivalry between Maverick and Iceman, their respective musculatures and the alternative types of masculinity they represent. After the wide shot of the court a series of medium shots and close-ups are intermingled, juxtaposing the gestures of competitive masculinity, such as Maverick and Goose doing 'high fives'; then there comes a sequence of three serves, followed by Iceman receiving and Slider winning the point, prompting him to celebrate. A couple of these shots – for example, Iceman receiving serve – are slowed down slightly, the alternating between fast and slow creating the rippling effect that has become a regular feature of contemporary Hollywood action films.[16]

Slider's celebration coincides with the beginning of the song's chorus, the most repeated and hence most familiar section of the music. The images and sound accompanying the chorus are cut in time to the music and go like this: Slider's whoop as he wins the point, a sound almost camouflaged by the similar crescendo in the song; a reverse shot of Maverick looking annoyed; Goose placing his arm around his buddy's back as they walk away from the camera and the net; Goose looking back over his shoulder as the image reverts to Slider, who appears to be striking a bodybuilding pose, three-quarters on and tightening his stomach muscles and those of one arm; Iceman spinning the ball on his finger again, this time front-on; Maverick doing his motivational clap again to indicate he is ready to receive; a rally comprising various close-ups of Iceman gritting his teeth, Slider lunging for the ball and Maverick high-fiving again, their celebration – the climax of the rally – coinciding precisely with the climax of the chorus. The volleyball game ends as Maverick – bathed in the golden light of late afternoon (fully emphasised by Scott's over-attachment to pink filters) – leaves, puts on his obligatory white t-shirt, jacket and aviator shades and roars off on his motorbike to dine with Charlie to the more romantic strains of 'Take My Breath Away'. The most significant factor of *Top Gun's* portrayal of masculinity is that it is a performance, a show put on for the imaginary crowd watching; in this, the inference is always there that masculinity comes into being when it is performed for others and that without the need to perform such brash, confident masculinity would cease to exist. The performative elements of *Top Gun's* images of masculinity are not only emphasised by but also constructed through the deployment of music and editing: the songs are obviously performances in themselves and that the renditions of masculinity they accompany are likewise performances is underlined by the synchronous editing. The energy dedicated to the performance of masculinity draws attention to the lack and emptiness at its core, that the men's identities are not fixed and definite but rather fluid and unstable. For all their posturing, the 'top gun' pilots are vulnerable, a vulnerability that is confirmed by the awkward contrast between their exuberant performances (the high fives, the fists pumping the air, the glistening muscles) and what these might be repressing – a lack of identity, certainly, but also the spectre of queerness that lurks behind all this excitable homosocialism.

Some ten minutes later comes a test piloting exercise, the prelude to which is Maverick getting fired up upon being told that Iceman, ahead in the 'top gun' competition, has won another exercise. In flying gear, walking towards the camera and towards their jet, he turns to Goose and says, 'I feel the need…', Goose then joining him for '…the need for speed', as they inevitably slap their palms together for more 'high fives', before a hard cut to a jet roaring across the screen. The first part of this sequence is without music, but the boom of the first jet performs a similar starting gun function to the first beats of the musical track that announced the volleyball match. Maverick is meant to be staying on the wing of fellow trainee pilot 'Hollywood' (Whip Hubley), but he soon decides to depart from the plan and go after 'Viper' (Tom Skerritt), the most decorated and respected of the

Top Gun instructors. Maverick assures Hollywood, 'You're looking good. I'm going after Viper.' After a close-up of Maverick in his jet, there is another close shot of his hand on the control stick, a purposeful click as he changes the settings on it, proclaiming – much as a cowboy cocking his trigger might do in a western – his readiness for a fight, an intention underlined with another quick shot of Maverick shunting the control stick as if going up a gear in a car (surely piloting a fighter jet is not so mundane?). Tony Scott then cuts from these tight interiors to an aerial exterior of two planes, the first (Maverick's) soon breaking the formation to soar almost vertically upwards as music starts up and Hollywood mutters 'God damn you, Maverick'.

Once more, there is the simple but affecting synchronisation of narrative trajectory, character, image and, this time, a drum- and bass-led instrumental track. The music continues, becomes more pulsating and strident and complements the fast-cut chase sequence comprising (as all the flying sequences do in *Top Gun*) a medley of close interior shots and wide exterior images of tense pilots and planes zipping across the limpid expanse of blue skies, not indicating exactly what is happening but suggesting most emphatically the strain and the effort such antics entail. The potential for likening such adrenalin-fuelled sequences to the single-minded trajectory of the male orgasm is great in *Top Gun*, particularly with the tumescence of its soundtrack, but here, just as the fraught and excitable Maverick thinks he has his man and is about to 'fire' at Viper, consummation is denied as another instructor's plane locks onto him from behind; had this been a real battle Maverick would have been killed. Throughout *Top Gun*, the veiled references to a stereotypical interpretation of the male sex act (the simple, linear trajec-tory of the music tracks and the actions they accompany, for example) comes to the fore, only to be undermined by its interruption, such as here, or by its evocation within a homosocial context. That *Top Gun* is so manifestly queerable consolidates the idea that masculinity (commonly glossed as heterosexual) is actually defined by its queerness rather than by its successful demolition of queerness. As in 'The Sexual Aberrations', the 'normal' sex act is an impossible ideal, dislodged by perversity. The music by the end of this flying sequence becomes subdued and finally peters out, as if marking the crucial interruption of the symbolic male sex act.

The synchronisation of music and editing is used consistently in *Top Gun* to frame mood and to offer a dynamic construction of masculinity that purports to repress such potentially disruptive forces. Cutting a sequence to the rhythm of a fast, beat-driven soundtrack ostensibly irons out nuances and complications. In relation to masculinity, such a transparent, synchronic editing style has the effect of imposing an over-simplified notion of masculinity, men's actions and men's motives; it also generates a comparably straightforward, uncomplicated and physical response in the audience. Much of the en-joyment of watching an action movie such as *Top Gun* depends upon our physical, active and not merely cerebral and passive engagement with it. It is a truism to suggest that the pounding beat of the soundtrack – slightly faster than an adult heartbeat – makes our heart race and adrenalin rise, but this is pretty much the feeling *Top Gun* induces, or at the very least aims to induce. These formal over-simplifications are intriguing, as they seem intent upon tarmacking over the strains and fissures that are so incompletely repressed throughout. *Top Gun*, however, is as deliciously receptive to being queered as it is devoid of irony.

The near-orgasmic training session is immediately followed by a locker room scene – camper than even the volleyball game – of minimal narrative purpose except to have Maverick chastised for his reckless though magnificent flying. It comprises little more than a series of tableaux of wet, half-naked men posing in their dinky identical white towels pulled tight around their taut waists (Figs 2.28–2.29). The spectacular narrative superfluity of the locker room sequence is underscored as Maverick, who had been posing against a pillar, moves away after his dressing down, to be replaced by a dripping Iceman, who takes up residence, with even less motivation, at the exact same spot. In case we have not understood that the two ace pilots (or is that torsos?) are being compared, Scott has the camera track smoothly round from further away to close-up, a move perfectly timed with the instructor's exit bottom frame left, Maverick walking away from camera and Iceman arriving at the pillar from screen right. The harmonisation once more of the various elements of Scott's

Fig. 2.28

Fig. 2.29

mise-en-scène ironically, though, draws attention to the fact that very little happens in this scene bar posturing and men putting themselves on display. Pauline Kael, in her characteristically pithy review observes about *Top Gun* that, 'It is as if masculinity had been redefined as how a young man looks with his clothes half off, and as if narcissism is what being a warrior is all about' (1986: 117). The ultimate irony for us as spectators of *Top Gun* is that the homosocialism and pent up desire of a scene such as this one queers or problematises our strong involvement and identification with the straightness of the fast action sequences.

Although *Top Gun*'s narrative concludes with the stabilisation of the heterosexual romance between Maverick and Charlie, the definitive affirmation of heterosexuality comes too late. As Kael noted, *Top Gun* is defined by its homosocialism – its attachment to and prioritisation of the bonding between men that derails the normative heterosexual union. In the end, the pumped-up action sequences are spectacular but can also be seen as the hysterical and fraught manifestations of internalised tensions between normality and perversity that the film never manages to reconcile. These action sequences thus function in tandem rather than at odds with the far more blatant camp and queerness of moments such as the locker room scene. The polarities – the macho and the closeted – come together in, for instance, the volleyball game, as masculinity becomes a hysterical performance. It is, however, too easy to use *Top Gun* as proof that all men's action cinema is queer at heart, so now this discussion will be balanced out by considerations of *Die Hard* (1988) and *Gladiator* (2000), two straighter examples of the masculine aesthetic – or at least two examples in which distinctions between heterosexuality and the perverse are demarcated more neatly.

Die Hard: the action sequence

In John McTiernan's *Die Hard* the distinctions between heterosexuality and perversity that define masculinity are made on the level of narrative and representation, for example via the differentiation between John McClane (Bruce Willis) and Hans Gruber (Alan Rickman), so that any latent perversity is linked to the 'bad' men with a liking for expensive couture and flowing hair like Gruber, whilst McClane remains the film's stabilising figure: a white father and cop in functional clothes. *Die Hard* establishes the relationship between sexual/marital fulfilment and success as an action hero very clearly. As the film begins, McClane is an estranged husband working as a cop in New York, going to Los Angeles to see his wife and children for Christmas. His wife Holly (Bonnie Bedelia) had left New York six months earlier to take up a senior position in the Nakatomi Corporation, where, much to McClane's annoyance, she works under her maiden name of Gennero. *Die Hard* revolves around McClane saving his wife and most of the other Nakatomi employees from a German terrorist group, headed by Gruber, which has infiltrated and demobilised the building. At the end of the film, McClane is reunited with Holly, who, when asked by a member of the LAPD what her name is, replies 'Holly McClane'. That success as an action hero restores McClane to his patriarchal role could not be more explicitly demonstrated, although by *Die Hard 2: Die Harder* (1990) their marriage is again in difficulty and by the later films Holly has disappeared altogether.

Die Hard's action sequences mirror the straightforward symbolism and linearity of the film's overall narrative. In terms of how the mise-en-scène is integrated into this dynamic, the spectacular visual style of the action sequences are driven by and have as their focus John McClane. Although many of the films so far discussed might invoke the sexual act metaphorically, very few feature sex explicitly; sex frequently emerges as a counterforce that could, if permitted a more dominant role, destabilise the action and its hero. That masculinity in cinema is so often predicated upon sexual frustration and equally often enacts the route to male triumph and satisfaction is one notable paradox of men's cinema. With so many heroes having to prove their masculine worth via conflict or battle, the action film's expressive and conventionalised mise-en-scène frequently becomes the means by which desire and sexuality become most actively expressed and eroticism comes to be displaced onto action.

Within this context the demise of Hans Gruber – the witty, intellectual German who heads a homosocial band of psychotic brothers – is inevitable, and the beginning of the end comes in an extended exchange of machine gun fire between McClane and Gruber's men, a sequence that starts just as Gruber had thought he had regained the upper hand by fooling McClane into thinking he was an ally. McClane had handed Gruber a gun, which, as it turns out, is not loaded. The prelude to the sequence is Gruber's attempt at shooting McClane at point-blank range, which concludes with McClane's remark (after Gruber has fired the gun) 'No bullets. You think I'm fucking stupid, Hans?' Gruber had, however, summoned his henchmen and a bell announces the arrival of the lift; there is a cut back to Gruber who asks smugly, 'You were saying?', at which moment the sound-track starts up and the camera begins to move – signalling the imminence of an action sequence, just as a song beginning over the end of the previous sequence had done in *Top Gun*.

One of the signature generic features of the contemporary action film is the con-struction of extended action sequences around the coupling of short shots and fast editing, a stylistic trope that fuels and is an integral factor in the films' pervasive, often remorseless, breathlessness. Another element of many action sequences is noise, pro-vided in this sequence from *Die Hard* by gunfire and the repeated shattering of glass.

Just after the stand off between McClane and Gru-ber, the camera tracks swiftly into the lift door as two of Gruber's long-haired collaborators emerge, immediately spraying the office into which they enter with bullets (Figs 2.30–2.33). There follows a reverse shot of McClane returning fire as he runs past the lift door, his machine gun emitting fluo-rescent clouds. Each shot is short (under or around a second) and slightly tilted, which is one of *Die Hard*'s recurrent visual tropes and one that adds to its breathlessness and urgency. The canted frames are ways of signalling firstly the prominence in *Die Hard* of the point-of-view shot (often from the per-spective of John McClane in hiding and trying to figure out what Gruber is doing) and secondly that all is not how it first appears on the surface. There follows the briefest of shot/reverse-shots between McClane and Karl (Alexander Godunov), the blond-est and most psychotic of Gruber's men, including two differently framed shots of McClane running by – one wider, one substantially tighter, both canted – and the repeated shattering of glass as Karl's bul-lets miss him. Then there is a cut to another tilted, low-angle frontal shot of McClane running round a corner, a fast-moving Steadicam in pursuit.

Repetitions are essential to such a frenetic sequence and as the two terrorists emerge from around the same corner, the camera tracking speedily into them, there is yet another canted re-

Fig. 2.30

Fig. 2.31

Fig. 2.32

Fig. 2.33

verse shot of McClane running, holding his gun aloft as he dives left into an anteroom, bullets raining around him. After a quick close-up of McClane crouched on the ground (a familiar position by now) there follows a floor level point-of-view shot of a third terrorist making his way towards McClane. From the same low angle we see his legs being shot through with bullets, and a wider shot shows him falling through another plate of glass. The mutual firing continues unabated between McClane and the other two, although there is the briefest of respites as Karl slithers behind a desk; a Steadicam shot appears to be paralleling his move, while in fact it is mimicking McClane's point of view as he tracks Karl. The machine guns blaze, the images get briefer and the filming angles multiply: explosiveness evoked as visual instability.

There is another short hiatus as Gruber (now also crouching behind a low piece of office furniture) and Karl talk in German. We may not understand this but then neither, it transpires, does Karl, at whom Gruber then snarls in English to shoot at the glass that is shielding McClane. Via further tilted point-of-view shots the sequence becomes reduced to its essence of noise and breaking glass. Its conclusion is arrived at as McClane, fearing he is done for, spies the inviting luminous green of a nearby 'Exit' sign. Karl – wanting to both smoke him out and finish him off – rolls a new-fangled grenade towards McClane's position (the anteroom in which he has been is, of course, his modern-day hide out) and, as Karl and Gruber look for but cannot see him, they presume they have won the battle. As Gruber finds the bag of detonators McClane had taken, he says triumphantly, 'We're back in business.' An edit to a television screen marks the conclusion of the sequence.

Victory, as it turns out, belongs to McClane who, though in pain from the shards of glass embedded in his feet, had escaped via the Emergency Exit. The uncluttered linearity of this sequence, its pace and its inevitable propulsion towards a definite climax are all features that, although they fall short of directly connoting the male sexual act, remain obliquely suggestive of it, down to the climactic ecstasy of freneticism and noise and the sharp withdrawal from it into the world of television coverage of the siege. Action in these circumstances (especially within a narrative such as Die Hard's in which heterosexual union and marital contentment are, at the outset at least, distant possibilities) supplants the sexual act. In Die Hard, McClane's successes as action hero then provide the route back into Holly's affections, so the perversity of the action sequences ('perverse' because their fragmented, fraught action becomes an eroticised substitute for the sexual act) is eventually repressed by the couple's rapprochement. This serenity, however, is only superficial as the urgent, passionate exchanges in Die Hard occur between men, whether antagonistic as between McClane and Gruber or supportive as between McClane and Al (Reginald Veljohnson), the cop who maintains a radio dialogue with him throughout the siege. I have here discussed an indicative action sequence, but in terms of what Die Hard tells us about masculinity and how mise-en-scène works to enforce this, the relationship between action and narrative is especially important. Energetic, heated action sequences and the protracted battle between McClane and Gruber are ostensibly the way for McClane to regain Holly; however, the action sequences in Die Hard (the all-male zones) are always more exciting, spectacular and enjoyable than the quieter, more tentative moment of the couple's reunion. I commented above that, unlike Dyer in his discussion of *Speed*, I do not believe the action spectator occupies an exclusively passive position, however pleasurable, in relation to the action itself. Passivity in *Die Hard* resides quite explicitly with Holly, held captive by the terrorists and only able to admire her husband's bravery from afar, and with the feminised Al who likewise can only look on and hope while McClane risks his life. Conversely, we the film's spectators, are permitted to identify with McClane by being propelled through the action sequences alongside him; in turn these sequences are leant both coherence and excitement via this proximity. So ultimately the short shots and fast edits engage us by making it possible for us to physically invest in the action sequences while the puncturing of them with point-of-view shots establish our collusion with McClane. Gruber and his men are always one step behind; we are not.

Gladiator: slow motion and the hero

The relationship between action, narrative and identification in *Gladiator* is slightly different as Ridley Scott's epic lacks the ultimate restoration of its hero, Maximus (Russell Crowe) as the patriarchal head of his family as well as the heroic slave who frees the Roman spirit by defying the corrupt Commudus (Joaquin Phoenix). However, Maximus's centrality is established from the outset via the mutual support of narrativisation and mise-en-scène. Reiterating the centrality of homosocialism to the action movie and the presence of perversity, one way in which the potentially perverse eroticisation of the male body in action films has been broken down is via the action itself – that one is looking, as Neale or Dyer (1982) would argue, not merely at the male body but at the actions that body is performing. Maximus's centrality in *Gladiator* is dealt with differently and if not quite unerotically, then certainly equivocally so. The directing of the spectators' look towards spectacle and spectacular mise-en-scène takes on, in *Gladiator*, added connotations, as our look is also diverted onto the film's use of computer-generated special effects, not merely more traditional cinematic methods of constructing action. Within this collision of old and new, what I will discuss in particular here is *Gladiator*'s specific use of fast cutting (including computer-generated images) and brief slow-motion close-ups of Maximus in the throes of battle or gladiatorial combat, intimate asides that privilege our relationship with a film's heroic protagonist. Pleasure in watching the spectacle of *Gladiator* stems from this blending of traditional and innovative modes of visual expression, and the distinctiveness of the film's aesthetic is most in evidence in the combat sequences: the battle at the beginning against the barbarian tribes resisting Roman colonisation in 'Germania' and the subsequent gladiatorial fights in the various arena, notably those contests in the Colosseum.

That Maximus Decemus Meridius is the most dynamic and significant of Marcus Aurelius's (Richard Harris) generals is emphasised right at the outset, before the battle against the barbarians has commenced, with the film's opening shots of Maximus's hand skimming heads of corn as he walks through them (an image that is repeated several times over and we later learn is Maximus fantasising about returning home to his family), swiftly followed by him echoing this action as he walks through his troops before battle, parting their lines as he had done the corn and preparing them for battle as Henry V might have done on the eve of Agincourt. Maximus then bends down and grabs a handful of dusty earth, which he smells as he looks over at his wolfhound. He mounts his white horse and issues the motivational command to a fellow officer: 'Strength and honour; unleash hell.' What is striking about this opening is the relationship between the masses (the sheaths of corn, the Roman infantrymen) and their natural leader; in essence, the two are complementary and have a traditional symbiosis, the many being dependent upon and commanded by one man. After Maximus has stirred up his troops with his inelegant and flatly delivered speech pregnant with slightly old-fashioned platitudes ('... what we do in life echoes in eternity'), catapults are cocked and fired, flaming arrows are lit and sent flying into the enemy lines and the music on the soundtrack quickens in expectation. This is the conventional prelude to the ensuing battle but also a rather more specific build up to a battle that will confirm Maximus's centrality.

The principal battle sequence begins with Maximus's dog (already established as the general's alter ego) hurtling through flames and trees into the fray, soon followed by Maximus charting a similar course (Figs 2.34–2.36). Swiftly, the manner in which *Gladiator* – in common with several other examples of contemporary action/epics – will represent combat is established, that is, via a disorientating, kaleidoscopic series of in-

Fig. 2.34

Fig. 2.35

Fig. 2.36

complete staccato images (the average shot during the more frenetic action sequences lasts barely a second) from a multitude of different perspectives and angles. In itself each image is an incoherent, inconclusive fragment, but edited together it comes to make sense, patchwork style, through its contex-tualisation. The entry of Maximus, careering down the hillside on his white steed to slice through the head and helmet of a Barbarian slumped against a tree, is the narrative intervention to give these ex-hausting images a focal logic. Ridley Scott adopts a variety of techniques to achieve the effect of rush and violence, for example alternating and changing shutter speeds or editing together truncated frag-ments of shots, often cutting mid-action. The effect is to make Maximus appear unstoppable.

It is interesting that, having established such momentum, Scott elects to slow the action down as Maximus decapitates his Barbarian foe, before resorting once more to a sea of panting close-ups leading to another encounter involving the Roman leader, this time on the ground as he has been thrown from his horse. The repeated interruption of this opening battle with brief slow-motion interludes of Maximus's involvement in it serves the purpose of making the sequence cohere around the trajectory of Maximus through it and so to make him its focal force and driving energy. These are crucial punctuations; the slow motion is slight, not exaggerated, but its effect is to draw us into Maximus, to believe that whatever happens around him radiates from him. As the refrain from the dominant piece of music on the soundtrack starts up (portentous, majesterial, inevitable strings) the images are slowed right down and the end of this monumental scene is signalled as, right at the end of the filming day, the natural light is fading leaving the flames on the torches to trail in a messy blur across the screen, part of a Bosch-like scene of chaotic carnage. This finale is, again, topped and tailed by Maximus, ending with the amplified sound of his exhausted breath being superimposed onto the soundtrack as he, once more in slight slow motion, raises his sword aloft in weary triumph.

Such a juxtaposition, as part of an action sequence, between short, almost violently abrupt shots and more leisurely, *largato* slow motion – usually close-up – images of the hero has become a relatively familiar trope of men's action cinema. Arroyo talks of the use of this contrast in *Mission: Impossible*, referring to sequences that involve 'quick cuts, to enhance the sense of danger and to give the impression of movement' and 'slow motion, to arrest and break down movement' (2000: 25). For Arroyo 'the combined effect is that of the sublime' but he goes on to dissect this generic use of contrast:

> The slow motion is thrilling to watch, but it's also fascinating because such a technique, so typical of the contemporary action/spectacle film, reduces difference into equivalence while divorcing an object from its properties. Here a drop of sweat and a knife are equally dangerous. (Ibid.)

The juxtaposition between fast and slow close-ups is not just an aesthetic affectation; it also creates an affinity between spectator and hero amidst all the active chaos of the surrounding scene and, through this proximity, establishes the idea that the action hero – able as he is to stand back for a moment from the freneticism surrounding him – controls his environment and dictates the course of the film's action. Maximus, while fully implicated in the violence and chaos of the Roman battles, is also singled out via the slow motion and becomes the epicentre of the conflict, the figure around whom it evolves.

What *Gladiator* adds to a film such as *Troy*'s (2004) use of a similar juxtaposition to emphasise the supremacy in the battle of Achilles, for example, is Maximus's symbolic as well as narrative centrality – that he is both a successful soldier and a good man, identified by Marcus Aurelius as his rightful successor (over his biological son, Commodus) following the triumph in Germania. Marcus Aurelius, in wanting Maximus to restore Rome to the Senate, suggests that his favoured general and surrogate son has a meaningful affinity with Rome and its own inherent morality and goodness – currently suppressed, but nevertheless latent. *Gladiator* is intensely patriarchal in its centralisation of Maximus, making him the epicentre of everything that is strong and good: he has an affinity with the men under his command, he is a loyal and loving father and husband, he is the protector of Rome and its temporarily lost republican morality, he is the leader and saviour of the gladiators, he becomes Commodus's nemesis.

These various facets of Maximus's narrative, formal and aesthetic significance come together in the protracted sequence in the Colosseum that concludes with the confrontation with Commodus (who thinks Maximus is dead) that makes up the symbolic core of the film. This sequence (that occurs a little over halfway into the movie) starts with the gladiators coming up from the dark bowels under the Colosseum and opens in a very similar way to the Germania battle, with Maximus rubbing soil in between his palms and smelling it (presumably as a means of gauging the omens for battle). There is then a close-up of Maximus donning a helmet before the gladiators march up into the light of the arena, Maximus's helmet being the one that is picked out by the sun's rays penetrating the shadows. As they emerge into the light and stare out at the vast crowd looking down at them, a circular Steadicam shot envelops the gladiators and mimics the spherical arena; as the men look up at the cheering crowds the sweeping circular move enhances the notion of solidarity between the gladiators and cements the bond between gladiators and crowd. The camera then comes to rest at a slightly low angle, literally looking up at Maximus. As Cassius (David Hemmings) announces the re-enactment of the 'Second fall of mighty Carthage' in which the gladiators are to play the 'barbarian hoards', a succession of individual chariots emerge through a set of gates. There is a close-up of Maximus as he recalls his days in the army and tells his fellow gladiators that they must work as a unit because 'if we stay together we survive'. Once again, through a combination of dialogue and mise-en-scène, the idea of unity and camaraderie is built up around the notion that such solidarity is only possible if Maximus is there to lead and orchestrate it. Once he has given his 'troops' his pep talk, as he had done in Germania, there follows an initial rapid montage of short shots from a variety of angles depicting the gladiatorial slaves' battle against the chariots (one chariot careering over almost into the camera, for example, or a female charioteer being sliced in half) interspersed once more with close-ups of Maximus telling his men to work 'as one'.

When the slow motion begins, its significance is not arbitrary or obscure. The re-enactment of the second fall or mighty Carthage is going better than expected for the barbarian hoards, and Maximus mounts one of the enemy's white horses (as this is his moment of renewal and affirmation, that this horse is reminiscent of his horse in Germania resonates with importance). This image is slightly slowed, continuing so as

Fig. 2.37

Maximus takes a spear (Fig. 2.37). What follows is a series of racing point-of-view shots of the chariots with Maximus in pursuit intermingled with sloweddown action shots. More so even than in previous confrontations, the action returns to Maximus after each altercation as he replicates his battlefield exploits, charging in slow motion in a straight line through the legionnaires' defences, sything off heads, blood dripping from his sword. In a direct parallel with the victory over Germania, the end of this gladiatorial conflict is marked by Maximus – in slow motion of course – on his adopted horse raising his sword aloft as the camera repeats its pan around the Colosseum and Hans Zimmer's soundtrack soars. This part of the sequence concludes with Commodus mocking Cassius as he remarks, 'My memory's a little hazy, Cassius, but shouldn't the Barbarians lose the battle of Carthage?' before deciding to go down into the arena to meet the hero he knows simply as 'the Spaniard'.

Gladiator is a measured and symmetrical film and what ensues is the middle of three big personal confrontations with Commodus, the first being after Commodus has committed patricide rather than have Maximus succeed his father and the last being the film's final scene in which a duel between them ends with both men dying (and Rome being restored, as Marcus Aurelius had wanted, to the Senate). Commodus descends from the royal box and enters the arena; he asks for the masked Maximus's name but Maximus refuses to give it, replying enigmatically (and with an allusion to *Spartacus*): 'My name is Gladiator.' It is here, in the moments leading up to Maximus's inevitable revelation of his face and name, that the over-determined importance of slow motion and close-ups is confirmed as bound up in *Gladiator* (as in other action movies) to identity and subjective agency; for Maximus's identity and power are bound up with his face – with hiding it, revealing it, seeing its expressiveness. For all the film's notable visual effects, *Gladiator* is an old-fashioned action movie inasmuch as its action is punctuated with insights into Maximus's character and the spectacle it generates understood in relation to him also and through our ability to access and feel affinity for him. Maximus transcends the banalities of the narrative and plot construction much as the 'Barbarian hoards' defied history as he is finally compelled to take off his helmet, turn around and face Commodus, whom he confronts with his defining speech:

> My name is Maximus Decimus Meridius. Commander of the Armies of the North, General of the Felix Legions. Loyal servant of the true emperor, Marcus Aurelius. Father to a murdered son, husband to a murdered wife, and I will have my vengeance in this life or the next.

Although there is no slow motion at this juncture, this is a comparably slow, powerful and portentous moment that segues into the momentous conclusion to the scene as the triumphant music, the cheers, the arms aloft and the circular pans around the spectators seated in the Colosseum all resume. The whole sequence is circular and closes as it began, with Maximus – once again the general – walking through lines of gladiators in the bowels of the Colosseum to the crowds' chants of 'Maximus! Maximus!'

Maximus's speech to Commodus lays out simply all that he embodies: father, husband, loyal servant, a man of morality and honour. The repeated use of certain tropes within the mise-en-scène – in particular the juxtaposition in the action sequences of fast editing and slow-motion interludes – are used to identify Maximus as the epicentre of every aspect of the film and to create a sense of unity between narrative, action, character, soundtrack and style. All aspects of *Gladiator* radiate out from Maximus and such at-one-ness with the film's meaning and style leads to an omnipresent collusion between masculinity and mise-en-scène. The contradictions and uncertainties of various other films discussed above have been replaced in *Gladiator* by an almost oppressive homogeneity of which I have discussed only one aspect or symptom. A consequence of this homogeneity, of everything having been tied into everything else, is the peculiar sense that *Gladiator* has not conceived of there being any such thing as offscreen space: everything is conceived of as spectacular and as part of Maximus.

Conclusion

Although action cinema has dominated much of chapter two of this study, I have never wanted to suggest that men's cinema is exclusively macho or even straightforwardly about fabricating an idealised, heterosexual, virile brand of masculinity. Men's cinema, often on the level of mise-en-scène, is preoccupied with these ideals but not merely in relation to spectacle, action or violence. I began this study by examining a beginning (the opening of *Mission: Impossible 2*) and I will close with a brief discussion of the ending of *Master and Commander* (2003) a film with a gently ambivalent and ironic attitude to masculinity. Captain Jack Aubrey (Russell Crowe) thinks he has finally won over the Acheron, the French ship he has been pursuing throughout the film; he has promoted one of his officers to Captain of it and sent it on its way, with the remaining French sailors under his command. With his mission accomplished, he imagines he can finally grant his own ship's surgeon, Dr Stephen Maturin (Paul Bettany), his wish to return to the Galapagos Islands to study the flightless cormorant he had seen there. However, Aubrey realises he has been gulled and that the captain of the Acheron is not dead as he had been led to believe, so he issues the order to go in pursuit of the French, once more, in the process dashing Maturin's hopes. This switch in course is matched by a shift in tone: from everything returning to normal after their presumed victory (the newly promoted Captain smiling as he leaves to take up his new command, the grumpy cook preparing dinner, Aubrey and Maturin tuning their violin and cello to enjoy a little duet before eating) to Aubrey issuing the command to change course.

Aubrey (a brute in comparison with his more cultured, refined friend) is not insensitive to Maturin's disappointment at not being able, yet, to return to the Galapagos Islands. Holding his violin he turns to the doctor and confirms that the cormorant cannot fly, concluding, with a twinkly eye and an arch of the eyebrow, 'well, it's not going anywhere', at which point he takes his fiddle and starts to strum bars from a movement of Luigi Boccherini's 'La Musica Notturna delle Strade di Madrid'.[17] Maturin is mollified, smiles back at Aubrey and sets himself to play his cello. The Boccherini is an apt accompaniment to this moment of manly rapprochement – playful and tuneful at the same time as being an intrinsically competitive piece structured around alternating solos by different instruments. This competition is indicated in the 'well, I'll show you what I can do' gestures and expressions the characters exchange as they swap solo and accompanist roles. The Boccherini is, however, unexpected in its lightness and delicacy for such an ostensibly purposeful juncture – Aubrey changing course in order to resume his battle with the Acheron. Once the duet is established,[18] the action cuts to a montage of short shots (at the start also speeded up) showing the sailors preparing once more for a possible confrontation – guns being loaded, sails being prepared. The music, switching from diegetic to non-diegetic, is continuous, the action returning – after this montage – to the Captain's quarters as Aubrey takes up his bow and takes over the musical lead from Maturin. As he hits his stride and as the Boccherini hits its concluding crescendo, the diegetic musical scene is replaced by an aerial shot of Aubrey's ship. The shot pulls out in an elegant arc, finally revealing the Acheron in the distance, and both film and music come to a close. Neither ends triumphantly or bombastically; this is an end pondering the realisation that the end is really just another beginning.

The tone of the conclusion to *Master and Commander* is ambivalent as it portrays masculinity as a mutable, unstable concept: at once authoritative, warmongering, refined and gentle. That the film ends on a quest with Aubrey's ship the Surprise in pursuit of the Acheron, is symptomatic of this lack of fixity. In addition, the decisiveness indicated by the synchronisation of music and action – the synchronicity between Maturin and Aubrey as they play (and are similarly able to understand and interpret each other's thoughts) and between music, images and editing more generally – or the commanding certainty of the final aerial shot around the HMS Surprise, all contradict the scene's initial suggestion that a real man like Aubrey would have been happy playing the fiddle all the way home. At various junctures in this study I have dwelt on the importance to masculinity of keeping any definition of it permanently beyond our grasp. The perpetual quest, therefore, may be the perfect state for real men to be in and may also be the most apt metaphor for masculinity itself: tantalisingly just out of reach, like the horizon (if not the Acheron).

I began by setting out to articulate something that seemed to be lacking within film studies, namely an extended discussion of masculinity and film style. I have argued, via a series of wide-ranging illustrations, for a liberating and flexible way of thinking about this relationship. The first chapter differed from the second; whereas chapter one focused on instances in which aspects of masculinity are particularly strongly evoked and articulated through visual style, chapter two sought to delineate the more concrete, definite category of what I have termed 'men's cinema' – not cinema for and by men (as women's cinema of the 1970s had been for and by women) but a by now conventionalised way of making films about men and masculinity that utilises certain recognisable tropes and abides by certain formalised ways of constructing a sequence or film. Many of the motifs or tropes identified in chapter two imply certainty and fixity (men striding forward, being a key example), yet ultimately what emerges through the discussions of the individual films is a far more mutable, unstable conception of masculinity – aware, maybe, of seeking or desiring linearity and purposefulness but also uncertain of how these were to be attained. For all the stridency of much men's cinema, masculine self-belief is more frequently undermined than validated, an ambivalence brought out most eloquently at the level of mise-en-scène. This core struggle is played out once more in *Master and Commander*, as Aubrey, at the end, is yet again in pursuit of a ship that, throughout the film, has possessed more symbolic value for him than it reasonably should have done. *Master and Commander* thereby ends poised between the surety of its arching closing shot and narrative inconclusiveness. Jack Aubrey, this ending seems to suggest, will rest and dedicate more time to playing the fiddle when he has achieved his goal, but will he ever get there? The end is just another beginning.

NOTES

1   *Mission Impossible* (1996) had been directed in a more traditional style by Brian De Palma whereas *M:I 2* was directed by John Woo, whose spectacular, stylised directorial style has had a major impact on Hollywood action cinema since he left Hong Kong and made films such as *Hard Target* (1993) and *Broken Arrow* (1996).

2   See Mandy Merck's analysis of 'Visual Pleasure and Narrative Cinema' as a manifesto in 'Mulvey's Manifesto' (2007).

3   This is the title of Dale Spender's 1982 book about patriarchy and language.

4   This is an intriguing use of the term 'sexual object' as Freud here is referring to what most readers would take to be the sexual subject. I am not going to dwell on this as later in the essay the term 'object' comes to signify that which is found attractive, so the problems could reside with a poor translation.

5   Cf. *Bringing Up Daddy: Fatherhood and Masculinity in Postwar Hollywood* (2005: 40–50).

6   In *The History of Sexuality* Michel Foucault referred to fetishism as 'the model perversion' (1976: 154), but as far as masculinity is concerned, this is homosexuality.

7   See *Hard Bodies: Hollywood Masculinity in the Reagan Era* (1993).

8   The only sequence in colour in *Raging Bull* is the home movie montage showing, for example, Jake and Vickie's marriage, that of his brother Joe and footage of their kids playing in the garden.

9   Gordon Cooper (Dennis Quaid) poses the rhetorical question, 'Who's the best pilot you ever saw?' to his wife several times, filling in the answer, 'You're looking at him'.

10 Just as certain cinematographers could be credited with pioneering aspects of the style of men's cinema, so certain composers – such as Zimmer – arguably have done the same. Zimmer scored *Mission: Impossible 2* and *Gladiator* as well as *Backdraft*, and several other examples of masculine and masculinist cinema. His familiar and rousing scores suit these films particularly well.

11 Tarantino is referring to Melville's remark that Jef Costello in *Le Samouraï* wears 'a suit of armour' (in Dargis 1994: 17).

12 As shown in Ron Howard's *Apollo 13*, the capsule window played a vital part in the pilots' safe return to earth.

13 Once one of Rainer Werner Fassbinder's cinematographers, Balhaus has of Scorsese's films to date shot *After Hours* (1985), *The Color of Money* (1986), *The Last Temptation of Christ* (1988), *The Age of Innocence* (1993), *Gangs of New York* (2002) and *The Departed* (2006), all of which share a characteristically extravagant, expressive visual style. In addition, a flourish such as the dynamic sweep of the Steadicam in *Goodfellas* is reminiscent of Balhaus's other work, such as the sweeping aerial shot over the water into New York that opens Mike Nichols' *Working Girl* (1988).

14 In *The American President* Sheen plays Andrew Shepherd's Chief of Staff.

15 Via the observation that 'The favoured position of hardcore fans for watching action movies in the cinema is slumped in the seat with legs slung over the seat in front. This is an excellent

position for anal sex as well as for cunnilingus and fellatio' (2000: 21).

16 Other notable examples amongst the films discussed in this book can be found in the fire-fighting sequences in *Backdraft* or battle sequences of *Gladiator*.

17 Boccherini instructed his string players to put their cellos – and presumably also their violins, as Russell Crowe does in *Master and Commander* – on their knees to play them as they might guitars.

18 Originally, the piece was written for a string quintet.

BIBLIOGRAPHY

Aaron, Michele (2007) *Spectatorship: The Power of Looking On*. London: Wallflower Press.

Arroyo, José (2002) 'Mission: Sublime', in José Arroyo (ed.) *Action/Spectacle Cinema: A Sight and Sound Reader*. London: British Film Institute, 21–5.

Berliner, Todd (2005) 'Visual Absurdity in *Raging Bull*', in Kevin L. Hayes (ed.) *Martin Scorsese's Raging Bull*. Cambridge: Cambridge University Press, 41–68.

Bovenschen, Silvia (1976) 'Is There a Feminine Aesthetic?', in Gisela Ecker (ed.) *Feminist Aesthetics*. London: The Women's Press, 23–50.

Bruzzi, Stella (2005) *Bringing Up Daddy: Fatherhood and Masculinity in Postwar Hollywood*. London: British Film Institute.

Butler, Alison (2002) *Women's Cinema: The Contested Screen*. London: Wallflower Press.

Charity, Tom (1997) *The Right Stuff*. London: British Film Institute.

Cixous, Hélène (1997 [1975]) 'The Laugh of the Medusa', in Robyn R. Warhol and Diane Price Herndl (eds) *Feminism: An Anthology of Literary Theory and Criticism*, revised edition. Basingstoke: Macmillan Press, 347–62.

Cohan, Steven (1997) *Masked Men: Masculinity and the Movies in the Fifties*. Bloomington and Indianapolis: Indiana University Press.

Cook, Pam (1982) 'Masculinity in Crisis?', *Screen*, 23, 3/4, September/October, 39–46.

Dargis, Manohla (1994) 'Quentin Tarantino on *Pulp Fiction*', *Sight and Sound*, 4, 11, November, 16–20.

Dawson, Jeff (1995) *Tarantino: Inside Story*. London: Cassell.

Dyer, Richard (1982) 'Don't Look Now: The Instabilities of the Male Pin-up', in *Only Entertainment*. London: Routledge, 103–20.

_____ (1985) 'Male Sexuality in the Media', in Andy Metcalf and Martin Humphries (eds) *The Sexuality of Men*. London: Pluto Press, 28–43.

_____ (1993) 'Homosexuality and Film Noir', in *The Matter of Images*. London: Routledge, 52–72.

_____ (2000) 'Action!', in José Arroyo (ed.) *Action/Spectacle Cinema: A Sight and Sound Reader*. London: British Film Institute, 17–21.

Elsaesser, Thomas (1987 [1972]) 'Tales of Sound and Fury: Observations on the Family Melodrama', in Christine Gledhill (ed.) *Home is Where the Heart Is: Studies in Melodrama and the Woman's Film*. London: British Film Institute, 43–69.

Foucault, Michel (1976) *The History of Sexuality: Volume 1: An Introduction*. Harmondsworth: Penguin.

Fraiman, Susan (2003) *Cool Men and the Second Sex*. New York: Columbia University Press.

Freud, Sigmund (1991 [1905]) 'The Sexual Aberrations', in *On Sexuality* (Penguin Freud Library, Vol. 7). London: Penguin, 45–87.

Gledhill, Christine (1995) 'Women Reading Men', in Pat Kirkham and Janet Thumim (eds) *Me Jane: Masculinity, Movies and Women*. London: Lawrence and Wishart, 73–93.

Jeffords, Susan (1993) *Hard Bodies: Hollywood Masculinity in the Reagan Era*. New Brunswick: Rutgers University Press.

Johnston, Claire (1976 [1974]) 'Women's Cinema as Counter-Cinema', in Bill Nichols (ed.) *Movies and Methods*. Berkeley and Los Angeles: University of California Press, 208–17.

Kael, Pauline (1986) 'The Current Cinema: Brutes', *Village Voice*, 31, 26, May, 114–17.

Kaplan, E. Ann (1983) *Women and Film Noir: Both Sides of the Camera*. New York: Methuen.

Kirkham, Pat and Janet Thumim (eds) (1993) *You Tarzan: Masculinity, Movies and Men*. London: St. Martin's Press.

Klevan, Andrew (2005) *Film Performance: From Achievement to Appreciation*. London: Wallflower Press.

Krutnik, Frank (1991) *In a Lonely Street: Film Noir, Genre, Masculinity*. London: Routledge.

Lacan, Jacques (1993 [1958]) 'The Signification of the Phallus', in *Écrits: A Selection*, trans. Alan Sheridan. London: Routledge, 1–7.

Lehman, Peter (2001) *Masculinity: Bodies, Movies, Culture*. London and New York: Routledge.

Merck, Mandy (2007) 'Mulvey's Manifesto', *Camera Obscura*, 22, 3, 66, 1–23.

Mulvey, Laura (1985 [1975]) 'Visual Pleasure and Narrative Cinema', in Bill Nichols (ed.) *Movies and Methods II*. Berkeley and Los Angeles: University of California Press, 303–14.

Neale, Steve (1993 [1983]) 'Masculinity as Spectacle', in Steven Cohan and Ina Rae Hark (eds) *Screening the Male: Exploring Masculinities in Hollywood Cinema*. London and New York: Routledge, 9–22.

Nowell-Smith, Geoffrey (1987) 'Minnelli and Melodrama', in Christine Gledhill (ed.) *Home is Where the Heart Is: Studies in Melodrama and the Woman's Film*. London: British Film Institute, 70–8.

Powrie, Phil, Ann Davies and Bruce Babington (eds) (2004) *The Trouble with Men: Masculinities in European and Hollywood Cinema*. London: Wallflower Press.

Rowbotham, Sheila (1973) *Women's Consciousness, Man's World*. Harmondsworth: Penguin.

Schrader, Paul (1990 [1972]) 'Notes on Film Noir', in Paul Schrader and Kevin Jackson (eds) *Schrader on Schrader and Other Writings*. London: Faber and Faber, 80–93.

Sedgwick, Eve Kosofsky (1985) *Between Men: English Literature and Male Homosocial Desire*. New York: Columbia University Press.

Spender, Dale (1982) *Man Made Language*. London: Routledge and Kegan Paul.

Stacey, Jackie (1987) 'Desperately Seeking Difference', *Screen*, 28, 1, Winter, 48–61.

Tasker, Yvonne (1993) *Spectacular Bodies: Gender, Genre and the Action Cinema*. London: Routledge.

Thomas, Deborah (1992) 'How Hollywood Deals with the Deviant Male', in Ian Cameron (ed.) *The Movie Book of Film Noir*. London: Studio Vista, 59–70.

Wood, Robin (2003) *Hollywood From Vietnam to Reagan ... And Beyond*, revised and expanded edition. New York: Columbia.